Where Is Our Responsibility?

William F. Hartford

WHERE IS OUR
RESPONSIBILITY?

Unions and Economic Change in
the New England Textile Industry,
1870–1960

University of Massachusetts Press ∎ Amherst

Copyright © 1996 by
The University of Massachusetts Press
Printed in the United States of America
LC 95–45291
ISBN 1–55849–022–1
Set in Galliard and Copperplate by Keystone Typesetting, Inc.
Printed and bound by Braun-Brumfield, Inc.

Library of Congress Cataloging-in-Publication Data

Hartford, William, 1949–
    Where is our responsibility? : unions and economic change in the New England
textile industry, 1870–1960 / William F. Hartford.
        p.   cm.
    Includes bibliographical references and index.
    ISBN 1–55849–022–1 (cloth : alk. paper)
    1. Textile industry — Massachusetts — History.   2. Trade-unions — Textile workers —
Massachusetts — History.   3. Plant shutdowns — Massachusetts — History.
4. Deindustrialization — Massachusetts — History.   I. Title.
HD9857.M4H37   1996
331.88′17′009744 — dc20   95–45291
                                                                                CIP

British Library Cataloguing in Publication data are available.

IN MEMORY OF MY GRANDPARENTS

Albert and Veronica Andrews
and
Joseph and Loretta Hartford

Contents

Acknowledgments

As with all historical studies, this was a collective effort that could not have been completed without the assistance of numerous individuals and institutions. Acknowledgment of these debts must begin with the archivists and librarians who eased the burdens of research. I am especially grateful to Harold Miller of the State Historical Society of Wisconsin; Jessica Randolph of the Museum of American Textile History; Eartha Dengler and Ken Skulski of the Immigrant City Archives; and Uta Bargmann, Michael Wileski, and Linda Seidman of the University of Massachusetts at Amherst. While he was at the latter institution, Ken Fones-Wolf not only acquired several relevant manuscript collections, but helped me to clarify some early thoughts on the project.

Although this project was an independent effort, support from the Amalgamated Clothing and Textile Workers Union made my task considerably easier than it otherwise would have been. The organization's Rieve-Pollock Foundation provided financial aid for a research trip to Wisconsin; President Jack Sheinkman gave me permission to read TWUA records that have not yet been opened to the general public; and Research Director Keir Jorgensen not only offered timely encouragement but furnished a variety of documents that proved extremely helpful. He also arranged to have two former TWUA officials, President Sol Stetin and Research Director George Perkel, read the manuscript. I am very appreciative of their comments.

I owe an especially large debt to another former TWUA research director. At a time when I was still uncertain whether I would see the study through to its conclusion, Solomon Barkin forced me to sort out my intentions. After I had stopped procrastinating and returned to work, his detailed remarks on several versions of the manuscript rescued me from various errors of fact and interpretation. He also put me in touch with Donald Stabile, who generously allowed me to read his then unpublished study of Barkin's economic thought.

My interest in deindustrialization began more than a decade ago while attending a three-day symposium on the subject organized by Bruce Laurie of the University of Massachusetts at Amherst. Since that time, Bruce has aided my development as a historian in ways too numerous to recount. At several critical junctures in the preparation of the present work, I encountered conceptual problems that threatened serious delays. On each occasion, Bruce's comments provided the perspective needed to resolve the dilemma.

At the University of Massachusetts Press, I benefited from the editorial assistance of Clark Dougan, while Pam Wilkinson and Catlin Murphy helped guide the study through to publication. I am also grateful for Michael Burke's careful copyediting of the manuscript.

Lastly, I must thank my brother and parents. Over the years, Philip Hartford listened to endless monologues on the New England textile industry with a patience that only a best friend could muster; and Francis and Julia Hartford were a vital source of support throughout. Having dedicated a previous work to them, this one is for some of the most important people in their lives: my grandparents.

WHERE IS OUR RESPONSIBILITY?

INTRODUCTION

"The story of the New England cotton industry is the story of the industrialization of America." So wrote Caroline Ware in the introduction to her seminal account of the industry's beginnings. Though her claim is somewhat overstated, there is much evidence to support it. That industry is now largely gone, and of its passing one might make a similar assertion: the collapse of textile production in New England is the story of the deindustrialization of America. Once considered an aberrant exception in an otherwise glorious tale of uninterrupted economic expansion, what happened to the New England textile industry is now occurring throughout the nation's industrial heartland. This work seeks to tell that story from the perspective of the textile unionists who have been blamed for the industry's disappearance.[1]

The ideas that led me to pursue this study began taking shape more than a decade ago. Since that time my then-primitive notions about deindustrialization have evolved considerably. I initially thought—as many New Englanders still do—that the industry's decline was a simple case of corporate efforts to evade unionization; and as the unions moved in, the mills moved out. I soon found, however, that this interpretation did not bear close scrutiny. Some mill owners were deeply committed to maintaining regional operations and believed unions could help them to do so; many others would have liquidated their plants regardless of whether they were organized. I also found that after World War II New England manufacturers faced an extremely tight labor market that made it difficult for them to recruit new workers during periods of even modest prosperity. A tradition of low wages, unattractive working conditions, and uncertain employment had given textiles an unenviable reputation that was widely at variance with the rising aspirations of mill workers' children. From this I concluded that the industry's demise could be attributed to a contradiction between a changing New England labor market and persisting interregional labor cost differentials.

1

This was certainly an advance from my earlier position, but a number of problems still remained. After presenting the above argument, I was asked whether, given the bleak picture I had outlined, there was any reason why New England would have wanted a textile industry. Although I did not then have a ready response, it was a good question. If the answer was an unequivocal no, there was no reason for New England to have wanted a textile industry, then my best course of action would have been to stop research, sort out my note cards, write a final paper or two, and move on to something else. Interpretive models that view deindustrialization as "decline is decline is decline" have limited instructional value. With further research, though, I came to realize that it was not enough to ask: Did the people of New England want a textile industry? This was not the question textile unionists posed as they set about trying to save the region's still-viable mills and at the same time make the industry a better place in which to work. Rather, they were seeking answers to a much different sort of query: What kind of textile industry can New England have? And once I began asking the same question, it was no longer possible to view deindustrialization as a process of uninterrupted decline. Such a framework cannot account for, much less explain, the struggles that invariably arise when unions attempt to confront the problems caused by economic transition — struggles that in our case not only pitted labor against capital but involved competing groups of mill owners as well.

I must hasten to add that I am not the first historian to examine the collapse of the New England textile industry. Most previous studies, however, were narrowly focused economic analyses that ignored the post–World War II period. And those that do look closely at the people involved — for example, Mary H. Blewett's excellent collection of interviews with Lowell workers and Laurence F. Gross's fine account of the demise of that city's Boott Cotton Mills — have little to say about union initiatives to halt the process of decline. The same can be said of an earlier book of my own on Holyoke. This work is intended to fill that vacuum in the literature. In so doing, I also hope to provide perspective on labor's current woes, as the problems textile unionists faced in New England are today shared by broad elements of the labor movement.[2]

As should be apparent by now, this is an institutional history. Although rank-and-filers will appear at numerous junctures in the narrative, the focus will be on union leaders. I recognize that such an approach has its hazards. But as Leon Fink and Brian Greenberg explain a similar decision on their part: "It is, after all, around institutions and through individuals acting together that social conflicts are both fought and contained. And it is through unions that working-class Americans have most often exercised leverage over society." Moreover, the U.S. industrial relations system is no longer the unproblematic structure that it appeared to be during the heyday of the American Century. After making a similar observation, David Brody noted that the disappearance of that structure has begun to influence the writing of labor history by prompting a "subtle but definite reorientation toward institutions, politics, and power that the era of mature collective bargaining had enabled the new labor historians to bypass." This study is part of that reorientation.[3]

The story begins in Fall River. Prior to the 1930s, no textile workforce in New England could match the degree of organization achieved by Fall River unionists. These advances, which were made possible by more than three decades of struggle, did not come easily. But by the early twentieth century, the city's British-born union leaders had established a stable system of industrial relations that would govern local affairs until the 1940s. Although the Fall River model of unionism benefited a broad range of Spindle City workers, its limitations became apparent well before its demise. When union leaders — steeped in the Fall River tradition and unable to communicate effectively with industrial populations dominated by new immigrants — attempted to extend the system, their efforts produced more misunderstanding than organization. And when economic crisis devastated large segments of the regional industry during the mid-twenties, the response of Fall River unionists was confused at best. These developments are examined in Chapters One and Two. Chapter Three looks at the emergence and consolidation of the Textile Workers Union of America (TWUA) during the late thirties and war years.

The remainder of the study focuses on TWUA efforts to save jobs and shield workers from the consequences of economic change during a period of continuing deindustrialization. Chapter Four, which covers the immediate postwar years, establishes the framework for this examination. Among mill owners, there were two main groups: a small but influential band of persisters who were committed to maintaining productive operations in New England and willing to work with the TWUA to achieve that end; and an assortment of interregionalists who already had plants in the South and were waiting for the right moment to liquidate their remaining northern factories. Similar divisions existed on the shop floors of regional mills. There a group of veteran operatives — for whom age and experience made employment outside textiles impossible — were joined by a shifting collection of younger workers with no binding ties to the industry. TWUA leaders faced the unenviable task of stimulating a level of investment sufficient to modernize aging regional plants, while securing the kinds of benefits that would convince rank-and-filers that they too had a stake in the industry. In the end, they failed. A series of events, beginning with the 1949 recession and culminating in the mid-fifties, ended all hopes of preserving a viable basis for continued production. Chapters Five and Six deal with these developments.

The final chapter examines the politics of economic transition. As union leaders came to recognize how little workers in declining industries could expect from the postwar structure of industrial relations, they sought to use the legislative process both to restore their faltering leverage at the bargaining table and to reduce the social costs of economic change for wage earners. We will take an in-depth look at two of these initiatives: corporate tax law reform and area redevelopment legislation. The first was intended to regulate corporate flight and impose responsibilities on footloose entrepreneurs; the second was designed to help regional communities adjust to the consequences of deindustrialization. Although the results of these efforts proved disappointing, TWUA political policy nevertheless exhibited the intelligence and foresight that characterized so many of its actions during these years.

Before beginning, I should note that although the study draws on material from throughout New England, much of the narrative centers on developments in three cities: Fall River and New Bedford, the region's premier cotton districts; and Lawrence, which occupied a similar place in woolens and worsteds. During the postwar years, TWUA agreements with the Fall River and New Bedford manufacturer's associations established a pattern for regional cotton producers, as did the American Woolen pact in that industry. By concentrating on these locales, I was able to give the study greater focus and at the same time examine events that had regionwide significance.

THE FALL RIVER SYSTEM OF UNIONISM

The history of labor organization in the New England textile industry prior to the 1930s is largely a history of Fall River unionism. From the political and economic initiatives of the Lowell mill women to the epic battles that made Lawrence a synonym for labor militancy during the 1910s, textile operatives outside the Spindle City made memorable contributions to the development of the American labor movement. In making such a claim for Fall River workers, it is not my intention to diminish their achievements. But in a number of important respects, Fall River operatives stood apart from their counterparts in other regional textile centers. One was continuity of resistance and organization. In no other city or town in New England did textile workers so persistently band together to demand their rights; and nowhere else did they create and maintain the degree of organization found in Fall River. Moreover, unlike the agreements that protected small groups of craft workers elsewhere in the industry, the Fall River system of industrial relations regulated wages and working conditions for broad segments of the workforce. Its benefits extended — though not in equal measure — to the nonunionist majority as well as the organized vanguard. At a time when most New England textile workers could choose between compliance and dismissal, as managers typically framed such choices, significant numbers of Fall River operatives were able to make their voices heard. Their ability to do so rested on a form of unionism that combined conciliatory gestures, market-based economic demands, and shop-floor militancy.

This model of unionism not only shaped the development of industrial relations in Fall River and its sister city, New Bedford. It also influenced organizational drives in Lawrence and other regional textile centers during the early twentieth century. As we will see in the next chapter, the Fall River system did not travel well, and efforts to apply the model elsewhere did more to retard than to advance the cause of textile unionism in New England. Before we do so, however, it is necessary to understand how the system evolved and why it was so successful in Fall River. We will begin by looking at a feature of local history that attracted considerable attention from Gilded Age observers: the city's reputation as a center of industrial conflict.

APPEARING BEFORE A congressional investigating committee in 1883, Gilbert B. Whitman, the agent at a New Hampshire mill, said that he knew of no city in New England that had experienced as much labor conflict as Fall River. Whitman's views were by no means unique. Not only did other witnesses express similar sentiments, but just a few years earlier the Massachusetts Bureau of Statistics of Labor (MBSL) had conducted an extensive investigation to answer the question: "Why is it that the working people of Fall River are in constant turmoil, when at Lawrence and Lowell they are quiet?" A fascinating mixture of anecdotal observations, idle speculation, and hard analysis, the bureau's report provides a useful starting point for an examination of Fall River textile workers.[1]

In attempting to determine what made Fall River so different from other regional textile centers, bureau investigators explored a broad range of explanations. One promising area was comparative living conditions. In Lowell and Lawrence, the report observed, "there is a certain spirit of refinement about the people; their clothing indicates care and taste, while in Fall River the air of slovenliness denotes a condition of poverty that is remarkable, considering the size of the city and the resources." Bureau staffers found added support for this line of analysis in one of those statistics that Gilded Age social investigators so assiduously gathered: Lowell and Lawrence operatives lived longer than Fall River workers. There was also a simple explanation for why living conditions in Fall River lagged behind those of Lowell and Lawrence. Compared with the relatively gradual development of the two northern centers, industrial expansion in Fall River had been extraordinarily rapid — so rapid in fact that even Fall River manufacturers believed this "sudden and abnormal growth" was the root cause of local tensions.[2]

This interpretation seemed equally compelling to bureau investigators, and they too concluded that differential growth rates best explained the greater prevalence of industrial unrest in Fall River. In so doing, however, they mistook context for cause. Earlier in the century, Lowell had expanded almost as swiftly as Fall River did after the Civil War without a similar degree of labor turmoil. Yet context is important, and it would be worth our while to pause for a moment and examine Fall River's abrupt emergence as a major textile center.

By any measure, the pace of industrial development in Fall River was truly phenomenal. Between 1865 and 1880, the number of spindles in local factories increased fivefold, and by 1883 Fall River mills housed one-seventh of the country's cotton spindles. They also produced 60 percent of the nation's print cloth. During the same period, population rose nearly threefold from 17,481 to 48,901. There were a number of reasons for this dramatic growth. One was the city's coastal location in southeastern New England, which enabled manufacturers to transport cotton and coal more cheaply than mills operating at interior points could. Reducing coal costs became especially important after 1860. As Thomas Smith observed, the decade of the fifties ended the "frontier days" of New England water power. Henceforth, most new factories were coal-consuming, steam-powered plants, and Fall River was well positioned geographically to take advantage of this development.[3]

Fall River's relatively close proximity to New York was another advantage. By 1865 New York had become the primary market for textile goods, and few other locales in New England could ship products there as quickly and as cheaply as the Spindle City. A final factor influencing Fall River's growth was the local climate. Compared with inland, more northerly textile centers, Fall River had a higher relative humidity. Moist air added to the elasticity and strength of cotton fibers, which reduced yarn breakage and provided what the English described as "good weaving weather." It also made the area a suitable location for the production of finer yarns, a circumstance that aided Fall River's early development during a period when Lowell had a stranglehold on the coarse goods market. By century's end, the invention of artificial humidifiers and the advent of more efficient, cheaper rail transportation would diminish these advantages. But they were of the utmost importance in the years immediately following the Civil War, when Fall River experienced its most rapid growth.[4]

No discussion of Fall River's postwar expansion would be complete without mentioning the manufacturers who owned and operated local mills. The most notable feature of the city's corporate structure was the extent to which the economy was dominated by a relatively small, inter-related group of Fall Riverites. During the 1870s, a close-knit band of seven families controlled between thirty and forty cotton mills. These same people also appeared on the boards of local banks, insurance companies, and transportation firms, over which they exercised a similar degree of control. Although increasing amounts of outside capital would be invested in Fall River concerns, this tradition of local hegemony remained intact well into the twentieth century.[5]

The Fall River system of ownership was not without its liabilities. There was always fear that a single setback affecting one or a small number of concerns might topple the entire structure, which nearly happened during the early seventies when a torpid real estate market provided a stern lesson in the hazards of speculation. More relevant to our purposes are the ways in which mill owners used the system to impose their will on local workers. The MBSL investigators who sought to uncover the sources of industrial discord in Gilded Age Fall River asked similar questions, and we would do well to follow their lead: by examining the operation of Fall River's Board of Trade.[6]

Formed in 1870, the board performed a variety of functions. On one hand, mill owners used the board to set cloth prices and regulate the output of local mills, which they were able to do with some effectiveness because of Fall River's dominant position in the national print cloth market. The board also sought to control labor conditions in local plants by fixing wages, mobilizing and coordinating mill-owner resources during strikes, and maintaining a blacklist designed to prevent worker organization. Said one mill owner, "We never employ a man who belongs to a trades union if we know it."[7]

Fall River workers claimed the Board of Trade had an additional function: to maximize the work pace in local mills. At board meetings, one operative remarked to MBSL investigators, "superintendents are told that the mills must produce more cuts per loom; that such and such a mill is producing more, and they must equal if not surpass it. Word is immediately passed to the overseers, and the operatives are again crowded." Another operative, then working in Lawrence, asserted that if a Fall River overseer "cannot drive his help, then he is immediately discharged." Local manufacturers denied these charges and maintained that the board made no effort to keep track of the pace of production in member mills. But Fall River producers did have an unenviable reputation for grinding their workers. "There is no interest there in keeping things up," a Manchester mill agent told a U.S. Senate committee, "everything is driven to the utmost there." By comparison, operating conditions in Lawrence and Lowell were reputedly more relaxed because, as one Lawrence citizen explained, "The mills are mostly owned and run by Boston men of large means, who give their agents considerable latitude in regard to their help."[8]

Whether such distinctions were as significant as these observers suggested is open to question. It is true that owners of Lowell companies were less likely than their Fall River counterparts to adopt common policies on wages, output, and the like. But in other matters, there do not appear to have been substantial differences among the three centers. Blacklisting was just as prevalent in Lawrence and Lowell as in Fall River and had been since the earliest days of the industry. Similarly, observers familiar with the early Lowell mills were startled by the increased work pace of later years; and there were frequent departmental-level strikes in the northern factories, many of which almost certainly resulted from worker objections to changes in the pace of production.[9]

What distinguished labor unrest in Fall River from workplace actions in Lowell and Lawrence was the capacity of operatives to shut down the entire city. We therefore need to ask: What made Fall River workers so different from operatives in other regional textile centers? By all accounts, it was the comparatively large number of English immigrants in the workforce. A New Hampshire mill agent claimed that Fall River "comes nearest to an English town with its strikes, its help, and its class of people." A Lawrence operative added that the main reason the city had fewer strikes than Fall River was "the absence of the English element, which was always harmful." And a Lowell textile worker contended that local operatives constituted "a better class of help" than could be found in Fall River mills. "Here we have but few English," he explained, "while Fall River can be called a second England." These observations duly impressed MBSL investigators, who concluded that the "class of help" employed in Spindle City factories was the second most important cause of industrial conflict in Fall River. And well they should have. Just two years earlier the bureau had reported, "It is now an established fact, that by the combined efforts of English manufacturers and English trade unions, or by their separate efforts, troublesome strikers and industrial malcontents are shipped to this country."[10]

Not all the British immigrants who flooded Fall River after the Civil War were militant trade unionists. But most did possess a well-developed sense of their class interests. As industrial veterans, schooled in the intricacies of workplace struggle, they believed that as workers they had certain rights, and they had no intention of seeing those rights compromised. This sense of class consciousness was so pervasive that it extended into the middling ranks of immigrant society. When a U.S. senator asked John Keogh, a former textile worker who operated his own print shop in Fall River, if he was a capitalist, Keogh replied, "No, sir." Only after the senator said he was not using the term "in the large and offensive sense" did Keogh concede that he might indeed be a capitalist.[11]

Although British operatives time and again demonstrated a remarkable capacity to act as a class during crises, they were only able to do so by surmounting certain divisions that were part of their industrial heritage. The most important of these stemmed from a tradition of craft separatism in which different occupational groups charted their own course, and which would become an integral feature of the Fall River model of unionism. Of these groups prior to the 1890s, the mule spinners most influenced the evolution of industrial relations in Fall River. Not only were they the best organized, but to local mill owners they were also the most troublesome. They were so less because of their militancy — which often paled beside that of weavers during strikes — than because of the challenge they posed to managerial control of the shop floor. Compared with other operatives, mule spinners had a broader conception of their rights. They also had more to lose. As Isaac Cohen has argued, the Fall River struggles of the 1870s can best be "understood as an attempt of recent Lancashire immigrants to retrieve 'the rights of craftsmen' that they formerly possessed in the Old World." By reviewing Cohen's instructive account of these disputes, much can be learned about an important phase in the development of the Fall River system of unionism.[12]

Cohen begins by examining a major technological breakthrough that transformed the production of mule-spun yarn: the replacement of common mules by self-acting mules. On the traditional common mule, spindles were mounted on a forty-five- to fifty-foot-long moving carriage that weighed as much as 1,400 pounds, and spinners manipulated the spindles so that the cotton roving they received from the card room was simultaneously drawn and twisted, thus producing a fine and even thread particularly suitable for use as the crosswise system of yarns (or weft) in the weaving process. As he was performing this operation, a spinner regulated the winding of the yarn with the left hand, varied the speed of the spindles by adjusting the handle of a flywheel with the right hand, and with his knee and left hand pushed the carriage on which the spindles were mounted back toward the frame. To do the job well required exceptional skill and more than ordinary strength. Spinners were also responsible for maintaining their machines, which necessitated a thorough knowledge of the equipment that could only be obtained through an extended training period of three years or more.[13]

With the adoption of self-acting mules by British mill owners, a process that began in the 1840s and extended into the 1880s, mule spinning became a simpler job. Although spinners still needed to exercise attentiveness and some degree of dexterity, newcomers required only a brief period of training to learn the craft. These changes thus placed British spinners' claims to craft status in dire jeopardy, and they adopted a number of expedients to protect their privileged position on the shop floor: they insisted on the right to perform such maintenance functions as oiling the spindles and repairing the straps and bands that drove the machine's moving parts; they preserved the authority to recruit helpers; and most important, they maintained the power to supervise their helpers without managerial interference.[14]

Even though British manufacturers could have employed the new technology to strip spinners of these traditional prerogatives, they apparently made no serious effort to do so. There were several reasons for their reluctance. One was the intense degree of competitiveness that characterized interfirm relations in the largely nonintegrated British spinning industry. Employers were seldom able to match the disciplined unity of worker organizations, and any firm that chose to go it alone faced the threat of extinction. Moreover, from the mill owners' perspective, the mode of shop-floor organization thus established functioned reasonably well. Not only did the spinners ensure that their helpers produced acceptable levels of output, but changing the system would have required investments in new managerial structures that most manufacturers were unwilling to make.[15]

This was the system of productive relations to which Lancashire spinners were accustomed, and which they sought to replicate in American spinning rooms. But unlike their English counterparts, Fall River manufacturers had no intention of relinquishing control of the shop floor — to mule spinners or anyone else. As one local mill owner characterized the 1870 strike, "I think the question with the spinners was not on wages, but whether they or the manufacturers should rule." Even more important, mill owners' efforts to preserve that rule rested on a degree of unity unknown to English employers. Bound together by a broad range of business and family ties, Fall River manufacturers used the Board of Trade to meet all challenges with a coordinated deployment of their formidable resources.[16]

At the same time, Fall River millowners were not the least bit reluctant to establish the managerial structures needed to maximize output in spinning rooms. By the 1870s, one overseer, assisted by four second hands, directed the work of nine spinners and their helpers in local mills — a mode of organization that differed markedly from staffing procedures in Lancashire spinning rooms, where one foreman supervised twenty or more teams of spinners. Nor was this all. To ensure that overseers exercised appropriate diligence, Fall River employers linked supervisory wages to departmental output. The result, as the 1882 MBSL report observed, was a system of productive relations in which spinners were "considered to be the hardest worked of any class, running two or more mules, and walking a distance variously estimated at from 15 to 25 miles a day." And when spinners questioned workplace irregularities, their complaints often fell on deaf ears, which further reminded them of how far they were from Lancashire. As one immigrant operative told MBSL investigators, "We could always make a complaint of any grievance there; but here, if we dare to do such a thing, we are told that if we don't like it we can get out."[17]

With this information in hand, it is now possible to answer the question posed by MBSL staffers in their 1882 report: "Why is it that the working people of Fall River are in constant turmoil, when at Lowell and Lawrence they are quiet?" Unlike the bureau's conclusions, which stressed the importance of differential growth rates, our interpretation focuses elsewhere: in the efforts of English-born operatives, particularly mule spinners, to re-create customary forms of productive relations in Spindle City mills. Compared with Lowell and Lawrence, not only did Fall River attract a markedly greater number of English immigrants, but mule spindles also comprised a much larger proportion of total spindlage in local mills: 90 percent in 1870, compared with 43 percent in Lawrence plants and 26 percent in Lowell factories. When the industrial heritage of these immigrant workers collided with the intransigence of Fall River employers, conflict was inevitable.[18]

Although this explanation disposes of one question, it raises others. How, for example, did Fall River workers and mill owners move from the state of affairs described above to the system of industrial relations mentioned in the chapter's introduction? Given the bitter nature of class relations in Gilded Age Fall River, it would not appear to be the kind of locale to develop the region's most successful system of collective bargaining. But it was; and ironically, the struggles of the 1870s helped make it so. These conflicts established a tradition of worker militancy that did not go away. There would be more strikes in the next two decades, and with each one manufacturers would become progressively less resistant to worker demands for union recognition. The outcome of these early battles was also important. Having established their authority on the shop floor, manufacturers were more willing to discuss other matters. While they considered control issues nonnegotiable, they became more flexible as worker grievances increasingly focused on the wage-effort bargain.

Indeed, evidence of this shift toward increased interclass dialogue was already discernible in the early 1880s. It can be seen, for example, in the seemingly confused observations of a Fall River mill treasurer interviewed by MBSL investigators. After stating that the secretary of the mule spinners' union was paid fifteen dollars a week "to look out for the interests of the Union and to stir up trouble," this executive inexplicably added: "He is a good enough fellow, and we understand him and he us." We can clear up this confusion, and at the same time deepen our understanding of the Fall River system of industrial relations, by taking a closer look at this union leader: no one did more to shape that system than Robert Howard.[19]

ROBERT HOWARD WAS a Lancashire Irishman — though apart from his Catholicism there was little about the man that was identifiably Irish. Not only did he speak "in the choppy dialect of old England," but the content of what he had to say invariably reflected the views of a son of the English working class. Long after he had departed Lancashire, Howard would — with a regularity that was almost instinctual — preface his statements about labor and industry with some reference to English conditions. The main sources of Howard's attachment to the Old Country were his craft and his union. After entering the mills at age eight, he began spinning seven years later and within a decade had become president of the Stockport Spinners' Union. Offered employment as an overseer, Howard declined "because he could not do the domineering required." The pride and satisfaction he derived from his work may also have been a factor. As he later remarked, some years after he had left the mills and become a full-time trade union official: "I was an extraordinary good spinner — if I do say it myself — and I left with some reluctance."[20]

However able a spinner Howard may have been, he is best remembered as a trade unionist. Blacklisted for his union activities in England, Howard came to Fall River in 1873; five years later he was secretary of the Fall River Spinners' Association. As a union leader, Howard was often the target of criticism. Sometimes it was quite harsh, as happened in 1880 when he ran for a seat in the state legislature against George Gunton, editor of the *Labor Standard* and spokesman for Fall River weavers. In a series of savage attacks, Gunton verbally assaulted Howard's personal character and professional competence, claiming that he had "sold out" local workers. Howard responded by urging workers to vote for "men who are not agitators by profession, but who are actuated by a principle acquired through patient toil and life's rigid struggles." This sober and restrained message proved effective. And if the results of the 1880 election were any measure of Howard's popularity among Fall River workers, he was very popular indeed. In a three-way contest, Howard trounced Gunton by a decisive margin, 3,349 to 304, while the third candidate received 1,924 votes.[21]

Our main concern here is how Howard sought to help workers deal with "life's rigid struggles." Over the years he had much to say in this regard, but above all else he repeatedly stressed the importance of organization. "By organization," he observed, "capital gets the lion's share of profits from products; and labor should not complain, if it has the same opportunity and neglects to use it." During his tenure as head of the Fall River Spinners' Association, Howard continued efforts begun during the 1850s to organize spinners in other regional textile centers. He also urged workers in other crafts to follow the spinners' example, though he was less likely to provide direct assistance for such drives. And during the 1890s, he not only persuaded the American Federation of Labor (AFL) to begin organizing southern textile workers, but made two organizational tours of his own during the fall of 1896 and the spring of 1898.[22]

For Howard the benefits organization conferred on workers extended well beyond the workplace and union hall. By joining a union and participating in its affairs, workers as a matter of course developed a host of salutary characteristics that made them better people: "They learn self-respect for each other. They become acquainted with the forms of procedure. . . . They become greater readers and reasoners. Where [unions] become firmly established, reading rooms become multiplied, and the drinking saloons are less patronized." But simply forming a union was not enough. The quintessential business unionist, Howard insisted that to be effective labor organizations required a solid material foundation. Unions that lacked such a basis were not only ill equipped to conduct strikes; they were more likely to find strikes necessary, because employers would not take them seriously. "The same respect that is shown to wealthy corporations," Howard contended, "is shown to the wealthy organization of workers as a rule." "The great hindrance to the success of labor organizations in this country," he added, "is due to their poverty."[23]

In these comments, Howard expressed opinions that would become enduring characteristics of the Fall River model of trade unionism. On one hand, his remarks illuminate important shortcomings of the system. The stress on organizational self-sufficiency meant that the industry's least-skilled and worst-paid operatives could expect little help from their more affluent and better organized coworkers. Insistence on these rigorous standards also prevented Fall River unions from fully participating in broad-based organizations such as the Knights of Labor and the United Textile Workers (UTW). Ever fearful that they might be called upon to subsidize weaker unions, they joined such bodies but ultimately went their own way. By the 1910s, Spindle City unionism comprised a small federation of craft locals whose influence was largely restricted to the Fall River–New Bedford area.

At the same time, though, Howard's observations exemplify the hardheaded pragmatism that made Fall River unionism more effective than organization elsewhere in the region. This was especially evident in the ways Spindle City unionists reacted to the market. As industrial veterans, Fall River's British-trained union leaders knew they worked in a competitive industry; they also knew that shifts in the business cycle influenced the size of employer earnings and their capacity to improve the wage-effort bargain. For them the question was never one of accepting or rejecting the market. Instead, they claimed an equal right to interpret what the market was saying, and they were constantly gathering and assessing price data as part of an effort to make the market work for them. They were, as Eric Hobsbawm aptly put it, people who had learned "the rules of the game."[24]

There is abundant evidence of this preoccupation with market conditions. The 1870 strike resulted in part from the spinners' belief that "the state of the markets does not warrant so great a reduction as now offered to us." On other occasions, market signals called for restraint. In 1875, George Gunton attempted to prevent a weavers' strike by warning that the depressed state of the industry gave employers an insurmountable advantage. Although the weavers did not listen to Gunton and other union leaders in 1875, Fall River workers generally took such warnings very seriously. Their views were perhaps best expressed by a local operative interviewed by MBSL investigators: "The market is very low now, and the profits are small, so, happily, the help are contented; but we think, and I think rightly, that when profits are large we ought to share in them. This may be a foolish notion, but it is one we have been brought up to, and we cannot very well rid ourselves of it." This is a fascinating statement that reveals the double-edged nature of what engaging the market meant to Fall River workers; how it induced caution, but how it also expanded worker definitions of labor's rights in a capitalist society.[25]

Among local unionists, none demonstrated a greater interest in market developments than Robert Howard. In trade union circles, his reputation as a market analyst was so widespread that one could learn of his prowess in a midwestern labor journal. "He keeps so close a watch on the market price of the raw material and of the manufactured article," an 1888 story in the *Detroit Advance* said of Howard, "that he knows just when to ask an advance or to resort to a cut-down." Howard's response to the market closely paralleled that of the Fall River operative quoted above. During periods of recession, he strongly and repeatedly advised restraint, urging union members to base their actions on a "dispassionate discussion of market conditions." Although some spinners doubtless grew weary of such counsel, they rarely challenged him. At the same time, Howard sought to use the market to increase labor's share of employer earnings. To realize this aim, Howard pointed to the Lancashire example and recommended adoption of standard price lists that related wages to changing market and workplace conditions. With such lists, he told a U.S. Senate committee, "I think we could get a fair week's wages for a fair week's work." "All manufactures would then stand on an equality with each other," he explained, "and we would all know what the profit was that was being made, and the proper share that each party was entitled to." The English system also provided safeguards against chiseling. Whenever a problem occurred there, Howard related, workers notified their union secretary, who in turn contacted the secretary of the Manufacturers' Board. Together they would then visit the mill in question to examine the indicators used to determine wages, "and if they find that there has been any cheating or anything wrong, they have got to come down to the fair thing."[26]

Howard hoped to establish a similar system in Fall River, and throughout the 1880s there were growing indications that he might succeed. Although local manufacturers did not share Howard's concern about doing the "fair thing," his constant invocation of market principles was a language they well understood. Mill owners were also beginning to realize that the spinners' union had staying power, and that neither blacklists nor threats to replace mule spindles with ring frames was likely to destroy it. In November 1886, they finally granted Howard his wish and agreed to a sliding scale arrangement that based spinners' wages on the difference between the market price of raw cotton and print cloth.[27]

As it turned out, the establishment of the sliding scale marked the high point of Howard's tenure as a union leader. The following decades witnessed a marked decline in mule spinner fortunes. One problem was that the sliding scale seldom worked as well as Howard had hoped. Because of the ever-increasing variety of cloth types produced in Fall River mills, together with differences in operating conditions among plants, establishing mutually acceptable margins proved much more difficult than anticipated. The result was constant suspicion that manufacturers, rather than doing the "fair thing," were manipulating the plan to their own advantage. Moreover, Howard's efforts to maintain the agreement, which applied only to mule spinners, widened the breach between them and other operatives. When the latter complained, Howard bluntly informed them that he was paid to represent the spinners, and they did not expect him "to imperil their interests while looking after the interests of others who won't become organized to try to help themselves."[28]

Much more troubling, for Howard at least, was the dwindling proportion of mule spindles in Fall River mills. By substituting ring frames for mules, manufacturers could fill their spinning departments with women and children, who were paid about half of what mule spinners received and who were considerably less demanding. As ring-spinning technology improved and existing mules wore out, local mill owners did just that. Where mules had accounted for 90 percent of total spindlage in 1870, they comprised only 24 percent in 1904. Although mule spinners would not be totally displaced for some decades yet, their influence among Fall River unionists inevitably declined. Labor would make further advances — advances that built on spinner achievements. But these initiatives no longer originated in local spinning departments. As workers began to look elsewhere for leadership, they increasingly found it in the weave rooms of Spindle City mills. And it is now time to take a closer look at the weavers' world.[29]

IN 1938, THE National Association of Cotton Manufacturers asked member mills for data on the amount of time needed to train various groups of workers. Responding to the request, Walter Whipple of the Nashua Manufacturing Company was able to furnish relatively precise information for most occupations: picker tenders and card tenders, for example, required one month, while spinners generally needed three. But when he reached the weaving department, Whipple was no longer so specific. "In regard to weavers," he wrote, "we have no idea." "[A]s in all cases," he added, "it is a question of promotion from battery hand to weaver, and those operatives who work as battery hands very readily become weavers after having become familiar with the motions of the loom." Just how long this took, however, Whipple could not say. All he really knew for certain about weavers was that Nashua Manufacturing used "very few learners as such."[30]

Walter Whipple's uncertainty is not surprising and should not be seen as evidence of professional incompetence. Weavers occupied an anomalous position in shop-floor hierarchies that makes them difficult to classify. The standard categories of skilled and unskilled obscure more than they clarify. Weavers received neither the pay nor the prestige associated with such male-dominated crafts as mule spinning, loom fixing, or slasher tending. Yet they were better compensated and more skilled than most other operatives. Comprising one-third of the workforce in a typical textile mill, they played a vital role in the production process.

The best way to understand that role is by looking at what they did. On traditional power looms, weavers had four main tasks: replenishing the weft yarn in shuttles; repairing broken warp yarns; correcting cloth defects by "picking out" weft threads that broke the weaving pattern; and monitoring the operation of looms. Although the installation of automatic looms at century's end eliminated some of these tasks, weaving remained a complex job. As one Lowell weaver recalled: "It's a job that you had to like. I liked it because it was very difficult. You have to like it in order to want to do it. There are ways of looking at cloth so you can pick up imperfections just like that. You don't even have to have a good eye if you know how to do it, if you know how to walk at it and shade it, you can do anything." For other weave-room veterans, what one heard was just as important as what one saw. "You've got to know your section," a Fall River weaver observed. "When you get close to a loom, it sounds different. It comes to you, the longer you're on. To me, the loom, I can tell if it's functioning right just by the sound." Listening to these operatives, one can see why an experienced mill executive like Walter Whipple discussed weaver training with such uncertainty: people did not develop this kind of shop-floor savvy overnight.[31]

For many weavers, work was more than a paycheck; it was also a source of great personal satisfaction. Many of the women weavers with whom Jessie Davis worked in a Lawrence woolen mill preferred factory labor to housework, "partly because of a real pride in [their] trade." Expressions of that pride are not hard to find. "You feel that you have accomplished something when you have finished the day," said one New Hampshire weaver decades later. "You know that you've done something and that you are using your head to do it." The reasons why weavers found their work so satisfying were perhaps best stated by labor economist Gladys Palmer: "Just as a good machinist enjoys working with metals, a good weaver knows about the construction of fabrics, wants to make a perfect product, and is interested in design. Many weavers are craftsmen in spirit." Lawrence mule spinner Anthony Parolisi not only agreed, but placed weavers in the same category as members of the industry's male-dominated crafts. Although it is unlikely that Fall River's British-born spinners would have made a similar concession, this really did not matter to most weavers. In textile mills, they were important people — and they knew it. Compared with most other mill occupations, one English visitor observed, labor turnover tended to be higher among weavers because they realized there was "always a demand for a good weaver."[32]

It is also noteworthy that whatever their differences — and they were sometimes considerable — weavers and spinners developed similar views of industrial relations. In 1889, for example, during the midst of one of numerous campaigns to unionize New England weavers, Lawrence Weavers' Protective Union No. 1 issued a declaration of principles that could have been written by Robert Howard. In addition to calling for a just wage and reduced hours, the weavers expressed a desire to "cultivate by all honorable means a friendly feeling between employer and employee." They also resolved to promote their "elevation in society as men." These were all sentiments that Fall River spinners could readily endorse. But mule spinning was a male-dominated craft. This was not the case in weaving departments, where women typically constituted half or more of the workforce. Although the statement may only have been an unconscious expression of the masculine biases so deeply embedded in Gilded Age trade unionism, it does raise questions about the nature of gender relations in New England weave rooms — questions that assume more than passing significance when it is further noted that some male weavers wished to reduce the proportion of women operatives in the industry.[33]

One such weaver was James Green of New Bedford. In testimony before an 1898 session of the Massachusetts legislature's Joint Labor Committee, Green recommended passage of a law that would bar married women from working in textile mills. Taken aback, committee members raised a number of objections. But Green was ready for them. Asked about the hardships such a law might create for families dependent on multiple incomes, he responded, "my wife don't work in the mill and it don't work any hardship on her." He further contended that the measure "would materially benefit our wage system."[34]

It is possible that Green was only expressing his own cranky version of the family wage doctrine that became increasingly popular in trade union circles at the turn of the century. None of the other weavers who testified before the committee seconded his proposal. Moreover, as Marc Miller has observed of Lowell, so can it be said of all regional textile centers: "no rigid ideology had ever kept women out of the factories; local custom only restricted their *competing* with men when the labor market tightened." It may also be coincidence that Green was a weaver. Yet there are reasons to believe otherwise. As noted, weavers occupied a peculiar position in shop-floor hierarchies: above the majority of textile operatives but below the male-dominated crafts. For women, weaving presented an opportunity to move beyond the low-paid, semiskilled occupations to which they were confined in most mass-production industries. But for men — especially those who had little hope of becoming loom fixers — weaving could be something quite different: having to work with so many women may have been a constant reminder that other males stood above them in the occupational structure. If so, this certainly explains why Lawrence weavers were so concerned about their "elevation in society as men." It also gives meaning to James Green's vague remark that enacting his proposal "would work such a change in the minds of men that things would become very much better."[35]

This is all speculation of course. But there are good reasons for raising such questions. Although no one ever doubted the willingness of weavers to take their grievances into the streets, many observers believed they were unorganizable. As one Fall Riverite, W. B. McCauley, remarked at an 1867 meeting to organize Spindle City weavers: "Some say it can't be done; there are too many women among the weavers." McCauley himself did not share this opinion. All obstacles can be surmounted, he declared, "and we want the women to understand the matter and work with us. God intended that we should work together, in a spirit of unity and sympathy." But the history of weaver unionism indicates that such barriers as existed were not easily overcome. One reason may have been the reluctance of male weavers to exhibit that "spirit of unity and sympathy" of which McCauley spoke.[36]

This was by no means the only problem confronting organizers. Because weavers constituted so large a proportion of the workforce in most plants, mill owners viewed weaver unionism with particular alarm. It was one thing to recognize the spinners, who comprised a small and declining fraction of the workforce. Dealing with weaver representatives was another matter entirely, because it could easily lead to a broad-based unionism that would drive up wage costs in all mill departments. No betting person would have wagered that effective weaver organization could be accomplished peacefully.[37]

The first of several major confrontations that preceded the creation of a stable weavers' union in Fall River began on March 11, 1889, when the recently formed Weavers Protection Union struck for higher wages. Local mill owners conceded that they could afford the increase, but they had no intention of making any concession that might legitimize the weavers' organization. As one manufacturer bluntly put it, "We positively will not recognize the Weavers Union if the mills remained closed until the belts rot on the shafts." Although such intransigence was no surprise to the weavers, several other problems cut the strike short. Not only did the union lack the financial resources needed to support an extended walkout, but the mule spinners' refusal to cooperate with the striking weavers reinforced the mill owners' resolve to stand firm. In late March, union leaders decided that further resistance would be futile and called off the strike.[38]

Afterward, the Weavers Protective Union fractured into shop organizations and appeared ready to add its name to an already lengthy list of groups that had unsuccessfully attempted to organize Spindle City weavers. But this time it would be different. In 1890, the weavers reorganized and formed the Weavers Progressive Association, which began laying the material foundation for future conflict. Two years later, the *Labor Leader* reported, "Never since that memorable year 1875, when the Weavers' Protective Association numbered 5,000 members in good financial standing, have the [Fall River] weavers been so well equipped for a fight." This was high tribute, given the *Labor Leader*'s ardent promotion of business unionism, and the weavers were determined to put these accumulating resources to use. In 1892, they organized a successful thirteen-week strike when the Narragansett Mill lengthened weaving cuts without a commensurate increase in wages; and during the depression year of 1894, they responded to a 10 percent wage reduction by shutting down nearly all of the city's mills.[39]

The strike began in mid-August and lasted until late October. Again, however, Howard's spinners went their own way. After joining the weavers in September, when improved market conditions provided a firmer basis for resisting the reduction, the spinners later arranged a separate settlement with local mill owners. Howard claimed that weaver unreliability justified such action, and that had the mule spinners not withdrawn, they "would have been left holding the bag in their traditional lonely position as the sole opponents of management." This may have been true at one time. But it was no longer so, and the weavers saw Howard's remarks for what they were: the self-serving rationalizations of a once-powerful union that feared the future. They also recognized that it was now time to take matters into their own hands.[40]

On one hand, Spindle City operatives helped spearhead a regionwide revival of weaver unionism. In 1895, they joined representatives from New Bedford and Clinton to form the Massachusetts State Federation of Weavers. Two years later, the organization widened its scope and changed its name to the New England Federation of Weavers. As weavers' locals began to appear in cities and towns throughout New England, the federation again broadened its ambitions and in 1898 became the National Federation of Textile Operatives. At the same time, Spindle City weavers were becoming the most powerful body on the Fall River Textile Council. Formed in 1895, the council was a federation of five unions that included a sizable number of low-paid, semiskilled operatives as well as such male-dominated crafts as the mule spinners, loom fixers, and slasher tenders. Not only did women comprise five-sixths of the carders' 1,200 members, but in 1898 the mule spinners initiated a drive to organize local ring spinners. Despite such efforts, the spinners' decline continued. And at century's end, the weavers had by reason of their numbers and militancy assumed a dominant position in council affairs: in 1900, one of every two Fall River textile unionists was a weaver, and their vanguard role in every major strike since 1884 had earned them a reputation for aggressiveness that no other local union could soon hope to match.[41]

MEANWHILE, THERE WERE indications that Fall River manufacturers had begun to reassess their views of textile unionism. This at least was the opinion of Robert T. Davis, who was president of three local mills. "For years," Davis told the U.S. Industrial Commission in 1900, Spindle City owners had believed "they should control the situation." Over time, though, manufacturers gradually recognized that neither capital nor labor "could get along without the other." A major turning point, according to Davis, occurred in 1897, when representatives of both sides met formally in citywide negotiations. At this conference, union leaders agreed to accept a 10 percent wage reduction; and the following year, when New Bedford operatives shut down that city's mills, it was the first time in a generation that a pattern-setting regional strike had originated outside Fall River. Not surprisingly, Davis assured the committee that local mill owners had every intention of continuing the meetings.[42]

For our purposes, the fact that the 1897 conference took place at all is more significant than its immediate consequences. As Davis noted, the meeting marked an important step in the creation of the Fall River system of industrial relations. We thus need to ask: What had changed? Why were local mill owners now prepared to negotiate citywide agreements with union leaders? One contributing factor was the appearance of a major split within their own ranks. Where manufacturers, acting through the Board of Trade, had traditionally presented a cohesive front on labor matters, such unity could no longer be taken for granted. The main reason was Matthew C. D. Borden of the Fall River Iron Works. Between 1889 and 1895, the Iron Works constructed four mills; and by the latter year, it was the city's largest employer. In his labor policies, Borden charted an independent course. His practice of advancing wages at the earliest sign of improved market conditions not only enabled the

Iron Works to secure the "best class" of workers; it also put pressure on other manufacturers.[43]

What made Borden's policies particularly unsettling to other mill owners was the changing state of product markets for local goods. Because Fall River had long dominated the national print goods market, strikes had often benefited local producers by reducing output and thus driving up cloth prices. In 1871, for example, Isaac B. Chase of the Tecumseh Mills told MBSL investigators that he thought the previous year's walkout had aided manufacturers "so far as money-making is concerned." When we note that Fall River mill owners had no greater concern than "money-making," it is easy to understand why they were so willing to adopt this course of action. By the 1890s, though, this too had changed. Although Fall River still held a commanding position in the print goods market, expanded local production of other fabrics meant that fewer mills would benefit from changes in print cloth prices. At the same time, the rise of the southern textile industry increased the potential costs of strikes. With these developments, manufacturers doubtless reasoned, dealing with the Textile Council might not be such a bad thing after all.[44]

These new conditions were certainly important. But they do not fully explain the changing consciousness of mill owners described by Robert Davis — why they had come to believe that capital and labor "could not get along without the other." There were other, equally important reasons for this change, and they are to be found in the double-edged nature of worker responses to capitalist development. For all their militancy, Spindle City operatives had always maintained that their foremost aim was to establish a peaceful and prosperous industrial environment based on the principles of reciprocity and justice. Manufacturers had never totally ignored these declarations, and during the 1890s they had more reason than ever to listen. They may also have had greater occasion to hear what workers had to say, as there is some evidence of increased social contact between the two groups. One institution that provided opportunities for such intercourse was the Coffee Tavern, a temperance dining hall and reading room manufacturers provided for their workers. According to Jonathan Thayer Lincoln, a local mill executive, some of the city's largest employers met weekly at the tavern during the nineties to discuss labor problems over dinner. Afterward, Lincoln recalled, mill owners and workers "smoked their pipes and played games together, and each returned to the factory with a higher regard for the opinions of the other."[45]

Because Lincoln sometimes tended to romanticize industrial relations, his observations should not be accepted at face value. But we should not dismiss them, either. Temperance lodges had a certain attraction for Fall River labor leaders, given the strong emphasis they placed on promoting working-class respectability; and they may well have participated in these gatherings. Even more important, their views on labor relations contained much that appealed to mill owners. This was nowhere more evident than in their remarks before the U.S. Industrial Commission. All five secretaries of the Textile Council unions testified, and each contended that the road to industrial peace ran through the union hall. Joseph Jackson of the slasher tenders described how the council's actions had averted conflict in 1898, while others maintained that union recognition had reduced the number of "impulsive" strikes in Fall River mills. "Twenty or more years ago in this city, when organizations were very rare," Thomas O'Donnell of the mule spinners observed, "it was a common thing to have strikes more or less every week." That this state of affairs no longer existed was mainly attributable to a new willingness on the part of manufacturers "to meet us to consider our grievances." And well they should, James Tansey of the carders added: "The organization, in my opinion, has become educational to the operative, and . . . where there is no organization there is nobody to control them, nobody to give them advice, and they become impulsive, and the first thing you know they are out on strike."[46]

Following the example set by Robert Howard, Fall River union leaders also continued to monitor market conditions. Although they did so mainly to prevent unjustifiable wage reductions by chiseling mill owners, reference to the market did provide labor and capital with a common language for the discussion of their differences. And whenever the two sides reached similar conclusions, union interest in market fluctuations became an additional source of industrial peace. As Thomas O'Donnell observed, "there are times when competition is so severe that for our own welfare and that of the community we live in we are willing to make the sacrifice and continue at our employment." At such moments, O'Donnell added, union leaders returned to their organizations and recommended acceptance of proposed wage reductions.[47]

This did not mean that Fall River union leaders had become thor-

oughgoing collaborationists. For one thing, they did not totally re-
nounce strikes. Thomas O'Donnell, for example, strongly advocated
arbitration and believed work stoppages were "a great injury both to the
employer and to the employee and to the community at large." "Still," he
added, "they are what I call a necessary evil, and although loss results,
pecuniarily speaking, at the time, still good results accrue afterwards."
Even where strikers did not achieve their aims, O'Donnell explained,
walkouts prompted "a more careful consideration of the question at
issue" and thus reduced the likelihood of future conflict. In short, reconciling the oftentimes disparate interests of capital and labor required a
certain degree of worker militancy.[48]

It would be equally erroneous to infer from James Tansey's remarks
that maintaining labor quiescence was the primary function of Fall
River's union secretaries. They did, as Tansey and O'Donnell observed,
make every effort to prevent "impulsive" strikes. But they also gave
operatives a means of questioning shop-floor irregularities without fear
of dismissal. "It was the terrible black list that brought about the necessity of men like myself," Joseph Jackson told the Industrial Commission.
And their presence in local mills meant that workers no longer had to
bring their grievances to overseers whose invariable response was: "If
you don't like it, get out." In addressing these complaints, union leaders
not only performed a vital and much-appreciated service for rank-and-
filers. Such activities served as constant reminders of the basically adversarial nature of the industrial order they were trying to reform.[49]

Finally, there were several important issues on which manufacturers
and union officials had serious differences. Perhaps the most significant
concerned technological change and the increased work assignments
that were the usual consequence of innovation. Their understanding of
industrial history made British workers instinctively suspicious of these
developments. As one Fall River operative observed during the early
eighties, "My father used to support his family of six off of the product
of one hand-loom, in England; with the improvements in machinery it
takes eight looms . . . to support two persons in this city." These views
were widely shared. Robert Howard was one of many immigrant workers who also believed textile workers would be better off "with the old
hand-loom." "I do not think that labor-saving machinery has been of the
slightest advantage to the operatives," he told a U.S. Senate committee.
"The tendency," Howard added, "has been not only to reduce wages,
but also to dismiss help."[50]

These were not simply the beliefs of a first-generation immigrant steeped in British industrial lore. Howard's successors in the regional labor movement expressed similar fears. This was certainly so among weavers. Speaking at century's end, Thomas Cahill of the Lawrence Weavers Association echoed Howard's views about the labor-displacing consequences of technological change; and James Whitehead of the Fall River Weavers Progressive Association observed, "If new and improved machinery means anything, it ought to mean a reduction in the hours of labor." But few believed that technological innovation would better workers' lives, either in terms of hours or compensation. Asked whether the increased loom assignments made possible by recent advances in weaving machinery raised wages, Matthew Hart of the New Bedford weavers' union remarked, "[Weavers] may receive a little more for their work, but they finally come down to the old standard." Responding to a similar question, Albert Hubbard perhaps said it best, at least so far as most textile workers were concerned: "If there is any good effect the manufacturer gets it."[51]

Weavers had ample reason to feel this way. At the turn of the century, technological change had a major impact on weave rooms. The most important innovation was the automatic loom. On traditional power looms, operatives had to insert a new bobbin of yarn in the shuttle at least once every eight minutes, which limited the number of looms a weaver could tend. The new looms not only removed this barrier to increased productivity by automatically replacing exhausted bobbins, they also introduced an improved stop-motion device that reduced the degree of vigilance weavers had to exercise by halting a loom whenever a warp thread broke. The result was an increase in loom assignments and a reduction in the skill needed to tend a loom.[52]

Although Fall River manufacturers were slow to adopt automatic looms, they did begin installing two surrogate innovations at the turn of the century: longer bobbins that reduced the frequency of bobbin replacement, and electrical warp-stop motions that performed the same functions as the stop-devices attached to automatic looms. They also increased machine assignments from eight to ten or more looms and reduced the price per cut by 30 percent. Under the best of circumstances, weavers would have had grave reservations about these developments. As it was, the manner in which mill owners introduced the changes reinforced the operatives' worst suspicions about the baneful effects of labor-saving machinery. Not only did the new devices fail to work as advertised, but weavers also complained that they were making less money than they formerly did. Moreover, some mills increased loom assignments without adopting the new stop-motions, a practice that had especially onerous consequences for the workers affected. "We never seen no electric stops at our mill—just got four more straight looms," one weaver stated. "It makes you crazy watchin' em."[53]

If Fall River manufacturers seriously sought better relations with their workers, this was not the way to go about it. And in July 1904, when they announced the second major wage reduction in a year, the mounting bitterness of local weavers could no longer be contained. Although the Textile Council advised against a strike, members of the three weave-room unions—the loom fixers, slasher tenders, and weavers—ignored their leaders' recommendations and voted overwhelmingly to take their grievances into the streets. On July 25, the last citywide strike in Fall River history began. With the exception of Matthew Borden's Fall River Iron Works and a few other mills that did not reduce wages, Spindle City textile plants would remain closed for six long months.[54]

The 1904 strike marked a major turning point in the evolution of the Fall River system of industrial relations. As journalist Herbert Francis Sherwood observed two decades later, "Out of it grew the determination on both sides that never again should there be a strike in Fall River if negotiation could prevent it." That a six-month walkout, which began with such anger and concluded without a restoration of wages, should end so amicably was not as surprising as it might seem. For one thing, union leaders made every effort to curb overt displays of worker hostility. They were apparently successful. According to an MBSL bulletin issued during the fifth month of the strike, everyone involved characterized Fall River labor leaders "as intelligent and conservative men[;]" and the strikers "have proved themselves to be law-abiding citizens."[55]

Even more important, local mill owners realized that, to achieve industrial peace, formal recognition of trade unions would have to be accompanied by substantive concessions that addressed worker yearnings for reciprocity and justice. A number of weavers, for example, had maintained that they were not opposed to improved machinery per se. But they believed manufacturers should share the benefits of technological change with workers; and, as an MBSL investigator observed, they objected to the installation of "devices which make the work harder without a proportionate compensating increase in wages." Influenced by Lancashire and mule spinner precedents, union leaders had attempted to establish a basis for such increases by negotiating a standard list. Prior to the strike, these efforts met stony resistance from Fall River mill owners. They afterward proved more accommodating.[56]

As noted, the settlement that concluded the 1904 strike did not restore recent wage reductions. But it did attempt to address weaver demands for a more equitable distribution of the corporate surplus by fixing piece rates on an eight-loom basis, and by establishing a sliding scale arrangement that related wage rates to the changing margin between the market price of cotton and that of certain standard cuts of print cloth. The new pact did not create the conflict-free industrial environment that mill owners desired. Some manufacturers refused to accept the agreement, while others attempted to evade its terms, thus prompting a series of small strikes; and in 1907 a major dispute over the standard length of weave cuts nearly resulted in another citywide shutdown. Yet something had changed. During the 1907 disagreement, mill owners exhibited an unusual readiness to expand bargaining procedures. "Should the result of the conferences which we thus propose not be satisfactory," George Hills of the Cotton Manufacturers' Association wrote weaver secretary James Whitehead, "it might be proper to refer the matter to a committee of seven, three of whom shall be chosen by the Weavers' Progressive Association, three by the Manufacturers' Association, and the seventh member to be chosen by the six appointed as above." And as William Mass has observed, even the strikes that occurred during these years were settled by union committees in ways that indicated an increased routinization of bargaining.[57]

Despite these developments, the sliding scale arrangement worked no better for weavers than an earlier agreement had for mule spinners. One problem was that the crude measures used to determine margins neglected important factors that influenced the local industry's profitability. That the margin was based on print cloth prices — at a time when Fall River mills were beginning to produce an increasing variety of other fabrics — provided manufacturers with further opportunities for evasion. For these and other reasons, wage rates tended to move down much more readily than they moved up. By 1910, workers had seen enough and the experiment was abandoned.[58]

Because the weavers' experience with the sliding scale so closely paralleled that of the mule spinners, it is worth asking: Why did Fall River workers continue to put such great stock in an arrangement that had failed in the past and, given recent industrial developments, promised to be no more successful in the future? One reason, of course, was the greater stability of such agreements in England, where workers were able to establish industrywide standards for a broad range of cloth constructions. Beyond this, textile operatives saw the sliding scale as an effortless means of achieving equity and stability in a chaotic economic environment that provided too little of either. "The philosophy of the sliding scale," economist Stanley Howard observed in a contemporary assessment of the Fall River plan, "appears to be this: that it will eliminate from industry the friction of industrial warfare and its consequent social waste, at the same time giving reasonable assurance that the individuals and corporations concerned shall lose nothing which the operation of competitive forces would secure for them." This was an alluring vision; it was also an illusion. For, as Howard added and Fall River workers again learned, the construction of a sliding scale, "in the last analysis, is a matter of the comparative bargaining powers of employers and employees."[59]

Although Fall River unions lacked sufficient power to make the sliding scale work to their advantage, they still retained some strength. And the agreement's failure by no means returned them to an earlier state of impotence. This was clearly apparent in their day-to-day operation. The best available evidence of how unions acted to protect workers on the shop floor during this period is the minutes of the Fall River Loom Fixers Association, whose members were responsible for repairing and maintaining weave-room machinery. This is in one sense unfortunate. Because loom fixers were the best paid and most highly skilled workers in weave rooms, they exhibited a sometimes insufferable sense of craft exclusiveness that set them apart from other operatives. They were also, with the possible exception of the mule spinners, the most thoroughly organized group in local mills. This, coupled with the indispensable nature of the functions they performed, gave them a degree of leverage in their dealings with management that few other workers possessed. We must therefore be careful about what conclusions we draw from their records.[60]

Yet, for all their self-importance, loom fixers did not live and work in a vacuum. Because weavers were paid by the piece, their wages depended on the smooth operation of their assigned looms. And if a group of weavers became dissatisfied with a fixer's work, they could make his life miserable — by making incessant and unreasonable demands on his time, or worse yet, by making their discontent known to management. Furthermore, weavers were the only workers in a mill who could take the place of loom fixers during a labor dispute. Most loom fixers were well aware of all this and behaved accordingly. As one Lowell fixer later observed, "If you don't get along with your weavers, you're going to have a hard time."[61]

The Fall River Loom Fixers Association also shared many of the same aims and functioned in much the same way as other local unions. Loom fixers had a duty, one member declared at a 1900 meeting, not only to pay their dues, but to "stand together and put into practice what the secretary, and the executive board is trying to enforce. And that comes under the head of 'justice to the Loom Fixer.'" As long as the union existed, he added, there was no reason for any fixer to shirk his responsibilities to other members of the craft: "Come down to the board, they will instruct you how to act[;] after acting under their instructions, if you cannot accomplish that which is demanded, return and we will back you up."[62]

Within Fall River mills, the loom fixers' union performed a number of services for its members. One was to maintain a standard working schedule. In one incident, the executive committee warned a member that he might be expelled from the union if did not stop working during noon hours; and on another occasion, the board resolved that "brother Joseph Talbot be called down here and the secretary give him an ear ache for working overtime." The union also sought to regulate workloads in local factories. Sometimes this meant securing promises from management to reduce excessive work assignments or to hire spare hands to assist overworked fixers. At other times, it meant ordering fixers at a given mill to refuse increased workloads, even though the fixers were willing to accept the new assignments.[63]

There were also occasions that required a more forceful response. In 1912, for example, the superintendent at Borden Mill No. 1 only reduced the number of looms in the weaving department's Draper sections after the fixers had walked out. In another incident the following year at the Seacomet Mill, a fixer was dismissed after he refused to perform a task for which he was not being paid; and when the union called the other fixers out, the mill treasurer agreed to meet with the union's secretary to resolve the matter. On yet another occasion, a mill agent suggested that a dispute be submitted to a joint committee of the Manufacturers Association and the Loom Fixers Association for arbitration. These and other incidents provide further evidence of the increased routinization of bargaining mentioned above. But they also show that struggle remained an integral part of the Fall River system of industrial relations, and that conciliatory intentions, however frequently and sincerely stated, could not overcome the inherently adversarial nature of those relations.[64]

As noted, loom fixers were not a representative group, and we do not know if other unions were equally aggressive in pursuing their notions of industrial justice. But we do know that the weavers were not idle during this period. Their most noteworthy advances addressed the vitally important workload question. During the 1910s, they established job specifications that fixed a maximum number of operations for weave-room personnel. These agreements limited weaving jobs to forty loom stops per hour and set comparable limits on the tasks performed by battery hands and doffers. Manufacturers doubtless evaded these standards from time to time, particularly when setting up new jobs. But they did not ignore them altogether, and the agreements soon acquired the sanction of tradition — a tradition that would govern workload determination in Fall River weave rooms as late as the 1950s. When we observe that stretchouts and speedups, especially among weavers, were primary causes of worker distress and dissatisfaction after the mid-twenties, the significance of these pacts becomes all the more remarkable.[65]

These agreements added to an already substantial list of union achievements. In an industry in which most workers had duties but no rights, Fall River unions had established a system of industrial relations that imposed some obligations on employers. It is true that not everyone shared equally in these advances; only 20 percent of the local labor force belonged to unions. But to a much greater degree than was the case elsewhere, nearly all workers benefited from the system. Wage determination is one example. Unlike most regional textile centers, where organization was confined to a small craft elite who often cut their own deals with management, weavers set the standard in Fall River and the wages of other occupational groups were adjusted accordingly. Similarly, even though not all weavers held union cards, the job specifications negotiated by union leaders had citywide significance.[66]

This brings us to a major shortcoming of the Fall River system: its isolation from broader regional developments. Apart from New Bedford, where workers erected a similar system of industrial relations, Spindle City unions stood alone in their accomplishments. Moreover, where Fall River unionists had once spearheaded efforts to organize other New England operatives, by the 1920s they had become almost totally preoccupied with their own parochial concerns. So long as general industrial conditions remained relatively stable, they saw little reason to regret their isolation; some may even have viewed Spindle City localism as a mark of distinction that separated the sound business unionism of Fall River from the less orderly practices of workers in other textile centers. But when economic crisis flattened the regional industry at mid-decade, they received a painful lesson in the perils of unionism in one city. These and other matters will be examined in the next chapter.

2 CULTURAL CONFLICT AND ECONOMIC CRISIS

Whereas the previous chapter highlighted the accomplishments of Fall River unionists, this one focuses on their shortcomings. One problematic area was ethnic relations. The Lancashire-born workers who dominated Spindle City unionism were by no means inflexible bigots. Like Robert Howard, many were of Irish descent and had doubtless encountered British ethnoreligious intolerance before departing for America. Familiar with the baneful consequences of cultural divisiveness, they did not expect everyone to be exactly like themselves. But as industrial veterans, they did have certain standards that they felt other members of their class should embrace. When, for example, English workers demanded "a fair day's pay for a fair day's work," they believed they were speaking for all working people. And when they encountered workers from newer immigrant groups who had yet to internalize these standards, they believed they had both a right and a duty to instruct them in the ways of industrial society.

In a city like Fall River, where their large numbers and control of key positions on the shop floor enabled English workers to dominate the textile labor force, they carried out this tutelary role with some effectiveness. But Fall River was not a microcosm of New England. With the exception of New Bedford, no other textile center in the region offered such propitious demographic conditions. This presented a real problem. For, even though the organizing zeal of Spindle City unions ebbed after the turn of the century, trade unionists imbued with Fall River ideals continued to play an important part in the regional labor movement. But efforts to extend those ideals in areas where newer immigrants comprised an overwhelming majority of the workforce made little headway. The Fall River model of unionization — in which a craft elite established standards that other groups then adopted as they formed their own organizations — did not work in these communities. Yet, contrary to the claims of some union leaders, these workers were organizable, as their own union-building activities demonstrated.

Nowhere was this more evident than in Lawrence, the great "Immigrant City" on the Merrimack. And nowhere did mainstream unionism fail more miserably. We will examine that failure, as well as the attempts to create a radical alternative to the established organizations. During the 1910s in Lawrence, the IWW and the Amalgamated Textile Workers posed a profound challenge to the acknowledged rights of capital. In so doing, they also challenged accepted notions of unionism. Not surprisingly, they encountered bitter resistance from both established unions and other social institutions. Of the latter, none reacted more vehemently than the Catholic Church, whose own views of social relations had much in common with those of the mainstream unions.

The final section of this chapter looks at the economic crisis of the 1920s and its effect on textile unions. A half decade before the onset of the Great Depression, a massive wave of mill closings devastated textile communities throughout New England. In southeastern Massachusetts, the crisis not only bankrupted the city of Fall River. It also raised serious questions about the viability of the Fall River system of unionism — questions that foreshadowed and made necessary the development of a new unionism during the 1930s.

"I WENT INTO THE mills of Manchester when I was just a lad," a New Bedford worker recalled during the 1928 strike, "and my mother gave me a union card. I've carried it ever since, and I'll carry it to my grave." This was the voice of Lancashire unionism — forthright, steadfast, and totally convinced of the value of organization. But, this operative believed, not all wage earners shared such convictions. "These Portagee workers and a lot of the other chaps on the picket line," he complained, "don't know what a union means. We couldn't get them to pay dues to the union after the strike is over unless we used guns." This is a telling statement that reveals much about relations between English unionists and newer immigrants. The latter's militancy was plainly not an issue. The workers of whom this operative spoke were, as he conceded, making their presence felt in one of the decade's most bitter strikes. Instead, what he found upsetting was that they "don't know what a union means."[1]

When Lancashire workers talked about the meaning of unionism, they spoke not only of organized efforts to defend a given level of wages and hours. Unionism was also a state of mind: a conviction that workers should share in the economic advances of industry, that their condition should improve in tandem with that of the economy as a whole. Most newer immigrants knew, before emigrating, that American labor standards were higher than in their country of origin; that was the main reason many of them came. Once here, they quickly became familiar with current conditions and often demonstrated a readiness to defend a given standard. British workers understood this and recognized that they could generally rely on the newcomers' support in defensive strikes. But for the English, this was not enough. As Fall River union leaders explained to the U.S. Immigration Commission, newer immigrants "may resist a decrease in wages as energetically as anyone else"; the problem was that "they are not aggressively seeking their general betterment."[2]

Yet by 1911, the year in which the immigration commission published its reports, Fall River union leaders were no longer "aggressively seeking" to integrate newcomers into their organizations. With the consolidation of the Fall River system of unionism after 1900, Spindle City unionists became victims of their own accomplishments and gradually withdrew their support from both local and regional organizing efforts. Well before the 1928 strike in neighboring New Bedford, most newer immigrants in southeastern Massachusetts had begun to look elsewhere for support. Because developments in the Fall River area had region-wide significance, it would be worth our while to examine the process. This can best be done by looking at the different ways in which Fall River unionists interacted with the city's two main groups of newer immigrants, the French Canadians and the Portuguese.

The French Canadian exodus to New England began in earnest during the 1860s. High birthrates in a province that possessed limited areas of arable land and little industry created an economic crisis that forced increasing numbers of Quebecois to look southward for the means of survival. Between 1860 and 1870, 200,000 French Canadians crossed the border; by the turn of the century, another 300,000 would follow. In 1900, nearly one of every two operatives in New England cotton mills hailed from Quebec. Although Fall River was one of the few regional textile centers in which French Canadians achieved a reputation as reliable unionists prior to the 1930s, their initial reception was anything but cordial. According to the city's Lancashire-born unionists, French Canadians posed a grave threat to their well-being: by working for substandard wages; by sending their children into the mills at an early age; by resisting organization; and by refusing to support strike actions. When Fall River's leading French Canadian priest, Father J. B. Bedard, helped recruit strikebreakers during the 1879 walkout, English workers were enraged. And when Carroll Wright in his 1881 report for the Massachusetts Bureau of Statistics of Labor (MBSL) described French Canadians as the "Chinese of the Eastern States," Spindle City unionists readily adopted the characterization as confirmation of their own low opinion of these interlopers from the North.[3]

By century's end, though, Fall River union leaders viewed French Canadians in a much different light. In an 1898 appearance before the labor committee of the Massachusetts legislature, slasher tender secretary Joseph Jackson expressly disavowed the conclusions of the 1881 MBSL report: "[S]ome of you gentlemen may remember what Carroll Wright said and the slur he threw upon a certain class of people in the New England states, and today we have no better class of people in Fall River." Spindle City unionists interviewed a decade later by the U.S. Immigration Commission expressed similar sentiments. Although they believed most newer immigrants had yet to recognize the benefits of organization, this generalization did not apply to French Canadians, who were characterized as "strong trade unionists."[4]

What had happened? In part, Fall River union leaders had misjudged French Canadian workers. It was true that early immigrants had different standards, viewed unions with suspicion, and wanted no part of strikes. But they did have certain expectations, and they were not nearly as submissive as English workers believed. This was not always evident, because they employed their own nonconfrontational strategies for increasing wages. As one French Canadian explained at an 1881 MBSL hearing: "After a few months, and the children have learned a few words of English, being not satisfied with the wages, they ask for more, and, if refused, they move to another village to get more." More important, as increasing numbers of French Canadians came to realize that New England would be their permanent home, their views of unionism changed. Initial arrivals did indeed tend to avoid unions, a French-Canadian priest from New Bedford observed: "but when they had gone back to Canada and returned again, they were almost certain to join the organizations to which the workmen of other nationalities belonged."[5]

This happened in Fall River during the closing decades of the century. Between 1884 and 1894, Spindle City operatives engaged in three major strikes, and on each occasion French Canadians did their part to maintain solidarity, despite the resistance of some older workers and the anti-strike declarations of priests and other community leaders. Although local unionists were slow to allow French Canadians a leadership role in the Fall River Textile Council, they did appreciate their support of council initiatives and welcomed their participation in the social activities of local unions. And just as French Canadians learned about the value of organization from their relations with Fall River unionists, the experience taught the latter much about newer immigrants. The most important of these lessons was that the newcomers shared many of their aspirations. "They come here and know nothing at all about our institutions," Joseph Jackson remarked, "but they are not here very long before they want a little more." Jackson did express concern about the continued threat to existing labor standards posed by more recent arrivals, who were willing to accept "wages that would not support American citizens." Yet, he added, they were not "to blame, for their conditions here at the low rate of wages they receive are far better than their past conditions."[6]

Given this understanding attitude on the part of Fall River union leaders, one would expect that recent arrivals — such as the Portuguese who began entering Fall River in considerable numbers at century's end — would be readily integrated into local labor organizations. But this did not happen. Although individual Portuguese operatives joined unions affiliated with the Fall River Textile Council, the council made no effort to organize the newer immigrants as a group. In his study of Fall River workers, John Cumbler attributed union neglect of the Portuguese and other new immigrants to a combination of cultural aversion and craft exclusiveness. Compared with French Canadians, the Portuguese had darker skin, seemed willing to accept considerably lower living and working conditions, and appeared generally more alien to established Fall Riverites. Moreover, Cumbler adds, the Portuguese arrived during a period when textile unionists had begun to view themselves "purely as craft workers," which led to a sharp curtailment of the social activities that had done so much to facilitate the integration of French Canadian operatives.[7]

Cumbler's analysis is right on the mark and needs only to be restated here. Even though their adherence to *la survivance* — the commitment to preserve the language and customs of French Canada in a hostile Anglo world — made French Canadians more resistant to Americanization than the Portuguese, the latter did not achieve the same degree of acceptance in Fall River. The types of racist slurs hurled at the Portuguese — "dirty

Portuguese" and "Portuguese stinkfish"—provide clear evidence of the social distance that separated them from established groups. Meanwhile, as Fall River union leaders solidified their bargaining relationship with local manufacturers after the 1904 strike, they no longer felt obliged to seek the active involvement of newer immigrants in union affairs. They believed they could achieve their aims without this support, and that groups such as the Portuguese should be grateful for whatever benefits they might derive from unionism.[8]

The organizational structure that emerged might, for lack of a better term, be called "trickle-down unionism." Because wages for all workers were based on what weavers received, both union and nonunion operatives benefited from union-negotiated pay increases. This still left nonunion workers underrepresented. On important matters such as workload and incentive rate adjustments, for example, they had no one to handle their grievances. Yet, as newer immigrants rose in the occupational structure and became eligible for membership in one of the council's five unions—the loom fixers, weavers, slasher tenders, mule spinners, or carders—they too could enjoy the full benefits of organization. This at least was how union leaders viewed the situation. And for some newer immigrants, like the Portuguese workers who became loom fixers during the 1910s and 1920s, the system operated satisfactorily.[9]

But the vast majority of Portuguese operatives were not so fortunate. Confined to the least skilled positions in the carding and spinning departments, they had no protection against managerial impositions. As Portuguese union organizer John Campos recalled in a 1924 statement, "When I was a boy working in the mills as a sweeper, we had troubles and many times we would seek for advice." But no one was listening. Those "near-manufacturers," as Campos characterized local union leaders, "absolutely refused to do anything with the majority of the people." Whatever reasons council leaders might have had for neglecting these workers, rank-and-file submissiveness or an aversion to organization were certainly not among them. By the late 1910s, local manufacturers were complaining that the second generation of Portuguese operatives, having lost their "docility," constituted a "bad lot" in the mills. And when the Textile Council refused to organize them, they formed their own doffers' union under Campos's leadership.[10]

There were doubtless some newer immigrants who, as the British worker quoted at the outset of this section claimed, did not know the meaning of unionism. But they were not nearly as numerous as he believed; indeed, another observer of the 1928 New Bedford strike offered a much different interpretation of their behavior. According to Paul Blanshard, most newcomers were less opposed to organization per se than to the type of unionism that developed in southeastern Massachusetts. During the strike, Blanshard noted, Communist organizers made their greatest gains among Portuguese operatives, "who feel a craft and race barrier between themselves and the British and French skilled workers." Blanshard was by no means the first person to make such an observation. What happened in New Bedford in 1928 had occurred elsewhere during the previous two decades. Wherever newer immigrants had encountered the Fall River system of unionism or one of its offshoots, the result had all too frequently been dual unionism or no unionism. We can obtain an even better understanding of why this was so by taking a look at John Golden and the United Textile Workers' experience in Lawrence.[11]

DURING THE FIRST three decades of the twentieth century, the United Textile Workers of America (UTW) represented the most ambitious attempt to bring textile workers within a single union. Founded in 1901, the early UTW was dominated by delegates from Fall River and New Bedford. It was not long, though, before unionists in southeastern Massachusetts began to question the aims of the national organization. Having created a system of craft federalism that worked for them, they had little use for a union philosophy that called for the organization of all workers and threatened to blur craft distinctions. And having achieved considerable success on their own, they saw no reason why they should help subsidize organizational drives elsewhere.

The issue that brought these differences to a head was local contributions to the national organization. When the UTW raised per capita levies on local unions in 1908, the New Bedford and Fall River weavers' organizations decided to withdraw rather than pay the new tax. Afterward, relations between the UTW and the Fall River–New Bedford unions became even more strained. UTW efforts to have the weavers expelled from local textile councils not only proved futile, given the vital role weavers played in these bodies, but reinforced the localistic orientation of other unionists by raising the specter of national domination. In 1915, a year after the UTW had moved its headquarters from Fall River to New York City, another increase in per capita taxes precipitated the complete withdrawal of the Fall River and New Bedford unions. The

following year they formed the National Amalgamation of Textile Organizations (NATO), which in 1920 changed its name to the American
Federation of Textile Operatives (AFTO), so that it would not be confused with the radical Amalgamated Textile Workers of America.[12]

Although Fall River unions decided to go their own way, a number of
Spindle City unionists remained with the UTW. The most prominent
was John Golden, who as president from 1903 until his death in 1921
did more than anyone else to shape UTW policy during that period. A
Lancashire Irishman, Golden had emigrated to Fall River during the
early 1890s after being blacklisted in England for his activities on behalf
of the mule spinners union. In the Spindle City, he obtained employment as a spinner at the Union Cotton Manufacturing Company and
served as treasurer of the local spinners' union before becoming a full-
time officer of the UTW.[13]

Golden's main task as UTW president was to organize the unorganized, which in New England meant bringing the newer immigrants
who were then flooding regional labor markets into the union fold.
Though not the best man for the job, he was not the worst either. On one
hand, newer immigrants were always "the foreign elements" to Golden,
and as such plainly inferior to established ethnic groups. On the other
hand, he did believe that they could be organized. He further recognized
that special arrangements were needed to communicate effectively with
these workers, and at the 1905 UTW convention he urged the union to
employ foreign-language speakers as organizers in areas where newer
immigrants comprised a substantial part of the textile workforce.[14]

On a related matter, Golden rejected the craft exclusiveness that hindered the organization of newer immigrants in southeastern Massachusetts. As one might expect, given his own background, Golden did feel
that skilled workers made the best unionists. "I find them the most
intelligent and easiest to organize," he once observed. "They are also of
more value to us than the unskilled workers." It would not be unreasonable to substitute "English-speaking" for "skilled" and view the remarks
as further evidence of Golden's low opinion of newer immigrants —
asked in 1912 why an overwhelming majority of UTW members in
Massachusetts were skilled and "medium skilled" workers, he replied,
"The answer is simply the rapid changing of the nationalities." Yet there
were other, more practical reasons why he would make such a statement. Textile unionists believed that because unskilled workers had the
poorest jobs and were therefore constantly seeking to improve their

condition, they were much less likely than skilled workers to remain in an organization for an extended period of time.[15]

Despite his preference for organizing skilled workers, Golden over time abandoned the rigid craft perspectives of Fall River and his native Lancashire. One reason for this greater flexibility may have been the fate of his own craft, which was nearly eliminated by technological change during his lifetime. Clearly a more important factor was the disruptive influence of the Fall River and New Bedford craft federations, which began in 1903 and continued throughout his tenure as UTW president. Golden may never have become the industrial unionist that he once claimed to be, but he did develop a real aversion to the Lancashire–Fall River credo of "the weaver for the weaver" and "the spinner for the spinner." And during the 1910s, the proportion of UTW locals organized on a plant rather than a craft basis more than tripled: from less than 15 percent to over half. Although much of this expansion took place during the war years in the South, where there was no tradition of craft unionism in textiles, it did indicate Golden's willingness to accept whatever form of organization promised the best results. Yet, despite such openness on Golden's part, the UTW made few gains among New England's newer immigrants under his leadership. We can best understand why by examining the Lawrence strike of 1912, an event that left John Golden a changed man and set back UTW organizational efforts among regional newcomers for at least a decade.[16]

Located in northeastern Massachusetts, midway between Lowell and Haverhill, Lawrence was the nation's leading producer of worsted goods. In 1910 the plants in its mill district, an imposing chain of massive structures densely packed together along the Merrimack, provided employment to more than thirty thousand operatives. Lawrence was also the "Immigrant City." From its founding in 1845, the city experienced steady growth, as successive waves of immigrants entered Lawrence in search of a better life. Despite the low wages and long hours that were typical of textile employment everywhere, the first generations of newcomers were not entirely disappointed. Where some established small businesses of their own, others rose to skilled positions in local mills; and everyone benefited from the gradual but marked improvement in living conditions during the quarter century after the Civil War.[17]

Two decades later, Lawrence was a much different place. Between 1890 and 1910, the city's population nearly doubled, increasing from

44,000 to 86,000 inhabitants. At the same time, housing deteriorated, health standards declined, and the death rate skyrocketed. Everyone blamed the newer immigrants, most of whom were part of that prodigious flood of southern and eastern Europeans who made their way to America during these years. Even when they were seeking to appear open-minded, longtime residents could not disguise their distaste for the newcomers. "I am willing that they should all come," William Rae of the Lawrence Central Labor Union remarked in an 1898 statement, but only "if they should live in a good respectable manner." And Rae plainly had his doubts on this score. Besides expressing astonishment at the "Italians and Armenians who wash their clothes right in the mills" and voicing disapproval of the manner in which the newcomers lived, he believed their presence was a major cause of recent wage reductions. However grudging and qualified his acceptance of the newcomers, Rae conceded more than most older immigrants would, with the result that ethnic relations in Lawrence came to be characterized by a degree of bitterness that was exceptional even for that intolerant era.[18]

These differences spilled over onto the shop floor of local mills, where established workers kept to themselves and the chasm separating older and newer immigrants was nearly as wide as in the community. Just how broad that gulf was is evident in the comments of an operative interviewed by the U.S. Immigration Commission: "The little jests that break the monotony of millwork are impossible when a 'Dago' is working next to you; if you joke him, he will stick a knife into you." Aware of these divisions, overseers avoided mixing the two groups in workrooms where they depended on the experience of veteran operatives. If a mill began employing newer immigrants in a department, one supervisor observed, "it would mean hiring only immigrants." These practices, added to the already considerable handicap of their late arrival, sharply limited the advancement of newer immigrants in the mill hierarchy. Wage data compiled by the U.S. Immigration Commission showed that the average weekly earnings of British, Irish, and French-Canadian workers were substantially higher than those of the newcomers. Among male operatives, native-born British workers earned $11.39 a week, the Irish received $10.54, and French Canadians made $10.78; by contrast, South Italian immigrants earned $6.84 a week, Lithuanians received $7.82, and Poles made $8.01. Similar differentials existed among women wage earners.[19]

Had these divisions been the only problem union organizers faced in

Lawrence, their task would have been daunting enough. But there were others as well. The most formidable was the unrelenting opposition of local employers to any form of worker organization. Unlike their Fall River counterparts, most Lawrence manufacturers were absentee owners who cared little about the city and who saw no need to bargain with local workers. And unlike Fall River mill owners, they had the means to cripple organizing efforts without destroying themselves in the process. Where the manufacturing activities of Fall River producers were confined to Spindle City mills, leading Lawrence firms such as the American Woolen Company operated plants throughout the region, which enabled them to maintain production during periods of labor unrest by shifting work to other cities.[20]

For these and related reasons, worker organizations in Lawrence exhibited all the defects but none of the virtues of Fall River unionism. Apart from some continuity of organization among such skilled male crafts as the loom fixers and mule spinners, the vast majority of Lawrence operatives had no protection whatsoever. Local unions reported a membership of 2,500 in 1912, and even this paltry figure—which accounted for less than 10 percent of the textile workforce—was probably overstated; according to John Golden, the UTW had only 208 members in Lawrence at the beginning of the 1912 strike. The differences between Lawrence and Fall River were especially evident in weave rooms. At a time when Spindle City weavers were becoming a major force on the local industrial relations scene, the numerous grievances of their Lawrence counterparts all elicited the familiar refrain: "If you don't like it, get out." That Fall River unions provided real benefits to their members doubtless explains why newer immigrants there sought the textile council's advice before forming their own organizations. There is no evidence that Lawrence textile unions made a similar impression on newcomers. This in turn helps explain another important difference between worker organization in the two cities. Where the Fall River doffers' union remained within the mainstream of American trade unionism by affiliating with the UTW, newer immigrants in Lawrence looked elsewhere for guidance: to the radical unionism of the Industrial Workers of the World (IWW).[21]

As a revolutionary union, committed to the organization of the nation's most exploited workers, the IWW viewed Lawrence's immigrant masses in a much different light than mainline unions did. To Wobbly organizers, newer immigrants were not a barrier to improved labor standards, but a dynamic force capable of creating a new society in which workers controlled the conditions of their labor. Although the Lawrence campaign progressed slowly, by 1910 the IWW had begun to make some inroads among local wage earners, particularly Italian operatives. The following summer it staged a series of slowdowns in selected mills as part of an effort to moderate the pace of work and increase wages. And in January 1912, when manufacturers responded to a new law reducing the workweek from fifty-six to fifty-four hours by slashing wages and speeding up machinery, the Wobblies were ready to act. So were the city's textile workers. As soon as the reduction was announced, operatives streamed out of local mills into the streets of Lawrence. The ensuing strike was one of the most momentous conflicts in American labor history. In its wake, one radical journalist would claim that "Revolutionary Unionism is [now] a fact that the capitalist class must consider and deal with." This may have been an overstatement, but the strike did cause changes, most notably in the way newer immigrants were perceived — both by mill owners and mainstream union leaders.[22]

Among the many people who went to Lawrence during the struggle was the UTW's John Golden. Having participated in earlier campaigns to organize Lawrence workers, Golden was no stranger to the Immigrant City. But nothing in his past prepared him for what he saw. Moreover, despite his growing dissatisfaction with craft unionism and his awareness of the special problems organizing newer immigrants presented, Golden was still very much a product of Fall River unionism. This became clear in his reaction to the strike. Everything about it — from the lack of preparations on the part of striking workers to the revolutionary objectives of the IWW — violated his notions of what trade unionism was all about. Unlike Fall River, where everything was done in a "systematic manner" and "we give and take a month's notice" before striking, Golden told a congressional investigating committee, Lawrence operatives had no conception of the importance of such formalities: "there was not a living soul on God's earth who knew five minutes before the [pay] envelopes came around in the Washington Mills what was going to happen." It was for that reason, Golden added, that "we call this a revolution. . . ."[23]

This was a remarkable statement. Why "on God's earth" would Golden attach so much significance to this matter? He knew from his attempts to organize Lawrence operatives that local mill owners played by their own rules. Why did he expect workers to observe more elevated standards? The answer can be found in the way his early experiences in Fall River shaped his development as a trade unionist. Having arrived there during the early 1890s, at a time when manufacturers had already begun dealing with local mule spinners and were about to recognize other groups of workers, Golden had missed the two decades of unremitting struggle that had been a necessary precondition for these advances. He no doubt knew about Fall River's tradition of worker militancy, but he did not feel it, because he had not had to confront mill owners who were implacably opposed to any form of worker organization. And though he played an active role in the 1894 and 1904 strikes, their outcome only reinforced his belief in the basic reasonableness of capital.

All of which is to say that Golden believed fervently in the system of industrial relations that had developed in Fall River. A strong advocate of arbitration and the trade agreement, Golden envisioned a world in which capital and labor joined forces to advance their mutual interests. Despite repeated setbacks, he held firmly to the conviction that "the interest of one is the concern of all, and in order to be successful employer and employee must work in harmony." It goes without saying that there was no place in this world for revolutionary unions that denied the rights of capital. "When any organization of labor, men or women, wants to take the authority away from those in whom it is properly constituted, and any time class consciousness is put above justice to the employer," Golden asserted, "I am ready to hand in my union card." He further believed that his views were shared by the "great mass of textile workers," who desired an "American organization" like the UTW, which was respectful of "the rights of the employer, and ready to fight for the rights of the workers."[24]

Much to Golden's chagrin, the "great mass" of Lawrence workers in 1912 were looking for a much different type of leadership. And as Golden came to realize just how limited UTW support was outside the ranks of those older immigrants who dominated the upper reaches of the local occupational hierarchy, he attempted to further the interests of his own organization by adopting a two-track strategy: when he was not condemning the IWW in public, he was negotiating in private with local manufacturers at a series of conferences arranged by the New England Civic Federation. Golden later claimed that if Lawrence workers had followed his lead, they could have ended the struggle ten days earlier on the same terms that they ultimately accepted. But few were listening, least of all those newer immigrants whose militancy had sustained the two-month struggle. For them, the UTW's refusal to cooperate with strike leaders represented an act of betrayal that they would not soon forget. According to one-time AFL organizer Mary Kenney O'Sullivan, many of these workers viewed the UTW "as a force almost as dangerous to their success as the employers themselves."[25]

Consequently, even though the IWW failed to establish a lasting presence in Lawrence, Golden's organization was unable to fill the vacuum. In November 1918, when the UTW brought its eight-hour movement to Lawrence, the union had only two hundred members in the city; another six hundred workers belonged to an independent craft union. The subsequent campaign, which sought to reduce the workweek from fifty-four to forty-eight hours, exhibited the same divisions that had split workers in 1912. Where the UTW, backed by the better-paid older immigrants, was willing to accept a 12.5 percent wage reduction in exchange for shorter hours, the city's ill-paid newer immigrants adamantly opposed any such concession. Instead, they demanded fifty-four hours' pay for forty-eight hours' work and voted to strike if manufacturers did not submit by the end of January. As in 1912, UTW leaders denounced the ensuing strike, which was led by a diverse left-wing coalition of ex-Wobblies and Christian radicals. And once again, the strikers achieved their aims despite UTW opposition. They also formed the Amalgamated Textile Workers of America (ATW) under the leadership of A. J. Muste, a former Protestant minister committed to preparing workers for the day when they "shall own and control their own industries." This was a noble vision, though John Golden did not see it that way. What Muste considered industrial democracy, Golden viewed as bolshevism, and he attacked the ATW just as vehemently as he had the Wobblies.[26]

Here we should note that there were practical as well as ideological reasons for Golden's antiradicalism. By presenting the UTW as a moderate alternative to organizations like the IWW and ATW, he hoped to persuade manufacturers that dealing with his union would end labor troubles. But Lawrence was not Fall River. Despite the occasional urgings of industry representatives who believed the leaders of mainstream unions were "far more conservative than the mass of their followers," Immigrant City mill owners wanted nothing to do wth any independent labor organization. Although they gladly used Golden's statements to play off the UTW against other unions, recognition was another matter altogether. When the Federal Council of Churches (FCC) claimed the 1919 strike could probably have been avoided if manufacturers had provided adequate machinery for discussion, the latter condemned the FCC statement as the work of men who "are upholders of radicalism, and who apparently wish to overthrow the present industrial system and substitute in its place the Russian-Soviet system." In an effort to improve industrial relations, while discouraging unionization, several firms afterward instituted employee welfare programs. They appear to have had little effect. This at least was the opinion of FCC official F. Ernest Johnson. Writing in August 1920, he informed American Woolen Company president William Wood that a recent FCC investigation of Lawrence workers indicated that industrial relations were no better than they had ever been: not only was there "practically nothing going on" in most companies, but he was "exceedingly doubtful of the value of any policies thus far inaugurated" at American Woolen.[27]

"Lawrence has long been a centre of labor unrest," one commentator observed during the 1919 strike, "but not a centre of labor organization." And so it remained. On one hand, UTW relations with newer immigrants could not have been worse. Lawrence CLU leaders believed the union no longer even wanted to organize the newcomers, "for fear it could not control them." They were not entirely wrong. The 1912 strike led John Golden to conclude that most newer immigrants arrived in this country imbued with radicalism; and in locales where they comprised a large proportion of the population, attempting to organize them "would merely be organizing for the IWW." Such workers were organizable, but only in places where they "come in small quantities and [where] the employers do not hamper the union" — which is to say in places like Fall River had been during his early years there. In 1922 Golden's successor as UTW president, the genial Tom McMahon, returned to the Immigrant City and urged his followers to make every effort "to harmonize the different elements that make up the workers in Lawrence." But he came away just as frustrated as Golden had been. "Any one who has any idea of the situation there knows they don't settle local problems in Lawrence," McMahon later remarked. "They settle other problems there and every 'ism' in creation runs riot amongst the people."[28]

Meanwhile, the ATW also faded from the scene. Following the strike, employer repression, ideological conflict within the union, and a sharp rise in unemployment during the 1920–21 depression combined to destroy the organization. Yet, even at the height of its influence in Lawrence, the ATW had faced obstacles that severely limited its potential for expansion. The most serious of these was the existence of two separate working-class cultures that were divided less by ethnicity — though that was certainly a factor — than by the way in which each defined industrial relations. As David Goldberg described them: "One was mainly composed of French-Canadian and Irish workers who were closely tied to the church, sympathetic to craft unions, and determinedly antiradical. The other was composed of workers who were often anticlerical, open to leftist ideas, and advocates of industrial unionism." Goldberg's description adds to our understanding of the two groups by underscoring the role of the Catholic Church in shaping social attitudes. The church did so not simply by decrying the spread of socialism, by telling workers what they could not do; in the major textile centers of New England, influential churchmen also disseminated a more positive message: one that spoke of the rights of labor, and of the responsibilities of capital.[2]

A good example is Father James O'Reilly, who from 1886 until his death in 1925 served as pastor of St. Mary's Church in Lawrence, where people of all classes applauded his ardent support of Irish nationalism and defiant denunciations of anti-Catholic activities. Even more important, O'Reilly was one of the few established residents who made a genuine effort to welcome newcomers to the city: Italians praised his sponsorship of Columbus Day celebrations; Greek, Syrian, Portuguese, and Lithuanian immigrants appreciated his patronage of their church-building initiatives; and everyone commended his attempts to restrain overzealous Americanizers. The renowned labor economist Selig Perlman was not exaggerating when he once referred to O'Reilly as the uncrowned monarch of Lawrence.[30]

Outside the Immigrant City, O'Reilly is best remembered for his strident antiradicalism. In 1912, he not only condemned the Wobblies for misleading their immigrant followers; he also organized a "God and Country" parade as part of an effort to "drive the demons of anarchism and socialism from our midst." Seven years later, ATW activities in Lawrence elicited a similar response from O'Reilly, who again spearheaded Catholic opposition to what he perceived as a mortal threat to the established order. "There is no labor question in Lawrence today," he said of the 1919 strike. "The battle in Lawrence is a test for the whole United States on the question of socialism. The movement in Lawrence is that of the Bolsheviki of Russia."[31]

Yet, as the Federal Council of Churches observed in its report on the

1919 strike, O'Reilly was by no means "blind to the economic issue." Nor was he unaware of the problems workers faced when they had to confront mill owners who refused to bargain with them. In 1894, after giving striking workers fifty dollars, O'Reilly told them he had made the donation to protest "the inhumanity of those who would rather lose one hundred thousand dollars ($100,000) in defeating you than allow it to you as fair compensation for your labor." And in a 1922 address condemning a recent reduction in wages, he set forth his own views of class relations. "On one side," he noted, "is the demand for justice on the basis of human rights; on the other the principle of economics on a basis of material profits." O'Reilly went on to reassure capitalists that they deserved a "reasonable profit," but at the same time he warned that "a reduction of labor's compensation to the breaking point and the maintaining of dividends to the [greatest] possible height means anarchy, revolution and death to our country." As it turned out, local manufacturers did not share this perspective. And when workers later voted to continue a strike undertaken to restore the pay cut, O'Reilly endorsed their decision, declaring that they would "remain out until they get the living wage they want."[32]

The foregoing is significant for two reasons. O'Reilly's willingness to back striking workers when he considered their cause just goes a long way toward explaining why radical leaders were unable to close the cultural divisions described by David Goldberg. Had priests like O'Reilly reflexively supported the claims of capital, labor dissidents might have been able to detach more practicing Catholics from their traditional loyalties. But few priests were ever so obliging. Their views on social relations were a good deal more complex than that, and most workers knew it. Moreover, where brick-and-mortar priests like O'Reilly were longtime residents who had shaped the institutional development of a given community, radical organizers were more likely to be newcomers — or as their local adversaries invariably asserted, "outsiders." That the IWW and ATW achieved the successes that they did, against such opposition, is a tribute to the commitment of their organizers. That they ultimately failed is not the least bit surprising.

Also noteworthy are the striking parallels between the structure of Catholic social thought and that of mainline trade unionists. Each was cast in a framework of reciprocal rights and obligations; and each accepted the hierarchical nature of the emerging industrial order. As Philip Silvia observed in his study of Fall River labor, it was surely "more than coincidental" that many of the city's union leaders — men such as Robert Howard, James Tansey, Thomas O'Donnell, James Whitehead, and John Golden — were Catholics. Even some Protestant unionists were impressed by Catholic social teachings. "As a non-Catholic," William E. G. Batty, the longtime secretary of the New Bedford Textile Council, remarked on one occasion, "I am amazed to discover how completely the encyclicals of Pope Leo XIII and Pius XI endorse the views I have expressed." The exact manner in which the church influenced the evolution of textile unionism is impossible to determine. It is nevertheless safe to conclude that, if nothing else, its teachings certainly reinforced the tendency, already strong among Spindle City unionists, to seek an accommodation with capital. It may also be no coincidence that three of the five public representatives who began attending labor negotiations in Fall River during the early 1920s were Catholic priests.[33]

For two decades following the 1904 strike, the accommodationist approach worked well for Fall River unionists. Unlike Lawrence employers, Spindle City manufacturers were willing to meet and bargain with workers. Moreover, the continued dominance of English-born operatives in the textile workforce enabled union leaders to present a united front. That they had failed to extend unionism outside southeastern Massachusetts did not seem to matter. Content to rest on their achievements, they largely ignored what was happening elsewhere. But these had also been years of relative prosperity for local producers; that period was now ending. As it did, Fall River unionists would find it increasingly difficult to maintain the structure of industrial relations that set the Spindle City apart from other regional textile centers. Faced with an economic crisis that shattered established bases for accommodation and for which they were decidedly unprepared, they were about to receive a harsh lesson in the perils of going it alone. Although the Fall River system of unionism persisted into the early 1940s, in many respects it died much earlier.

IN RETROSPECT, THE most remarkable feature of the textile crisis of the 1920s was its unexpectedness. Despite the 1920–21 depression, the early twenties was a time of extraordinary profitability for New England cotton producers. But this prosperity was illusory, in large part the result of cotton speculation. The short crops of these years had driven up cotton prices, thus enabling mills to reap enormous profits from an appreciation of their inventories. That these profits derived from a one-time boon made little impression on mill directors. As industry critics noted, many of them believed that "[i]t is not manufacturing skill but judgment in buying and selling cotton that makes a mill prosperous." And rather than using the windfall to modernize aging plants, they distributed it to stockholders: through 1924, dividend rates for regional cotton firms averaged 12.2 percent. This was shortsighted, for they would not have another such opportunity for nearly two decades. By the mid-twenties, the New England textile industry had entered a period of depression that would continue with varying degrees of severity until the onset of World War II. Between 1919 and 1939, the number of active spindles in regional mills declined to 5.4 million from 18.1 million; and nearly three of every eight production jobs were lost.[34]

The main problem was overcapacity. Because of the industry's labor-intensive nature and relatively modest capital requirements, textiles had long been a favored starting point of newly industrializing regions. With minimal barriers to entry, new firms were constantly coming into the market. At the same time, gradual improvements in technology further added to the industry's output, as did the practice of double-shift operations inaugurated by southern producers during the war years and continued into the 1930s, despite trade association efforts to curb the practice. These developments might not have been serious in an expanding market. But this was not happening. National demand for cotton goods flattened out at mid-decade and remained stagnant thereafter. Meanwhile, the emergence of strong domestic industries in China, Japan, and India prevented U.S. manufacturers from dumping surplus production in traditional export markets.[35]

New England producers were almost totally unprepared to meet the challenges of this new era. They had been aware of the potential threat posed by southern manufacturers since at least the depression of the 1890s. During that decade, several firms had built branch plants in the South; and in 1898 New Bedford mill owners tried to use southern competition as justification for the wage reduction that precipitated that year's strike. Other warnings were occasionally voiced in later years, but most regional producers did not take the threat seriously. Reassured by the writings of industry analysts like T. M. Young, who contended that a dearth of skilled operatives in a tight labor market would eliminate whatever advantages the South then enjoyed, New England mill owners believed they had little to worry about. Robert T. Davis of Fall River probably spoke for many northern employers when he told the U.S.

Industrial Commission in 1901 that the problems presented by regional labor differentials would be resolved within five years. "The more vigorously [southern producers] extend the business the quicker that will come," he explained, "because labor will be in greater demand, and like any other commodity, when there is a large demand the value of that labor in the market will rise."[36]

Two decades later, the adjustment of which Davis spoke had still not occurred. Despite occasional shortages, southern manufacturers found sufficient supplies of labor to keep wages well below northern standards; and just as important, the general skill levels of southern operatives steadily advanced throughout the period, thus enabling mills to produce increasingly higher yarn counts. As a result, not only did regional wage differentials remain wide, but growing numbers of southern firms were able to challenge the northern monopoly on medium and fine goods production — and at a time when rayon and silk producers were already making incursions into those markets. On top of all these problems, most northern plants were older than those in the South. As early as 1902, for example, a consultant at Lowell's Boott Mills urged "the entire demolition of the present structures": "Your old buildings have perhaps served well in the past, but they were long ago out of date, and are of no value now even if they can be considered safe to work in." Most northern manufacturers also lagged behind their southern counterparts in the installation of new machinery, as they entered a period in which it would become increasingly difficult for many of them to generate the earnings needed to replace obsolete equipment.[37]

To maintain their competitive position in national markets, New England employers undertook a variety of initiatives. Nearly all of them were directed at the industry's workers. One was a campaign to repeal state labor laws that prevented the enactment of further measures without substantially changing current legislation. A second line of attack occurred on the wage front. Between 1924 and 1930, wages for all classes of textile operatives steadily declined. Meanwhile on the shop floor, many manufacturers took steps to increase work assignments, often without installing the new machinery that would have made expanded workloads bearable. These developments had terrible consequences for working people. Everywhere he went in the mid-twenties, UTW organizer Thomas Reagan encountered "that feeling of unrest amongst the workers, brought on by the reduction in wages and the adding on of more machinery, which I find is carried on in some of our New England mills to such a point that it is injurious to the health of the men and women who work in our industry." And everywhere he was asked the same question: "How are we going to stop it?"[38]

Reagan had no real answer to such queries; nor did other UTW leaders. The union's membership, which had soared to 105,000 during the war years, fell to 30,000 afterward. Subsequent communications from New England were unrelievedly grim. "We are shot to pieces in New Hampshire," William Courrette of Manchester reported in 1927. "I was actually representing nothing on the Board." A year earlier Francis Gorman had found that the situation was no better in Maine. Even some of the major strikes that took place during these years evinced more desperation than hope. In 1925, for example, more than 2,500 workers at American Thread's Willimantic plant walked out to protest a wage cut. They remained out for more than two years, throughout which time UTW leaders fully supported the strikers. But one reason they did so was because the Willimantic local was the only organization the union had in Connecticut.[39]

Although these were awful years for the UTW, the union did retain some basis for a revival of organization during the early thirties. The same cannot be said for the craft federationists of the Fall River Textile Council. For them, the decade was an unmitigated disaster. In 1920 Fall River had 111 mills that contained nearly one-eighth of the nation's total spindlage and employed thirty thousand workers, but more than half of these mills were gone a decade later. By 1931 the city of Fall River was bankrupt and a state-appointed board was managing its finances. That same year an industrial improvement organization was formed to aid exploited workers in local sweatshops. But the association quickly discovered that substandard working conditions were much more widespread than it had imagined. When the operators of these small businesses contended that their employees were paid as well as cotton mill workers, an investigation by union officials found that there was some basis for the claim. Fall River had indeed become, in Thomas McMahon's words, "a tragic city."[40]

There were a number of reasons for the Spindle City's collapse. Some firms had ignored the increasing shift from coarse to medium-grade production in southern mills and continued to focus on the manufacture of print cloth. They were among the first to go under. A more common problem was the failure of local mill owners to replace outmoded equipment. As one former union leader told Louis Adamic: "The trouble with this place is that the machinery in all these big mills which you see is archaic. In some of them the equipment has not been replaced since the mills were built, thirty and forty years ago. Of course, they cannot compete in productive efficiency with mills equipped with modern machines, each of which produces with the aid of a single worker more than twenty machines here used to produce with ten workers." Spindle City corporations were also hampered by their localistic orientation. When Fall River dominated the print cloth market, local producers could afford to go their own way, secure in the knowledge that the level of output from their mills would dictate the prices they received for their goods. But that day had passed, and if Fall River was to remain a textile center, they would have to adopt a new outlook.[41]

This at least was the opinion of their most outspoken local critic, Monsignor James E. Cassidy. The self-proclaimed spokesman for three-quarters of Spindle City workers, Cassidy was one of the leading Catholic progressives of his era. Never afraid to take a stand, he was the only priest in New England who publicly supported women telephone operators in their 1919 strike. He also possessed an acid wit, which he most often exercised in ways calculated to delight working people and outrage their social betters. When, for example, the Fall River Chamber of Commerce asked an official of the New Haven Railroad to address a 1924 meeting, Cassidy expressed surprise at the choice. Such a person, he said, "ought to be the last man to be invited to cheer us on as we patiently struggle through the difficulties and disasters begotten in the cotton business and due to the same dumbellism, dis-honesty and mis-direction that stripped the New Haven road and pulled down its stock valuation from $250 to $15 a share." Observations of this sort did not make Cassidy a popular figure among the local business elite. But he did not seem to care; nor was he easily intimidated. Of the heated response to one blistering attack on Fall River mill owners, he simply observed: "my remarks, as the truth always does, provoked a variety of comment and criticism."[42]

Like other Catholic leaders, Cassidy placed social relations in a framework of reciprocal rights and duties. The operative, he said, "must work for his employer, not loaf on the job. He must save for his employer, not waste. He must be careful, not careless. He must be a help and not a hurt to the efficiency of the mill." Mill owners also had duties, the most important of which were to provide steady employment and a living wage to their workers. As he put it in a 1924 address: "We want mill conductors and not mill undertakers. We want mill runners and not mill stoppers. We want mill savers and not mill killers. We want mill executives whose heads and whose hearts are susceptible of impressions from conditions and modern requirements, and not those whose heads and whose hearts are as hard as flint."[43]

By 1924, though, Fall River mill owners were no longer meeting their obligations to either workers or the community. And with each mill closing, Cassidy's rage grew. He was particularly incensed by the seeming indifference of local business leaders to the suffering around them. "In Fall River," he angrily remarked, "there is much material for the starting of a new organization known as the Ostriches, hiding their heads under the sand and making themselves believe there is no storm, while devastation is all about us in the form of staggertime and fallen and dying and dead mill corporations." No less upsetting was the series of wage reductions imposed on those operatives fortunate enough to keep their jobs. "The future of this city," he declared in a 1928 address entitled "Mills That Burn and Mills That Grind," "depends upon the willingness of capable cotton manufacturers to pay their employes, men, women, and children, a living wage." Until they did, he said on another occasion, the National Association of Cotton Manufacturers should adopt as its motto: "We give when we must, we take when we can." At decade's end Cassidy was contending that local mills must be reopened, even if it meant operating them at a loss to their owners.[44]

In all this, Cassidy was more often than not disappointed by the response of the Fall River Textile Council. On one hand, he believed union leaders had not taken the southern threat seriously and criticized them for not doing more to help improve the competitive position of Spindle City producers. At the same time, though, he chided them for their inaction on the wage front. When the council passively accepted a pay reduction in 1928, Cassidy could barely contain his dismay: "I do not say it was necessary to strike but they should have told the manufacturers if they put the reduction in effect the unions would fight it with every dollar, instead of walking away and saying, 'Well, let it be done.'" Three years later, when the city's largest employer announced that wages would be slashed at five plants the firm planned to reopen, Cassidy took the lead in spurring resistance to the cuts.[45]

As Cassidy's remarks suggest, Spindle City unionists were just as unprepared for the new era as local manufacturers. One problem was technological innovation. They recognized that mills had to install new machinery if they were to stay in business. Yet they also feared the consequences of such changes. Although there were good reasons for these fears, change was going to occur, and standing in the way would only hasten the demise of those local plants that still had a future. The question was whether they would remain on the sidelines as passive observers, immobilized by their ambivalence, or whether they would attempt to formulate an approach that both facilitated change and protected workers from its social costs.

It was also apparent that, like Spindle City manufacturers, Fall River unionists had to discard their provincialism. And they had to do so for the same reasons. Just as southern mills now competed with local corporations, the substandard wages and working conditions of southern workers posed a potentially mortal threat to the well-being of Fall River operatives. In these circumstances, the practice of unionism in one city was as obsolete as the hand-loom. The struggles of southern workers were now their struggles, in ways they had never been before. To meet this challenge, textile unionists needed to abandon their complacent localism and revive those notions of labor solidarity that had once made Fall River the center of organizational activity in New England.

Meanwhile, the Fall River system of unionism was coming apart at the seams. In a 1924 address, a local mill treasurer stated that manufacturers were on "the pleasantest terms" with officials of the Fall River Textile Council: "All these men are our best friends." This was no doubt an overstatement. But to the degree that it was true, council leaders needed new friends. The year before members of John Campos's doffers' union had criticized them for not acting more vigorously to restore earlier wage reductions; in 1925 a group of weavers deserted the council after it passively accepted a 10 percent reduction; and in 1928 the council's failure to contest yet another cut caused further defections. These developments underscore the paradoxical nature of the challenge that union leaders then faced: on one hand, mill modernization required new forms of cooperation with capital; on the other, the protection of workers' rights in this changing industrial environment necessitated a rekindling of older traditions of militancy.[46]

As it was, the early thirties was a decidedly inauspicious time for bold new undertakings. "There is, perhaps, more destitution and misery and degradation in the mill towns of New England today," Louis Adamic wrote in 1930, "than anywhere in the United States." Many of the workers who had to endure these conditions were more concerned about economic survival than social justice. "We see human nature at its worst,"

William E. G. Batty of the New Bedford Textile Council observed. "Workers consent to things that normally would be strenuously objected to, and employers resort to practices that they justify upon the grounds of commercial necessity, which under normal conditions would never merit serious consideration." Yet, there was a point beyond which working people could not be pushed; and as another New Bedford unionist remarked: "Revolt will come, and with it better and more permanent organization." It was a prescient observation.[47]

THE EMERGENCE
OF THE TWUA

3

The New Deal era was a period of enormous growth and achievement for the American labor movement. The changes that took place during these years were not simply quantitative. Where, with a few notable exceptions such as the miners and clothing workers, earlier organizations had shared the parochialism and craft exclusiveness of the Fall River system of unionism, the new industrial unions of the 1930s embraced all wage earners and tended to view labor's needs in national rather than regional or local terms. By 1945, the Textile Workers Union of America–CIO had displaced both the United Textile Workers and the Fall River–New Bedford craft federations as the leading voice of textile unionism. In so doing, it not only established a more inclusive form of unionism in New England; it also made important organizational advances in the South and undertook a variety of political initiatives designed to reduce interregional wage differentials. We begin our examination of these developments by looking at one of the more memorable struggles of those turbulent times, the general textile strike of 1934.

THEY BEGAN ARRIVING in New York City during the second week of August 1934, in groups of two or three, some alone. They came by train or automobile; others, because they lacked the money to pay for more conventional means of transport, had stuck out their thumbs and hitchhiked. They came from the mill villages of the southern Piedmont and the textile centers of New England and the Middle Atlantic states. They were in New York to attend a special convention of the United Textile Workers (UTW). A year earlier, on July 9, 1933, President Roosevelt had signed Fair Code of Competition No. 1, which set the minimum wage for cotton textile workers at thirteen dollars a week in the North and twelve dollars in the South, established a forty-hour workweek, and prohibited child labor under the age of sixteen. An accompanying executive order directed that steps be taken to prevent "improper speeding up of work to the disadvantage of employees." The code also contained the full text of section 7(a) of the National Industrial Relations Act, which guaranteed workers the right to form unions and bargain collectively with employers.[1]

It looked like the beginning of a new day for textile workers. This was especially so in the South, where the UTW had been trying to establish a foothold since the war years. Major campaigns in 1919–21 and 1929–31 had ended badly, producing more disillusionment than organization. With the passage of the National Industrial Recovery Act (NIRA), UTW organizers were back in the field. And southern operatives were responding to their message, despite lingering doubts about the union and the often haphazard nature of the understaffed UTW effort. In New England, workers watched these activities approvingly. Since the mid-twenties, increasing numbers of them had come to share the sentiments of a Salem, Massachusetts, local that had withdrawn from the American Federation of Textile Operatives because that organization's localistic orientation precluded the type of national organization needed to protect northern workers. In a world of cutthroat competition and capital mobility, they now knew, their own security was intimately tied to that of their counterparts in southern mills.[2]

As it turned out, worker hopes that the NIRA would usher in a new era were soon dashed. Although conditions improved somewhat during 1933, largely because of a brief spurt in production, this situation did not last. The 1933 boomlet, as Irving Bernstein observed, "stole production from the future," and by the summer of 1934 it was clear to anyone who cared to look that little had changed. A recent curtailment of production had reduced wages, the stretchout continued unabated, and nonunion mill owners in both North and South resolutely ignored section 7(a). Meanwhile, the government was either unwilling or unable to do anything about it. A major stumbling block was the Code Authority formed to administer the cotton code. Headed by George A. Sloan of the Cotton Textile Institute (CTI), the industry's leading trade association, the Code Authority was mainly concerned with curbing overproduction and had no intention whatsoever of abetting UTW organizational efforts. As worker grievances flooded in, they first went to the tripartite Cotton Textile National Industrial Relations Board, whose transparently promanagement chairman, Robert W. Bruere, sent them to the Cotton Textile Institute, which checked with the offending employers, who invariably reported that all was well.[3]

The 500 delegates to the UTW convention had seen enough. They believed it was now time to take matters into their own hands. According to union officials, membership had increased from 40,000 to more than 300,000 workers during the previous year, and many felt that if they did not act now, conditions would never improve. Few had any illusions about the magnitude of the task before them. When a worker from South Carolina asked UTW president Thomas F. McMahon if the union had sufficient funds to support a general strike, he responded, "No, sir." This knowledge had little effect on the delegates, only ten of whom cast dissenting votes on the final strike ballot. Voicing the dominant sentiment of the convention, one worker declared, "We have nothing to lose and everything to gain from a strike."[4]

The strike began on September 1. It would last three weeks and involve more than 400,000 textile operatives in states extending from Maine to Mississippi. New England mill owners had initially planned to close their plants because of heavy inventories. But some later changed their minds and, believing their workers would oppose the walkout, decided to test the UTW's strength. Most such manufacturers were in for a rude awakening. As flying squadrons of union activists moved from mill to mill and town to town, support for the strike spread and attempts to maintain production became increasingly hazardous. A number of locales witnessed violent confrontations between strikers and state and local authorities. In Saylesville, Rhode Island, when 3,000 strikers broke through militia lines and attempted to burn the Sayles plant, 132 people were injured in the ensuing struggle, four of them critically. Elsewhere in the state, efforts to shut down the Woonsocket Rayon Mill resulted in a night-long battle that pitted 8,000 to 10,000 rock-throwing workers against gun-toting guardsmen. When the smoke finally cleared, one striker lay dead and another fifteen people, including four policemen, had been taken to a local hospital. Less sanguinary but equally bitter confrontations occurred in Danielson, Connecticut; Lewiston, Maine; Ludlow and Pittsfield, Massachusetts; and other textile centers. Before the walkout ended, four of the region's six states had called out National Guard troops to protect mill property.[5]

Events followed an even more violent course in the South, where the National Guard was also mobilized, company thugs used tear gas to disperse pickets, sheriffs forcibly evicted worker families from company housing, and airplanes tracked the movements of flying squadrons. Many mill sites took on the appearance of military strongholds, surrounded by machine-gun nests and patrolled by company guards armed with shotguns. Although intimidated, strikers refused to back down. It was thus inevitable that some blood would be spilled. In one shocking incident at a mill in Honea Path, South Carolina, private guards opened fire on pickets, killing seven of them; another worker and a deputy sheriff died in a gun battle outside a Trion, Georgia, mill. Further bloodshed was narrowly averted at numerous other locales when an employer prudently decided to shut down or union leaders urged pickets to avoid provocative actions.[6]

In the end, worker solidarity and picket-line militancy were no match for the combined forces of capital and government. Nor could enthusiasm and courage make up for a lack of organizational preparation: few union leaders had experience leading large strikes and overall coordination was for the most part nonexistent; little aid was obtained from other unions, many of which faced problems of their own; and the fact that the strike occurred during a period of market contraction further undermined its viability. By late September, UTW officials recognized that time was running out. Trying to make the best of a desperate situation, they declared victory and accepted a settlement based on the recommendations of a commission appointed by President Roosevelt to resolve the dispute.[7]

Called the Winant Board, after its chairman, John G. Winant, a former governor of New Hampshire, the commission submitted a report that offered textile workers small recompense for their exertions. It did recommend investigations of a variety of worker grievances and urge that a new Textile Labor Relations Board (TLRB) be formed to replace the Bruere Board. But, as the northern-based National Association of Cotton Manufacturers immediately noted, the report's "most important" conclusion was that industrywide collective bargaining "between the employers as a group and the United Textile Workers is not at this time feasible. . . ." And while the TLRB was more favorably disposed toward labor than its predecessor, it proved unable to enforce its decisions. In short, the strike settlement left conditions virtually unchanged; and despite union assertions to the contrary, everyone knew it.[8]

For the UTW the outcome of the 1934 general strike was an unqualified disaster. Yet Irving Bernstein's conclusion that the strike "left no heritage beyond bitter memories" is much too harsh. It is true that in some areas of the South, where poststrike repression was often severe, the struggle created an enduring distrust of both government and unions.

The "AF of L has certainly failed to stand by us here in the South" was how one South Carolina unionist later put it in a letter to Emil Rieve. "On account of this I have heard many say they would never join another union." But this was not the case everywhere. In Woonsocket, Rhode Island, French-Canadian operatives poured into that city's Independent Textile Union in the months immediately following the walkout. And Solomon Barkin, who later became research director for the Textile Workers Organizing Committee, believed the strike generated the "bases and the leadership for unionism" in numerous other textile centers. It was a formative experience for many union activists, one that they did not soon forget. Nearly two decades later, Mariano Bishop could still vividly recall leading a flying squadron into North Dighton, Massachusetts, where the sheriff was reportedly on the Mount Hope Finishing Company payroll, and walking "right into a platoon of 150 goons, crouched behind street barricades, pointing guns down our throats."[9]

The strike also made an impression on New England mill owners. "Labor has demonstrated that it is most efficiently organized and ready to consolidate its position," an NACM bulletin informed member companies in late September. "This makes it essential for manufacturers to attain a degree of solidarity that they never had before." As it turned out, this observation was more a tribute to past militancy than an accurate description of the poststrike UTW, and cotton manufacturers had less to worry about than they imagined. By year's end, union membership had plummeted to about one-fifth of its prestrike strength, and there was little evidence that it would be on the upswing anytime soon. The union did attempt to expand its foothold in the woolen and worsted industry, but the campaign made little headway. It began in the summer of 1935 with an effort to increase wages and reduce workloads at the Uxbridge Worsted Company, a major secondary producer with mills in Massachusetts, Connecticut, and Rhode Island. The company resisted union demands, and in late June workers walked out. Four weeks later, Uxbridge paid off its foremen and threatened to move all of its six plants south if the strike continued. In light of past developments, this was the kind of threat that operatives took very seriously. And when the company opened one of its mills in early August, a number of workers returned to their jobs. Fearing that they might lose complete control of the situation, union leaders authorized a vote on a five-point agreement that they had earlier rejected. This time the strikers accepted the settlement. By now, however, UTW members at four of the company's plants had withdrawn from the union and formed independent organizations of their own. Thus it was that an initiative designed to bolster the union's position in the industry had in effect weakened it.[10]

In the meantime, UTW organizers were having no better luck in Lawrence, the nation's leading center of worsted production. The Immigrant City should have been an ideal site for such a drive. "We are living in this city on a human volcano that many erupt most any time and plunge the city into another strike," said one local unionist in 1932. Although conditions were only marginally better three years later, the UTW was unable to exploit the situation. According to Thomas Blackwood of the Woolen and Worsted Department, there was "a bad taste among the workers in Lawrence toward the UTW." In part a legacy of the UTW's divisive role in the 1912 and 1919 strikes, this animus had more recently been reinforced by the union's lackluster performance in a 1931 walkout. During the latter struggle, Edmund Wilson found that many rank-and-filers believed the UTW was more concerned about collecting dues than winning strikes. One can easily guess what all this meant in terms of organization. Asked at a November 1936 meeting of the UTW Executive Council how much of a membership the union had in Lawrence, one official replied, "practically none."[11]

Throughout these years there was also much talk of a new drive in cotton. But talk is all it was. Rather than making any serious effort to organize cotton operatives, the UTW instead shifted its attention to the political front. When the Supreme Court struck down the National Industrial Recovery Act in May 1935, the union responded by drafting legislation that provided for government regulation of the textile industry. In addition to outlawing unfair trade practices, the bill called for the creation of a National Textile Commission to establish minimum wage standards, guarantee collective bargaining, regulate workloads, and adopt measures to prevent overproduction. Speaking on behalf of the plan, UTW president Francis Gorman claimed that "the establishment of uniform labor standards in the textile industry [would] automatically do away with unfair competition."[12]

For a variety of reasons, the bill never had a chance. One was the mixed reaction of textile manufacturers. Although some northern mill owners supported the proposal, southern producers adamantly objected to government oversight of their labor practices. Another was the improved condition of textile markets in 1936, which enabled opponents of the measure to claim that private initiatives were sufficient to stabilize the industry. A third obstacle was the organizational weakness of the UTW. When, during the course of congressional hearings on the bill, a legislator observed that organization rather than legislation offered the "best solution" to the union's problems, Francis Gorman agreed. But, he added, because of employer opposition, "we cannot create those organizations. . . ." However truthful, Gorman's admission did little to advance the union's case. Congress was not prepared to do for the UTW what it could not do for itself.[13]

Moreover, Congress had already taken steps to aid labor. In June 1935, a month after the Supreme Court declared the NIRA unconstitutional, it passed the Wagner Act, which set up a permanent agency to determine appropriate collective bargaining units and prevent employers from engaging in unfair labor practices. And if the UTW was not able to make use of these protections, others were. That November John L. Lewis formed the Committee for Industrial Organization (CIO) to bring unionism to the nation's mass-production industries. The next eighteen months was one of the most exciting and tumultuous periods in American labor history. By the spring of 1937, the United Auto Workers had brought General Motors to the bargaining table, the Steel Workers Organizing Committee had signed a contract with U.S. Steel, and the United Rubber Workers had organized most of that industry's major producers.[14]

Meanwhile, there were indications that textiles might become the next major target of CIO organizers. In August 1936, UTW president Thomas McMahon asked the CIO to help his union put together an organizational drive in the South. Among those expressing interest in McMahon's proposal was Sidney Hillman, whose Amalgamated Clothing Workers (ACW) union was also threatened by the southern migration of runaway shops. After months of discussions, the CIO and UTW agreed the following spring to join forces under Hillman's leadership and formed the Textile Workers Organizing Committee (TWOC). There were then more than a million workers in the nation's textile plants, and if the new organization succeeded, it could create the largest union in the American labor movement.[15]

To do this, the TWOC would have to overcome formidable obstacles. One was industry structure. Textiles was in many respects an industrial unionist's worst dream. As Irving Bernstein observed, it was not really an industry at all, but a collection of industries, each of which "had its own geographic distribution, its own markets, its own technology, its own distinctive labor force." Textiles was also an intensely competitive economic environment, littered with marginal producers whose long-term prospects were as cloudy as their machinery was obsolete. Recent shifts in demand patterns further complicated matters. The displacement of traditional staple goods by style fabrics in a broad range of textile markets had focused productive capacity on product lines that had limited growth potential.[16]

The industry's fragmented structure had long been a barrier to effective organization. In 1921, for example, A. J. Muste had organized a conference of independent textile unions in an attempt to coordinate their activities. That there was interest in such an undertaking was evident from the turnout. Representatives from the AFTO, hosiery workers, lace operatives, silk workers, and a host of other unions attended the gathering out of a conviction that "something must be done in the way of getting together as closely as possible." At the same time, though, they all wished to maintain their autonomy because, as one delegate put it: "We believe that every individual unit knows more about its own affairs than anybody in a general capacity." Given the administrative incompetence of the UTW, which was the only broad-based organization with which most of the conference delegates were familiar, these concerns were perfectly understandable. And while Francis Gorman later initiated efforts to collect data on the industry's various branches, many workers remained skeptical about the extent to which any central body could capably represent their interests.[17]

Sidney Hillman was well aware of these problems, and one of his first acts as TWOC chairman was to recruit Solomon Barkin as research director. Barkin was one of those talented Jewish youths who had transformed City College of New York into a distinguished center of learning during the early decades of the century. Although only thirty years old at the time of his appointment, he was an experienced labor economist whose previous work included stints with the New York State Commission on Old Age Security and the Labor Advisory Board of the National Recovery Administration. As TWOC research director, he quickly demonstrated an ability to shape vast amounts of data from disparate sources into compelling arguments that both reassured textile operatives and impressed industry executives. Commenting on his testimony on behalf of the Fair Labor Standards Act, Russell T. Fisher of the National Association of Cotton Manufacturers observed, "Mr. Barkin consistently puts on an unusually good performance as a witness, as he not only knows his story but is able to tell it."[18]

The TWOC campaign began during the spring of 1937, several days after the Supreme Court affirmed the constitutionality of the Wagner Act. The New England drive enlisted organizers from a variety of backgrounds. Among them were UTW veterans like Horace Riviere, who directed the TWOC effort in western Massachusetts. An aggressive, broadshouldered man with a booming voice, Riviere had been in the forefront of every major regional struggle since the Nashua strike of 1915. Over the years, he had experienced much but learned little: "Times changed," a biographer noted, "not Horace." Stubborn, tactless, and a poor administrator, his younger colleagues sometimes found him "pretty hard to swallow" and felt he "should be kept in the background as much as possible." At the same time, though, Riviere exuded an infectious enthusiasm, and no one ever questioned his dedication. "[W]hen placed in a situation where I am going to have to choose between our organization going to pieces or a strike," he wrote Barkin, "the strike we shall have!"[19]

Where people like Riviere represented the old unionism and provided links to the past, the presence of others in TWOC ranks foretold a different future. In terms of personnel, the campaign's most significant feature — and what set it apart from earlier organizational efforts — was the energetic support it received from a group of young, ambitious newer immigrants who had never felt completely at home in the UTW, and who in Barkin's words had "gained their spurs" in the 1934 general strike. One was the Czech-born John Chupka, a stocky, blond-haired woolen worker from East Douglas, Massachusetts. As a youth, he had traveled the country, working in the nation's copper mines, oil fields, and lumber camps, before returning to East Douglas in 1928 and resuming his job as a woolen weaver. A one-time member of the IWW, Chupka possessed in ample measure both the experience and the toughness that an organizer needed to operate effectively in the company-dominated wool towns of central Massachusetts, where as he later recalled, "we often ran the risk of getting our heads busted." Another was Fall River's Mariano Bishop, a young man from the Azores whose burly figure soon became a familiar sight in regional cotton centers. Already well known among the Portuguese of southeastern Massachusetts for his youthful exploits as a soccer player, Bishop was a fearless organizer who exhibited a quiet determination that won over many undecided cotton workers.[20]

One of Hillman's main objectives was to use unionization to stabilize the textile industry by introducing uniform labor conditions, as the Amalgamated had done in men's clothing. TWOC strategy for achieving this aim was based on industry structure. In woolens and worsteds, where most producers recognized a single firm as the industry leader, the union would seek to negotiate pattern-setting agreements with American Woolen. In cottons, where the Fall River and New Bedford manufacturers' associations were New England's most influential employer groups and had citywide contracts with local labor organizations, the union would attempt to make these agreements the basis for regional negotiations.[21]

For a time, things appeared to be going according to plan. During its first six months in the field, TWOC won an election at American Woolen's Wood Mill in Lawrence, and while progress was slow in Fall River, the New Bedford Textile Council became an early affiliate. Organizers also established joint boards in Lowell, Webster, and Holyoke, Massachusetts, as well as the traditional UTW strongholds of Olneyville, Pawtucket, and West Warren, Rhode Island. But the drive stalled elsewhere. The main obstacle was a severe economic downturn, beginning in the fall of 1937, which ruled out new initiatives as union leaders worked desperately to preserve existing gains with a reduced staff, and nonunion operatives avoided taking any action that might jeopardize their positions. Although hard times lifted early in some industries, textiles was not among them. "The insecurity and caution of the depression still prevails," Solomon Barkin reported to a January 1939 meeting of the TWOC Advisory Council. "Workers are still generally depressed by the fear of losing their jobs or of finding that the bottom is removed from under them."[22]

Increased unemployment among industry operatives was not the only problem TWOC faced during this dark period. When Sidney Hillman fell ill in October 1937, his withdrawal from the campaign's day-to-day operations exposed a number of structural flaws in the TWOC effort that had not been apparent earlier. According to the original design, the regional directors in charge of field operations were experienced ACW officials who reported directly to Hillman; and the only national officer was research director Solomon Barkin, who also looked to Hillman for direction. As long as Hillman took an active part in TWOC affairs, the system functioned reasonably well. But his illness created a major vacuum at the top. As Barkin recalled, "we were in no position to know when he would return or the liberties that could be taken in his absence for changing or transforming the union." This dilemma would not be resolved until early 1939, when Emil Rieve was appointed executive director.[23]

TWOC operations were further disrupted by that perennial curse of the American labor movement, internal factionalism. The main source of discontent were former UTW officials who resented the privileged position of the ACW regional directors and who never fully accepted industrial unionism. One such dissident was Joseph Sylvia of Rhode Island, a veteran member of the UTW's Woolen and Worsted Federation. Sylvia joined the TWOC staff in March 1937 and from the outset demanded that the organization recognize the autonomy of the old UTW federations, while doing almost nothing to advance the union drive in Rhode Island. By the summer of 1938, TWOC leaders had had enough, and Barkin dismissed Sylvia in a letter that did little to conceal his personal dislike of and professional contempt for the man. "We find that despite the long period allowed you and the tolerance displayed to your many variant moods," Barkin wrote, "we have been met with rebuff." Worse, Barkin added: "Most of the agreements in your area have been lost. Many important elements in your district have been estranged. Besides failing to build strongly, you have sought protection behind insults which you have heaped one upon another. You have constantly disparaged the TWOC in the eyes of the textile workers in your area." Sylvia's dismissal was certainly no loss to the organization. Indeed, had he gone quietly, his departure might have been cause for celebration. But it was not in Sylvia's nature to accept rejection — or much else for that matter — uncomplainingly. Condemning what he characterized as the dictatorial practices of TWOC leaders, Sylvia immediately began urging other disgruntled UTW officials to follow him out of the organization.[24]

Of those who did, the most important was Francis J. Gorman. It has been Gorman's misfortune that he is best remembered for his inept leadership of the 1934 general strike. He deserved better. A longtime supporter of efforts to bring all textile workers within a single organization, Gorman had joined the UTW in 1922 and quickly demonstrated an ability to reconcile the ethnic divisions that were then so common among New England operatives. During the 1930s, he really came into his own, forming a research department in 1934 to counter the political advantages that their ability to gather information gave trade associations like the Cotton Textile Institute, and drafting legislation to stabilize the textile industry after the Supreme Court struck down the National Industrial Recovery Act.[25]

With this record of achievement behind him, Gorman expected to play a major role in the TWOC campaign. But this was not to be. Sidney Hillman, who neither liked nor respected him, believed old-line leaders like Gorman and McMahon were primarily responsible for the UTW's ineffectiveness and needed to be replaced. Gorman thus found himself cast aside, unable even to obtain current information about TWOC activities. When he demanded that Hillman restore the UTW federations, the differences between the two men deepened. And as it became clear during the course of 1938 that Hillman had no intention of allowing Gorman to succeed him as TWOC leader, the latter joined forces with Sylvia, taking about fifty old UTW locals with him. By year's end, he too was denouncing TWOC authoritarianism in wild-eyed pronouncements declaring that "textile workers are through with Hitlerism."[26]

The person whom Hillman did tap as his successor was Emil Rieve of the hosiery workers. Then forty-seven years old, Rieve had grown up in a small town near Warsaw, Poland, and in 1905 emigrated alone to the United States, where he obtained employment in a Pennsylvania hosiery mill. It was said that Rieve never worked in a plant that he did not try to organize. Often blacklisted, he was for many years always on the move, "not because he liked to travel, but because he had to eat." Rieve and Hillman had much in common. Both were former socialists who were constantly seeking ways to make government responsive to labor's needs; in fact, they had collaborated on several political initiatives during the previous decade. And like Hillman, Rieve believed unions had an important role to play in maintaining industrial stability. As head of the Hosiery Federation, he had initiated a drive to establish a uniform national contract, formed a research and publicity department, and helped create an industrywide arbitration system that became a model of its kind. He also assembled an able team of organizers, whom he sent into the South as well as the nonunion hosiery districts of the Middle Atlantic states. Appointed TWOC executive director in early 1939, Rieve became the first president of the Textile Workers Union of America (TWUA) at the organization's founding convention that May.[27]

With the leadership question finally resolved, textile leaders moved to consolidate their earlier gains. The union's most impressive accomplishment during this period came in February 1939, when it signed an agreement with the American Woolen Company, the "General Motors of the textile industry." The pact covered four plants, including the Wood and Ayer mills, two massive fortresses guarding the entrance to Lawrence. Well aware of American Woolen's place in both the industry and textile lore, union leaders celebrated the breakthrough with unabashed glee. "For the first time in its history," an editorial in *Textile Labor* declared, "the largest woolen company in the country has agreed to deal with a union. Even to a schoolboy, this achievement must come as an epic development in the textile industry." The paper later kept close track of union progress at the company's remaining plants. By May 1945, the scorecard read: twenty down, four to go.[28]

Although TWUA leaders had good reason to be jubilant, the American Woolen breakthrough was not an unqualified success. One problem was the stiff resistance of smaller mills that were reluctant to follow American Woolen's lead. On the eve of World War II, only about one-third of the woolen industry's 190,000 workers were dues-paying members of the TWUA. Another was ethnic divisiveness, which continued to be a major factor in Lawrence unionism. Where newer immigrants tended to embrace the CIO with enthusiasm, many workers from older immigrant groups kept their distance. At the Wood Mill, for example, the older immigrants who dominated the mending department resisted unionization until the mid-forties. "We have been handicapped in Lawrence, since we became the collective bargaining agency, because of the propaganda which pictured TWUA pretty much as a union of foreigners," TWUA vice-president George Baldanzi later explained. "We had never been able to break through the Anglo-Saxon groups in the region." For many local operatives, another observer remarked, "the AFofL is considered *the* textile union in Lawrence." And while important advances were made in all regional woolen centers during the war years, the UTW maintained a strong following in Immigrant City mills into the 1950s.[29]

As in woolens, progress on the cotton front was slow but steady. In March 1940, 2,000 workers at Pepperell's mills in Biddeford, Maine, where union efforts to cultivate the friendship of local merchants, public officials, and fraternal orders put the city in a "holiday mood for the election," voted by a 3–1 margin to join the TWUA; and just prior to the war, the union added 1,500 operatives from the Bates Manufacturing Company in Lewiston to its rolls. The TWUA further solidified its position in Maine during the early war years. After it won a relatively close election at Pepperell's Lewiston plant in September 1942, *Textile*

Labor reported that the city was "now 100% TWUA." Although numerically unimportant, these successes were of more than passing significance. Maine manufacturers had traditionally paid their workers less than mills in Massachusetts and Rhode Island, and it was imperative that the TWUA organize the state's major producers if it was to eliminate intraregional wage differentials.[30]

Having secured their northern flank, union leaders turned their attention toward the region's two primary cotton centers, Fall River and New Bedford. Here their main adversary was not local capital, but the "provincialism" of long-established labor organizations, which Solomon Barkin claimed was a major impediment to CIO progress in New England. Even though the textile crisis of the 1920s had discredited the Fall River Textile Council in the eyes of many operatives, it continued to maintain a strong presence in Spindle City weave rooms, where the loom fixers, slasher tenders, and knot tiers constituted the bulk of its membership. Still affiliated with the nearly moribund American Federation of Textile Operatives (AFTO), the council strongly resisted any organizational change that might diminish its independence or threaten the privileged position of its craft members in local mills.[31]

Vowing to bring real organization to local workers, the TWUA moved into Fall River during the summer of 1941. The drive was led by Edward Doolan, a loom fixer and Spindle City native who had begun work at age fourteen. Eager to get ahead, he spent countless evenings at the local library and attended night school to become a designer. He soon found, however, that people from his ethnic and class background had little chance of moving from the shop floor to the front office in Fall River mills. His ambitions thwarted, Doolan redirected his energies toward unionism, serving as a UTW business agent for a number of years before joining TWOC in 1937. As head of the Spindle City campaign, he based the TWUA appeal on two claims. One was the superiority of industrial unionism to the craft federalism of the textile council. Under a craft setup, Doolan asserted in a typical statement of the TWUA case, mill owners had "isolated the textile workers in small groups and gobbled them up one by one." With the CIO now in the field, there was no reason why this state of affairs should continue. Through industrial unionism, Doolan declared, "[T]he workers are united. The grievance of one becomes the grievance of all. The aspirations of one become the aspirations of all. An injury to one is an injury to all." Doolan also emphasized that the AFTO, which had no permanent organizers, was manifestly incapable of organizing southern textile mills. Only the TWUA, with its 160-member staff, possessed the resources and will needed to remove "those forms of oppression which for years have held the Southern worker in bondage," and that now threatened to destroy the wage and work standards of northern operatives as well.[32]

The TWUA message was apparently well received. In August, it won a contest at American Thread's Kerr plant, which was a well-chosen initial target in that thread mills did not have weaving departments. And that winter, after the NLRB had approved a TWUA petition for industrial rather than craft elections, the union obtained bargaining rights at the Border City, Richard Borden, and Arkwright mills. From the outset, though, organizers faced considerable resistance from AFTO members determined to protect their shop-floor status and organizational autonomy. During the Arkwright election, a loom fixer assaulted TWUA representative William Bowes while he was escorting an aged worker to the polls; and in March 1942 the loom fixers, slasher tenders, and knot tiers staged a walkout when the NLRB dismissed a petition for citywide craft bargaining units. This was among the first of a series of AFTO strikes during the war years, one of which resulted in a temporary government takeover of seven mills.[33]

The results of the Fall River campaign were mixed. On one hand, the TWUA successfully organized a substantial majority of local textile workers. According to *Textile Labor*, 80 percent of the city's fifteen thousand operatives were CIO members by September 1942. Workers at the two major holdouts, Pepperell's local plant and the Luther Manufacturing Company, voted to join the TWUA in March 1945. Just prior to these elections, however, the NLRB had approved a petition for a separate bargaining unit from the loom fixers, slasher tenders, and knot tiers. Thus permitted to preserve their independence, they would remain a thorn in the TWUA's side for years to come.[34]

Despite many similarities between the two cities, the situation in New Bedford was somewhat different from that in Fall River. Compared with their Spindle City counterparts, New Bedford mill owners and unionists had come out of the textile crisis of the interwar period with a greater appreciation of the need for change. Because it is important to understand why they did so, and because the next several chapters will focus increasingly on New Bedford, it would be worth our while at this juncture to step back and examine the TWUA drive there against the backdrop of the city's development as a textile center.

ORIGINALLY A WHALING center, New Bedford did not become a major textile producer until after the Civil War, when the decline of the whaling trade forced local capitalists to seek new areas of enterprise. Their decision to invest in textiles may well have been influenced by the example of Fall River. Like the Spindle City, New Bedford had a coastal location that enabled prospective manufacturers to save money on coal purchases and provided easy access to major markets, while its humid climate made the city an ideal site for the production of higher-grade fabrics. And like Fall River, New Bedford's locally dominated textile industry would experience dramatic growth during the Gilded Age. By the early twentieth century, the city's mills employed nearly fifteen thousand workers.[35]

From the outset, though, the New Bedford industry differed from that of Fall River in one important respect. Where Spindle City mills specialized in the production of medium-grade print cloth, New Bedford quickly achieved a reputation as the "home of fine spinning." As a consequence, New Bedford producers were less affected by southern competition than their Fall River counterparts, and the textile crisis of the 1920s had a delayed impact on the city. Between 1918 and 1927, the profits of local mills averaged 11.27 percent annually, which was a truly impressive showing for these troubled years. New Bedford manufacturers soon learned, however, that they were not immune to the changes then taking place in the cotton industry. The problem was that as southern mills began to produce higher yarn counts and turned out ever-larger quantities of medium-range fabrics, increasing numbers of northern manufacturers shifted to fine goods production. William W. Crapo of New Bedford's Wamsutta Mills had foreseen the results of such a development years earlier. In 1901 he told a congressional committee: "If the increase of spindles in the finer goods becomes largely in excess of the home demand, and a glut occurs, then follows the inevitable restriction of production through the shutting down of mills." This is exactly what had happened by the late twenties; and for New Bedfordites the decade after 1928 was a period of unprecedented misery.[36]

It began with a 10 percent wage reduction, which was the main cause of the 1928 strike. This struggle is most often used to illustrate the potential appeal of radical ideology to Depression-era cotton workers. It was here that Fred Beal, the Communist organizer and leader of the 1929 Gastonia strike, established his credentials as a champion of the disinherited. And it is true that the Communists maintained a presence in New Bedford for some years afterward. These were certainly noteworthy developments that merit the attention of researchers. In the end, though, the CP made no lasting gains in New Bedford or any other New England mill town of the period; and for our purposes, the strike had two other less spectacular but more enduring consequences.[37]

The first concerned the New Bedford Textile Council. Prior to the 1928 strike, the council was in many respects a carbon copy of its Fall River counterpart — a federation of crafts affiliated with the AFTO that cared little about what was happening outside New Bedford. It was also dominated by a group of English workers who still followed events in the Old Country, drawing inspiration from the achievements of the British Labour Party. But the onset of hard times prompted council leaders to reassess their localistic orientation; and during the strike, they withdrew from the AFTO and joined the UTW in order to fend off the Communist challenge and to deal more effectively with the economic changes that now threatened New Bedford workers. Although the council would continue to subordinate broader imperatives to local concerns, it had plainly moved beyond the navel-gazing provincialism of Fall River craft unionists. Where many AFTO members in the Spindle City never accepted the CIO, the New Bedford Textile Council became an early TWOC affiliate and generous supporter of the union's southern campaign.[38]

The second notable consequence of the 1928 strike concerned New Bedford employers. According to labor journalist Harvey O'Connor, a split developed among local mill owners during the course of the struggle. On one side, O'Connor observed, a "diehard group" of "old line manufacturers whose mills have been operating at 30 to 60 percent capacity" resolutely opposed making any concessions to the strikers. On the other side stood a group of owners who had been working full-time and wanted to settle the dispute. Although the full dimensions of the division are not clear, it is likely that members of the latter group arranged the compromise settlement that finally ended the walkout.[39]

It is also likely that they were responsible for a number of important changes in the way the New Bedford Cotton Manufacturers Association (NBCMA) subsequently dealt with local unionists. Maintaining peace with the textile council had traditionally been a major function of the organization. But, as C. F. Broughton of the Wamsutta Mills observed in a 1932 address, "There existed a lack of confidence, a certain distrust, and an apparent disregard of the opposite point of view." After the "costly mistake of 1928," Broughton added, mill owners recognized the inadequacy of existing industrial relations machinery. To correct the situation, they arranged a tripartite conference that included representatives from local unions, the NBCMA, and a Citizens' Committee. The main purpose of the gathering was to establish a means of increasing efficiency and reducing costs that would be jointly supported by capital and labor. Since that time, Broughton concluded, the struggle of local mills to maintain their competitive position in textile markets had been characterized by increasing cooperation between employer and worker organizations. Whenever a dispute arose, the Citizens' Committee stepped in, "and in every case its ruling was observed."[40]

Broughton no doubt overstated the degree of industrial harmony in New Bedford. The early 1930s was an awful time for local workers, and at least one company engaged in practices designed to intimidate union employees. Yet there is evidence that New Bedford unionists were truly concerned about the market position of manufacturers. Extant copies of the *Weave Room News Sheet* show that leaders of the Protective Weavers Union closely monitored developments that might influence the competitiveness of local producers. And in January 1938, the textile council broke ranks with TWOC and accepted a 12.5 percent wage reduction. According to council leaders, they did so to help mill owners secure orders in a contracting market; they also did not want "New Bedford to be the battleground for New England in 1938 as it was in 1928." Because New Bedford was the regional wage leader in fine goods production, the cut quickly spread to Fall River and other cotton centers.[41]

The council's decision created a serious dilemma for TWOC. On one hand, TWOC leaders knew that the recession had created tremendous pressure for wage reductions throughout the region, and if New Bedford had not given in, another locale almost certainly would have. Moreover, council secretary William Batty had genuinely tried to cooperate with TWOC. At the same time, though, TWOC leaders recognized that they could ill afford to let self-interested local groups determine general wage policy. The line had to be drawn somewhere, and on February 10 Emil Rieve suspended the council for violating a provision in the TWOC

Constitution that required local unions to submit all wage demands to the international.[42]

Although William Batty bitterly resented the suspension, he did not like dual unionism, and in January 1939 the textile council agreed to a truce with TWOC. Had TWOC leaders been able to deal with Batty alone, they might have brought New Bedford back into the CIO fold without having to undertake a major campaign. Unfortunately, the situation there was much more complicated than that. Not only was the reconstituted UTW on the scene, but there was also the formidable presence of Seraphim P. Jason, the tough-talking head of the local teamsters' union. Jason had little love for either the UTW or the textile council: the Sylvia-Gorman forces were "a gang of rats," while council leaders were "nothing but a bunch of sellout bastards." Yet, as vice president of the state AFL, he strongly opposed any development that might augment the strength of the CIO. And because Jason was the local unionist whom mill owners most feared — he could "shut down the mills at any time," said one textile executive — CIO leaders had to take him very seriously.[43]

The TWUA started distributing leaflets in New Bedford during the summer of 1942, but the main drive did not begin until the following spring. Emil Rieve believed the city would not be "easy to crack," and he first wanted to clean up Fall River so the union could go into New Bedford "with both feet." The campaign was led by Mariano Bishop and Antonio England. Despite their different backgrounds — Bishop had entered a Fall River cotton mill at age ten, while England had briefly attended Northeastern law school — they worked well together. England would later serve as Bishop's assistant after the latter's appointment to the cotton-rayon directorship. During the campaign, Bishop handled Portuguese-language assignments on the radio and in the streets, while England, a New Bedford native, performed similar tasks among the city's French Canadian workers.[44]

The nominal leader of AFL forces was UTW fifth vice president Lloyd Klement, but his efforts were often overshadowed by the activities of Seraphim Jason. In addition to threatening to call out his truckers and close local mills if the TWUA won, Jason handled the "brunt of the mud-slinging" prior to the election. Throughout the campaign, *Textile Labor* reported: "A squadron of frog-throated AFL goons captained by Jason toured the city every day for a week, broadcasting the opposition's lies and slanders on four amplifying units mounted on pleasure cars and station wagons. At change of shifts, the loudspeakers parked at mill gates and hurled obscenity and low-comedy wheezes at TWUA-CIO representatives, organizers, and others who were at the mill gates morning, noon, and night talking to the workers." As the TWUA's house organ, *Textile Labor* was not the most objective source on such matters, and in fairness it should be added that CIO organizers did little to elevate the level of discourse when they urged operatives "to get rid of the company-dominated, do-nothing, inefficient leaders of the New Bedford Textile Council"; or when they accused council officials of using "their positions to get jobs and favors for their relatives." In the end, of course, it mattered little which side circulated the most palpable falsehoods. Here we need only note that, however much labor veterans accepted such bombast as an inevitable part of organizational work, the use of these tactics created bitterness that did not bode well for the future.[45]

On March 31, workers in eleven mills went to the polls. It was the second-largest election in TWUA history, and as voting officials began counting the 11,500 ballots it soon became evident that New Bedford was no longer what *Textile Labor* called the "rock-ribbed Gibraltar of AF of L textile unionism" — if indeed it ever had been. Operatives in ten of the eleven plants involved in the contest had opted to join the TWUA. Afterward, union leaders thanked local activists for their assistance and rubbed a few final grains of salt into AFL wounds as they recalled the ineptitude of certain UTW orators: like the speaker whose favorite expression was "get thee behind me, Satan," but who invariably pronounced "'Satan' to rhyme with 'Latin'"; and the "gas-artist" who declared, "Two heads are better than one but the two heads must pull together." What the latter probably intended to say, a TWUA journalist quipped, "was that a stitch in time gathers no moss."[46]

As it turned out, the UTW presence in New Bedford could not be laughed away. On the shop floor, small groups of AFL supporters hindered union development; in the courts, UTW lawyers challenged the validity of TWUA contracts with employers; and before the NLRB, craft units like the loom fixers occasionally sought separate bargaining rights. The UTW also mounted major election challenges in 1945, 1951, and 1953. Although the TWUA won these contests by decisive margins, the campaigns nevertheless took their toll. Within the mills, disgruntled wage earners sometimes tried to use these occasions to settle old scores with plant-level union leaders. In a 1945 incident, "A true member of your local" wrote joint board director Antonio England that workers in the Wamsutta twisting department were turning against the CIO because of inept shop-floor leadership on the part of union officials: "wouldn't it be much nicer and to your own advantage to put in a shop steward who possesses at least the average intelligence and one that doesn't use the method of threatening everyone he comes in contact with. 'I mean Tony Barboza.'" A business agent investigated the complaint and found not only that Barboza was well liked by most workers, but that the letter had probably been written by a second hand whom Barboza had prevented from doing special favors for a female operative in the department. In this and numerous other ways, UTW election challenges diverted union time and resources from matters of much greater significance to local wage earners.[47]

Nevertheless, the TWUA was in New Bedford to stay and local mill owners made little effort to aid UTW dissidents. Seeking shop-floor stability in a tight wartime labor market, the New Bedford Cotton Manufacturers Association signed a preferential union shop agreement with the TWUA shortly after the 1943 election. In an August arbitration case concerning a worker who refused to join the CIO, the association's main spokesperson, Seabury Stanton, showed no sympathy for either the operative or the mill involved and declared: "We are not going to hold with any breaking of that contract." The association was even more opposed to attempts to revive craft unionism. "We are always afraid that [the loom fixers' union] will come in and gum up the works," one textile executive later remarked, "even though they have been defeated on three or four occasions before the NLRB." The association acted as it did not out of any love for the TWUA, but out of a keen regard for its own interests. Manufacturers like Stanton, who was deeply committed to maintaining textile production in New England, knew that regional producers would have to modernize to stay in business. These mill owners also believed that, despite the past cooperation of the New Bedford Textile Council, craft unions were more likely than industrial unions to stand in the way of such developments.[48]

By war's end, the TWUA had thus established solid footholds in the New England cotton and woolen industries. But as union leaders recognized, signed agreements alone would not long satisfy the workers they represented. They now needed to infuse these pacts with real meaning. On one hand, they had to establish a system of shop-floor jurisprudence that would give workers some measure of control over their work lives. Because this was a protracted process that carried over into the postwar period, the development of grievance procedures will be examined in the next chapter. Here we will focus on wages, a matter of no small concern to textile workers, given the industry's low pay traditions.

BEFORE THE POSTWAR period, raising wages in the northern textile industry was rarely a simple matter of sitting down at the bargaining table and negotiating a mutually acceptable adjustment. Apart from the impact of the 1937 recession, which touched off a series of wage reductions, interregional wage differentials also had to be considered. Before the late forties, when woolen and worsted producers began moving south, this was mainly a problem for cotton workers. During the 1920s, the wage costs of New England cotton manufacturers were more than 50 percent higher than those of southern mill owners. Adoption of the NRA textile codes in 1933 reduced the spread to less than 20 percent, but the differential again widened after the Supreme Court declared the NIRA unconstitutional.[49]

One way in which CIO unionists hoped to resolve the problem was by organizing southern workers. In the spring of 1937 TWOC mounted what F. Ray Marshall has called "the best-planned textile organizing campaign ever undertaken" in the South. Well financed and making extensive use of southern-born organizers, the drive made impressive early gains. As in the North, however, the recession severely hampered southern field operations. Between October 1937 and March 1938, TWOC reduced its southern staff by half, and the union made little additional progress before the war years. As late as 1941, TWOC had only twenty-nine southern contracts covering a mere 27,750 workers.[50]

Despite persistent setbacks, union leaders knew they could not afford to write off the South. During the war years, they were able to expand the organization's presence in the region with the aid of National War Labor Board (NWLB) orders that required mill owners to bargain with the union. The TWUA's most important southern breakthrough during this period was at Virginia's Riverside and Dan River cotton mills. The focus of a 1930 southern campaign by the UTW, Dan River claimed to be the "World's Biggest Cotton Mills." The drive began in June 1941, when the TWUA dispatched an organizer to Danville at the request of local workers. As the effort progressed, with assistance from the railroad brotherhoods and AFL motion picture operators as well as area CIO unions, organizers encountered stiff resistance from a red-baiting Anti-CIO Association that questioned their character and motives, claimed they could not obtain a contract, and asserted that unionization would lead to a reenactment of the unsuccessful 1930 strike. Company operatives had doubtless heard it all before, and the propaganda appeared to have little effect on them. That at least was the conclusion of one frustrated association leader, who during the midst of the campaign declared, "the damned workers are no good anymore." Meanwhile, on the shop floor of Dan River mills a group of about two hundred committeepeople was signing up family and friends in preparation for an NWLB-sanctioned election, which took place in June 1942 and which the TWUA won by a decisive 7,207 to 4,716 margin. With further pressure from the NWLB, Dan River agreed to a contract the following spring.[51]

The union also made important advances in North Carolina during these years. At the Erwin Mills in Durham, company efforts to increase workloads caused rising tensions throughout the late 1930s. A subsequent membership drive by the TWUA culminated in a 1941 ruling by the National Defense Mediation Board that ordered Erwin to sign a contract with its Durham workers. Elsewhere in the state, the union obtained agreements at four mills in the important Cone chain, and by war's end more than seventy thousand southern operatives were carrying TWUA cards. Although this figure represented only one-eighth of the southern textile workforce, it was nonetheless a solid beginning, given the staunch antiunionism of regional producers.[52]

New England manufacturers watched these developments closely. The union's southern campaign was of particular interest to mill owners who had either moved part of their operations south or were considering such a move. What they saw was not encouraging. For example, American Thread's Dalton, Georgia, plant was the scene of a series of strikes throughout the 1930s and was organized by TWOC years before most of the company's northern mills; Dalton workers would later spearhead a drive to organize American Thread wage earners in neighboring Tallapoosa. Equally unsettling was the experience of Pacific Mills, which in 1916 had begun transferring its cotton operations to Columbia, South Carolina. During the late thirties and early forties, Columbia workers not only joined the TWUA but engaged in several walkouts when Pacific refused to adjust workloads to their liking. The union also organized Nashua Manufacturing's Cordova, Alabama, plant in late 1939, following a seven-month strike. Events such as these were not enough to deter mill owners intent on moving south; they were sufficient, though, to make many northern employers think twice and adopt a wait-and-see attitude. In an interview conducted for her 1940 book on Lowell, two manufacturers with plants in each region told Margaret Terrell Parker that southern labor "has of late been very insistent in its demands and that the results have practically eliminated the greater profits formerly obtained from their southern mills."[53]

In terms of wages, the significance of these organizational advances would become apparent after the war, when regional earnings became closely linked to union-negotiated pay scales at Dan River. In the meantime, union leaders had to find other ways to boost southern wages. Their main efforts focused on the enactment of minimum wage legislation and the presentation of several important wage cases before the National War Labor Board (NWLB). Union initiatives in these areas deserve attention for several reasons. They not only illuminate wage strategy during the period, but also shed light on both inter- and intra-regional relations among textile producers.[54]

Sidney Hillman was an early and ardent advocate of the Fair Labor Standards Act and worked hard to help guide the bill through Congress. Passed in 1938 following more than a year of acrimonious debate, the measure prohibited the employment of child labor in interstate commerce and established wage and hour criteria for industrial workers. From the outset, southern conservatives, worried about preserving regional wage differentials, raised cries of federal despotism and insisted that the law was as unnecessary as it was unconstitutional. According to South Carolina's Cotton Ed Smith, workers in his state could exist comfortably on fifty cents a day. Fortunately, not all southerners shared Smith's views, as the act might never have become law without the support it received from liberal legislators like Florida's Claude Pepper.[55]

Some also contended that pressure from northern capital was no less essential. At the time of its enactment, Walter Lippmann argued that northern industrialists viewed the Fair Labor Standards Act (FLSA) as an internal protective tariff. Although there is evidence to sustain this interpretation, Lippmann was not entirely correct. It is true that nearly all northern textile manufacturers supported the measure, but they did so for a variety of reasons. Where woolen producers backed the bill as a moderate alternative to federal licensing legislation, cotton manufacturers were not certain what to expect from it or how best to use it to their advantage.[56]

This was evident in the way New England cotton producers approached the question of an appropriate initial minimum. The FLSA provided for the establishment of a forty-cent minimum by 1945 without specifying how quickly that figure had to be reached; the pace at which the minimum would be raised was to be determined by tripartite committees appointed for each branch of the industry. Not surprisingly, the TWUA called for an immediate forty-cent minimum. To set a lower limit "would cause unemployment in areas paying higher wages," Solomon Barkin declared. "It is a matter of choice as to where unemployment might result — in high wage areas because of migration or shifting of business to low wage areas, or in low wage areas because of advancing wages too rapidly." There was a good deal of support for this position in northern textile circles. Some manufacturers such as Johnson and Johnson joined Barkin in demanding a forty-cent minimum; E. F. Walker of the Rhode Island Textile Association stated that it "would have comparatively little effect" on mills in his organization; and the Fall River Cotton Manufacturers Association hoped for at least a thirty-five-cent limit. In the end, though, the National Association of Cotton Manufacturers (NACM), with support from both the Fall River and Rhode Island groups, settled for 32.5 cents.[57]

As it was, even this compromise figure proved too high for some southern producers. One group of mill owners, led by Charles Cannon, the baron of Kannapolis, North Carolina, and president of Cannon Mills, demanded a twenty-five-cent minimum. However much they may have equivocated up to this point, NACM officials had no intention of accepting less than 32.5 cents. They immediately began assembling data on southern living costs and collecting briefs on the effects of unfair interregional competition from public officials in New England's leading cotton centers. They also sought and obtained support from major interregional producers such as Pepperell, American Thread, and Pacific Mills. The latter testified that a 32.5-cent minimum, though it would force them to raise wages slightly in their southern plants, would have little or no effect on sales and employment. In voicing his approval of minimum wage legislation, Pepperell's Russell H. Leonard stated that the FLSA "may be expected to make the road more difficult for the unregenerate employer who chisels on his hours or wages, or both."[58]

In October 1939, FLSA administrators adopted the 32.5-cent minimum. As TWUA leaders had hoped, the new wage standard had a salutary impact on regional wage differentials. Where the increase affected only 6 percent of northern operatives, it raised the pay of 44 percent of southern textile workers. Because a higher initial minimum would have had a more substantial impact on the differential, it is worth asking why New England mill owners did not back the TWUA's forty-cent demand. The reasons for their hesitance appear to have stemmed mainly from practical considerations. Certain groups of wage earners in regional plants did not even receive 32.5 cents an hour, and manufacturers feared that boosting their pay would have an unsettling effect on the entire wage scale. NACM officials may also have believed that a forty-cent minimum would alienate the New England–based inter-regionalists, who still had some lingering commitment to the region and whose support might yet be essential on other legislative matters.[59]

Although TWUA leaders could derive some satisfaction from their efforts to boost southern pay scales through minimum wage legislation, much work remained to be done. With the coming of war, wage policy became the province of various government regulatory bodies. This presented new opportunities for textile unionists and they were quick to grasp them. In a 1942 case before the NWLB, the TWUA conducted a frontal attack on regional wage discrepancies. Its main argument was that southern cotton operatives received ten cents an hour less than their northern counterparts, despite the fact that they were equally efficient, faced similar living costs, and often worked in the most modern and profitable plants in the industry. It was further noted that recent decisions involving the bituminous coal industry and Aluminum Company of America provided ample precedent for reducing regional wage differentials. The TWUA thus asked that southern wages be raised twenty cents an hour and that northern workers be given a ten-cent increase.[60]

On this occasion, New England manufacturers abandoned their earlier vacillation and lined up squarely behind the TWUA. Testifying on behalf of the NACM, Charles B. Rugg sounded more like a born-again New Dealer than the Yankee Republican that he was. The main thrust of Rugg's argument was that, while collective bargaining had become the centerpiece of national labor policy, most southern textile mills remained unorganized. As a consequence, any board ruling that granted the same wage increase in the South as in the North would "constitute a repudiation of the whole philosophy that has dominated labor legislation in this country since the earliest days of the New Deal." It would also be a grave injustice to northern mill owners, who are "simply asking that production costs be equalized, so that managerial skill, not geographical location, will determine the outcome of the competitive struggle for the textile market."[61]

The NWLB was apparently unimpressed by these contentions and, refusing to deal with the regional differential, granted a 7.5-cent-an-hour general wage increase. However disappointed they may have been by the decision, union leaders were not about to sit on their hands. During the next eighteen months, as evidence accumulated that low wages were the primary cause of persisting labor shortages in textiles, the TWUA made plans for another assault on the regional wage differential. Now aware that the NWLB would not accept arguments that directly challenged long-standing differentials, the union this time asked for a sixty-cent minimum wage and ten-cent general increase for all cotton-rayon workers, both North and South. In another departure from its earlier effort, the TWUA focused on the substandard living conditions of southern operatives rather than the comparative efficiency of regional producers. The research department created a solid empirical basis for the union's case by preparing "emergency sustenance budgets" for workers in three northern and two southern textile centers. These showed that southern operatives ate less, wore cheaper clothes, lived in less comfortable homes, and were unable to provide their children with the same amount of education as northern wage earners.[62]

This time, however, New England mill owners refused to back the TWUA initiative. According to an NACM study, not all southern producers had granted their employees the 7.5-cent-an-hour raise mandated by the earlier NWLB decision, and the association now opposed any further wage increases. Despite this opposition, the case moved forward. In September, an NWLB fact-finding panel both endorsed the research department's family budget approach and upheld major contentions presented in the union brief. Southern employer groups reacted by stepping up their lobbying campaign to bury the case. The union was cognizant of these activities and somehow managed to obtain correspondence documenting the effort, which it made public in the pages of *Textile Labor.* Of particular interest was a letter written by William P. Jacobs of the Print Cloth Group of Cotton Manufacturers, which stated, "From conferences which I held I know that Justice Byrnes, Senators George, Maybank, Russell, and Governor Gardner and perhaps others have insisted that [Judge Fred Vinson, director of economic stabilization] do nothing which will wipe out the traditional North-South differential."[63]

Judge Vinson was not pleased by the revelation, as he soon made clear in a letter to Jacobs. "Evidently you feel that the only flaw in your report was its indiscretion," Vinson wrote. "I cannot agree." He added that he "deeply resent[ed] any intimation" that he was "subject to political pressure." What effect all this had on the subsequent decision is impossible to determine. But a few days later the NWLB issued a ruling that established a fifty-five-cent minimum for cotton workers and granted a five-cent general wage increase. Although the TWUA had wanted more, what it obtained was nevertheless quite a lot. The order cost southern manufacturers twice as much as it did their New England counterparts and, as Lloyd Reynolds and Cynthia Taft observed, "produced for the first time a standard wage schedule in the South." By 1946, the interregional wage differential stood at 12.4 percent in cottons, the lowest ever recorded and half of what it had been three years earlier.[64]

As TWUA leaders looked ahead to the postwar period, they could take great satisfaction from this and other achievements. Having created a solid organization in the North and established a base from which future drives might be launched in the South, they had some reason to believe textile workers might soon enjoy the same benefits that CIO unions were then obtaining for their members in other northern industries. Yet, however much cause there was for optimism, they also recognized that they could not rest on their laurels. Aware of just how tenuous many of these advances were, they knew how quickly they could be lost. In a number of important respects, their struggle had only begun.

YEARS OF HOPE, 1945–1949

4

As World War II neared its close, organized labor looked forward to a period of industrial peace and economic prosperity. In March 1945 CIO leaders joined William Green of the AFL and U.S. Chamber of Commerce president Eric Johnston in endorsing a "Labor-Management Charter" that committed unions to a defense of the free enterprise system and capital's right to manage. In exchange, union leaders expected corporate America to adopt an economic strategy based on high wages and employment security. Many of the nation's leading manufacturing firms would ultimately do just that, as they came to recognize that such an accord offered them real benefits. But this did not happen immediately. With the exception of a handful of progressive employers, in 1945 most manufacturers were in a decidedly uncompromising mood. Uncertain about the postwar economic outlook and determined to restore what they saw as a decade-long erosion of managerial authority, these industrialists wanted no part of a "Labor-Management Charter" or anything else that might restrict their freedom. And when Walter Reuther, then head of the UAW's General Motors department, demanded that the giant carmaker grant a 30 percent wage boost without raising auto prices, the stage was set for the greatest strike wave in American history.[1]

On November 21, 1945, 320,000 GM unionists hit the streets; in January they were joined by hundreds of thousands of steel, rubber, oil, meatpacking, and electrical appliance workers. Although Reuther hoped the struggle would provide labor with the leverage to play a major role in shaping the postwar social and economic order, other union leaders had more modest aims. CIO president Philip Murray, who feared that insistence on a wage-price formula might alienate the Truman administration, backed away from the demand for price ceilings after urging Reuther to do the same. In February Murray's steelworkers settled for 18.5 cents, a 20 percent increase, as did the United Electrical, Radio, and

Machine Workers, which represented 30,000 wage earners at GM's appliance division. Other unions agreed to similar pacts, thus isolating Reuther's GM workers, who after holding out for another month also accepted the 18.5-cent offer.

The 1946 strike settlement set a pattern that would endure for nearly three decades in the nation's core industries. On one hand, capital recognized the need to increase wages and fringe benefits; on the other, labor shelved any plans it might have had for restructuring industry and society. Even Reuther's UAW gradually backed away from its broad social and economic aims to focus on industry-specific bread-and-butter issues. In the decade after World War II, unions in mass-production industries such as autos and steel achieved impressive advances at the bargaining table. In addition to providing substantial wage increases, union-negotiated contracts contained provisions for paid vacations, health insurance programs, pension plans, cost-of-living allowances, and other security measures. It is true, as various historians have pointed out, that these gains were accompanied by the establishment of a rigidly legalistic system of industrial relations that limited worker self-activity and narrowly defined labor's role in society. Yet the benefits obtained were equally real. And with memories of the Depression still fresh in mind, numerous wage earners were more than willing to accept an arrangement that exchanged promises of industrial peace for a share of the fantastic earnings American corporations were accumulating during these heady years of economic expansion. To many workers, it doubtless seemed a small price to pay for membership in the "new middle class" that Walter Reuther declared the labor movement was then creating.

New England textile operatives had also been active in the 1945–46 strike wave. When Maine and Rhode Island cotton producers refused to follow the pattern-setting New Bedford–Fall River agreement, workers deserted their looms and spinning frames in an effort to force recalcitrant employers into line. But regional operatives would not become part of the new industrial accord. Textile manufacturers did not possess the market strength enjoyed by firms in the core industries, and New England producers were particularly disadvantaged. Indeed, looking back at the regional textile industry during the immediate postwar period from the vantage point of the 1990s, it is easy to detect those signs of instability that a decade later would result in a massive wave of mill closings. Viewed from this detached perspective, the whole process takes on an air of grim inevitability; the only surprise is that it took so long. At the time, however, it was not at all clear what the future would bring. A number of people, in the ranks of both labor and capital, felt there was much worth saving, and that they possessed the wisdom and diligence needed to save it. These union leaders and mill owners were by no means living in a fool's paradise: rose-tinted sunglasses never became fashionable among textile unionists, and whatever else they may have been, manufacturers committed to maintaining production in regional plants were not naive.[2]

More important, there was still good reason to believe textiles did, in fact, have a future and was not yet ready to join the whaling industry and other antiquated forms of regional endeavor in New England museums. Not only had interregional wage differentials been substantially reduced during the war years, but the launching of Operation Dixie by the CIO in 1946 promised a further equalization of labor conditions. The immediate postwar period was also a time of unimagined prosperity for textile manufacturers, both North and South. This was especially significant for New England, which had more than its share of outmoded plant and equipment. If mill owners truly wished to preserve the regional industry, the capital needed to modernize aging production facilities was available. And if the TWUA could prompt them to make such investments, it might extend to its membership more of the economic benefits then being obtained by auto and steel unions.

These were important opportunities. But, as TWUA leaders knew, that was all they were. In the South, they could anticipate fierce resistance from nonunion employers. And even if they succeeded there, it was by no means certain that New England manufacturers would make the capital improvements needed to assure the long-term competitiveness of regional mills. Moreover, those who did would undoubtedly demand increased work assignments, which could be expected to arouse discontent among a workforce that tended to equate changes in workloads with the dreaded stretchout, and whose younger members had little commitment to the industry. What this meant was that union leaders had to find ways of promoting economic innovation while minimizing the costs of change for rank-and-filers. It also meant that they would be forced to challenge some of the managerial prerogatives that textile manufacturers, like their counterparts in the core industries, so fiercely guarded. Under the best of circumstances, this would be no easy task.

Before proceeding, a few words of explanation are in order concerning the treatment of the cotton and woolen sectors of the industry in the chapters that follow. Although important developments occurred in both sectors during the immediate postwar period, such matters tended to surface sooner in cottons than in woolens. This was so for two reasons: cotton producers felt more threatened than woolen manufacturers; and TWUA relations with woolen employers centered on the American Woolen Company, where managerial lethargy delayed serious industrywide consideration of a number of significant questions. As a result, this chapter will focus on events in the cotton industry, and an examination of related issues in woolens will be deferred to Chapter Five.

CONTRARY TO EXPECTATIONS that textiles would again become an economic basket case at war's end, the most noteworthy feature of the industry during the immediate postwar years was its extraordinary profitability. The release of pent-up consumer demand at home, coupled with the wartime destruction of productive facilities abroad, created the kind of sellers' market that manufacturers dream about. As orders quickly absorbed inventories, output increased, prices rose, and textile producers made money — lots of it. Business journalists, amazed by the incredible turnabout in this long-depressed industry, struggled to find appropriate words to describe the phenomenon. According to one *Fortune* writer, the industry "leak[ed] profits from every seam, for anything woven or knitted was selling at prices from fair to outrageous." Another *Fortune* commentator characterized the 1946 earnings of cotton manufacturers as "positively embarrassing." The next year's returns were even more startling. The TWUA research department calculated that the $2 billion in before-tax profits for 1947 equaled "the total profits earned by the industry in the 14 years from 1929 through 1942."[3]

On one hand, these were cheering developments for groups interested in preserving the New England textile industry. Mill for mill the region had the oldest plant and machinery in the industry, and without substantial modernization there was little hope that producers could maintain profitable operations when market conditions returned to normal. The postwar boom thus provided the capital needed to upgrade aging facilities. There was some question, however, as to what proportion of this investment stream would flow into New England plants. These years also witnessed a major restructuring of the textile industry, particularly in the South, where it was estimated that 22 percent of existing textile capital changed hands during the period. The result was that by 1948 northern interests controlled eighteen of the forty-two largest concerns in the region.[4]

This expansion of interregional production was in part an extension of earlier trends. Pacific Mills liquidated the last of its northern cotton facilities during the early forties, and in 1945 began transferring its worsted operations to southern plants; that same year American Thread, which already had several mills in Georgia, obtained plants in the Carolinas. But this was by no means the whole story. Several wartime developments both prompted and facilitated the formation of new interregional concerns that would later play a major role in the decline of the New England textile industry. One was government price regulation, which placed tight limits on the prices charged for staple gray goods, but allowed finished products to be priced according to an open cost-plus formula. This led manufacturers to convert increasingly greater amounts of their own gray goods and significantly reduced the flow of unfinished cloth to converters who styled fabrics for the market. The latter, in an effort to ensure a steady supply of gray goods, began to purchase their own mills. Thus it was that by 1946 M. Lowenstein and Sons, Inc., a New York–based converting operation that would later buy New Bedford's Wamsutta Mills, became the owner of six plants valued at approximately $8 million.[5]

The fluid market conditions engendered by these events in turn affected selling agencies. Worried that they would be unable to protect their sales lines in so unsettled a situation, commercial houses began to buy the mills for which they sold. The most notable example was J. P. Stevens and Company, Inc., a Worth Street cotton sales agency with intimate ties to the Stevens family's New England woolen and worsted interests. In 1946, Stevens concluded a merger agreement that brought twenty-eight cotton, wool, and rayon plants under the company's control. Numerous other mills would later be added to this already sizable operation.[6]

The merger movement of the forties was also influenced by federal tax laws. A major reason that concerns like Lowenstein and Stevens could so easily acquire properties was that the federal tax code made liquidation a profitable undertaking for the former owners. Many of the latter made substantial profits during the war years, but had little interest in using them to undertake needed modernization programs; nor did they wish to pay the high personal income taxes that would be levied upon these earnings if they were distributed as dividends. By selling out, these mills had only to pay a 25 percent capital gains tax. The purchasers also benefited from the arrangement, because they often paid for these acquisitions with money taken from the liquidating company's till. The result was that the former owners received generous compensation for their plants and the buyers acquired the firms at what were in effect fire-sale prices.[7]

Of the new interregionalists, no one was more adept at manipulating the tax code than Textron's Royal Little. Little was a maverick entrepreneur who characterized himself as "completely unconventional." He was also an inveterate empire builder who sometimes seemed more interested in acquiring new properties than in producing goods. In 1943, Little was president of the Atlantic Rayon Corporation, a modest-sized Rhode Island concern then engaged in making parachutes for the government. Sensing that the war had opened up unique opportunities for expansion, Little obtained a line of credit from New England banks and quickly demonstrated an ability to acquire aging companies loaded with surplus cash at bargain prices. By 1947, he presided over a growing interregional network that included seventeen textile mills and twelve sewing and cutting plants.[8]

What impact the rise of the new interregionalists would have on the New England textile industry was not immediately clear. There was some hope that it would not be altogether baneful. The old-line family firms that they absorbed plainly had no stomach for the long haul and their departure for less demanding fields of entrepreneurial endeavor was scarcely cause for mourning. The new owners could be expected to operate their plants at least as long as the great postwar sellers' market lasted. What would happen then nobody yet knew: Would it be a repeat of the 1920s? Would it be possible to maintain production on a relatively stable basis without wholesale liquidations? These are questions to which we will return. In the meantime, we need to take a closer look at another group of manufacturers: the regional persisters who sought to preserve the place of textiles in the New England economy.

Exactly how many textile manufacturers could be characterized as persisters is impossible to determine. The group's most active and outspoken members were certainly few in number. Nevertheless, because they held prestigious positions in the regional industry and were the kind of people others looked to for advice, their influence was doubtless greater than their limited numerical strength would suggest. Included in the group were such people as Joseph H. Axelrod, owner of Pawtucket's Crown Manufacturing Company. Axelrod believed that, compared with the South, New England possessed numerous advantages as a manufacturing center: that its supply of skilled labor, research and training facilities, capital resources, and proximity to major product markets provided a sound basis for competitive operation. These beliefs were by no means unique among regional producers. What distinguished persisters like Axelrod from other New England manufacturers was a willingness to put his pocketbook behind his convictions. During the immediate postwar period, Crown outfitted its plants with the most modern machinery available, as did New Bedford's Wamsutta Mills after Axelrod acquired that concern.[9]

Another persister, and perhaps the most influential member of the group, was Seabury Stanton. As treasurer of New Bedford's Hathaway Manufacturing Company, a position his father had held before him, Stanton made the preservation of the New England textile industry his life's work. In rousing speeches that combined an appeal to tradition with a call to arms, he periodically urged other regional producers to do their duty. Though cynics might have their doubts, Stanton told a 1951 meeting of the Rhode Island Textile Association, "one of our great reasons for being determined to continue here grows out of our own innate character. Our roots are deep in New England soil; most of our mills were established 'way back in the last century; those of us who still remain have stood fast during the thirty years of general exodus from this area. From a standpoint of character and personality we are, I guess, stubborn men who like a fight and who refuse to give up under competitive difficulties." If the textile industry was to remain in New England, Stanton declared in another speech before the National Association of Cotton Manufacturers, mill owners needed to adopt a "broad new outlook and vigorous constructive action."[10]

Stanton's aim in these addresses, he wrote TWUA research director Solomon Barkin, was "to awaken the New England mill men to a realization of their responsibilities, and to arouse a desire on their part to hold this industry in New England." And while they were delivered during the crisis years of the early fifties, the sentiments he expressed in them reflected long-standing convictions. No one who knew him ever doubted Stanton's love of his native region. Nor did they question his willingness to undertake "vigorous constructive action." According to a 1952 report commissioned by regional governors, Stanton had a reputation as "one of the most enterprising business executives in New England." And well he should have. During the mid-thirties, he had directed a "five-year plan" that revamped Hathaway's productive capabilities and created a modern merchandising program, thus enabling the company to adjust to changes in fine goods markets. Afterward, he never ceased looking for ways to keep Hathaway a leader in its field.[11]

In their efforts to preserve the New England textile industry, the persisters received substantial assistance from William F. Sullivan, who headed the northern-based National Association of Cotton Manufacturers (NACM). A close associate and friend of Stanton, Sullivan shared many of his views. Through the NACM, he was able to provide valuable aid on a number of legislative matters that concerned New England producers. And during the early fifties, as intensified southern competition threatened to destroy what was left of the regional industry, Sullivan made it clear where his organization stood by having the NACM's name changed to the Northern Textile Association. The new name, he explained, "would emphasize that New Englanders must think in terms of one group of mills that are enterprising and are trying to stay in New England, and another group of mills that are not."[12]

Sullivan also aided persisters in their dealings with textile unions. Depending on the circumstances, these relations could be either bitterly adversarial or constructively cooperative. On one hand, their strong commitment to mill modernization made the persisters formidable opponents at the bargaining table. Having put their own money on the line, they acceded to wage demands grudgingly and exerted unrelenting pressure on union officials to increase workloads. In 1962, Solomon Barkin accompanied both Sullivan and Stanton to a trade conference in Geneva, Switzerland, after which he penned an assessment of their negotiating styles. Because Barkin's profile was doubtless based as much on his own previous encounters with the two men as what he saw in Geneva, it is worth quoting at some length:

> neither will give easily in negotiations [Barkin wrote]; they retreat slowly and want a full measure of blood. Stanton considers himself a "Yankee Trader" who always has a card up his sleeve and gives nothing. Stanton is dry but yielding; Sullivan is even harsher and colder. You cannot accept their first offer or statement. They play to give slowly. They invite counter-brinksmanship. There is some chance of playing a more honest negotiating game with Stanton, but not with Sullivan. With the latter, you're pitting steel against steel.

When union leaders sat down with these people, they knew they were in for a fight. As a group, persisters were ever mindful of their class interests and did not hesitate to do whatever was necessary to defend them.[13]

At the same time, though, they accepted unionism as a fact of life. Joseph Axelrod contended that New England's "more mature labor movement" gave it a competitive advantage over regions that had not yet "weathered the problems created by unionization." Although William Sullivan would not go quite that far, he had little patience with manufacturers who believed their employees longed for the open-shop conditions of an earlier era. "Despite the disintegration of the New England textile industry," he later told a meeting of regional producers, "workers in the mills cling to union representation and, in general, seek a more militant organization." One employer never afflicted with the delusion of which Sullivan spoke was Seabury Stanton. In 1948, when manufacturers mounted a campaign to pass state legislation that would undermine union security in Massachusetts, Stanton not only refused to support the effort but argued that many mill owners actually preferred the union shop. Enacting the proposed bills, Stanton added, would deprive these employers "of the right to bargain with their own workers on union security."[14]

Apart from an indisposition to flee reality, there were other reasons why the persisters accepted unionism. One involved the regional wage differential. During the war years, NWLB rulings, coupled with unprecedented competition for workers between southern textile mills and the war industries that located in the region, exerted upward pressure on wage scales and reduced the differential to 12.4 percent; it would fall to less than 10 percent in the late forties. The persisters acknowledged that the figure represented a historic low; they also knew that, given their vacillating approach to minimum wage legislation and the NWLB cases, they could take little credit for what had happened. By 1949, Seabury Stanton had joined the TWUA in its efforts to remove wages from interregional competition by raising the federal minimum. Stanton recognized that interregionalists opposed the initiative, but this did not stop him from forging ahead. Such action, he declared, "would limit this competition [between northern and southern producers] to its proper sphere, namely, management's ability and skill in purchasing raw materials, in manufacturing, and in merchandising, where it economically belongs."[15]

The seriousness with which Stanton approached the minimum wage issue is well illustrated in a 1949 letter to Joseph W. Martin, Jr., the Republican House minority leader from Massachusetts. That year Stanton had wanted a ninety-seven-cent minimum that would have completely eliminated the interregional differential, though he knew he would probably have to settle for less; and as it turned out, the proposed bill called for a seventy-five-cent minimum. Before it could be enacted, however, a coalition of southern Democrats and northern Republicans, led by Martin, sought a further reduction to sixty-five cents. As a Republican, Stanton appreciated the benefits of the conservative coalition; but as a New England textile producer he had his own priorities, and he believed Bay State representatives should share them. Writing Martin, Stanton mentioned the problems facing regional textile manufacturers, noted that he had been informed of the congressman's actions on behalf of the amended measure, and then concluded on this ominous note: "I realize that a coalition with the Southern Democrats would be of considerable advantage in many ways, but it does not seem to me that you should buy such an arrangement at the expense of your Northern Textile constituents, and I, therefore, hope that I have been misinformed." Though it is unclear what effect Stanton's intervention had, Congress subsequently passed the seventy-five-cent bill.[16]

On a related matter, the persisters were encouraged by postwar CIO efforts to organize the South. Begun in the spring of 1946, Operation Dixie promised to do for southern workers what the great organizational drives of the 1930s had accomplished for their northern counterparts. From the outset, organizing textiles was the campaign's first priority, and TWUA contributions in terms of both money and organizers surpassed those of any other participating union. Although everyone knew that employer opposition would be fierce, the drive began on a hopeful note. "On balance," a writer in *Fortune* observed, "there is little doubt that eventually the South can be organized. The question is not whether, but when." And it was with these developments in mind that Joseph Axelrod declared it "hard to conceive of any section of the country ringing about itself an iron curtain for the purposes of shutting out organized labor."[17]

Lastly, the persisters hoped that unions could help them deal with a labor recruitment problem that had first surfaced during the war years and continued to plague regional producers. At a 1948 meeting of the New England Council, Textron's Royal Little stated that the refusal of younger wage earners to seek employment in textile plants foretold a "gloomy future" for regional mills. "If you can't operate a plant on a three-shift basis," Little explained, "you can't afford to modernize it. It is wise to go to another section where you can be sure to operate three full shifts six days a week." However much they rejected Little's solution, the persisters knew that the problem was real. In response, Joseph Axelrod attempted to paint a more optimistic picture and expressed his belief that the industry could yet expand "if there is cooperative effort on the part of all community elements: management, labor, government." We will later see that regional manufacturers were able to obtain some measure of cooperation from the TWUA. Right now, though, it would be useful to examine the social dimensions of the labor supply problem that Royal Little found so troubling.[18]

IN 1950 HATHAWAY MANUFACTURING hired the Budge Company to conduct a survey of worker attitudes at its New Bedford plant. After interviewing a wide range of employees, the Budge consultants submitted a report that sharply distinguished between the firm's older and younger operatives. The former, the report claimed, were for the most part dependent, "submissive in nature," and extremely worried about maintaining their positions. This did not mean that older workers were incapable of dissent. Although they had the utmost confidence in upper management and were impressed by working conditions at Hathaway, "Fear of being taken advantage of is often deeply entrenched, at the least, lingering." Younger workers, on the other hand, were a different lot altogether:

> This new H_____ Company type has a strong sense of individual freedom, dignity, and independence. He has a tendency to rebel against authority if it seems to him to be applied in an authoritarian, undemocratic way.

> This type of employee is interested in *job satisfaction*, not just satisfaction at having a job. If in his work he is not afforded an opportunity to feel a sense of participation, to him there is something missing. On matters that affect him he likes to be consulted in advance.

Where older workers would only go so far in criticizing their superiors, the report added, "The new type is likely to blame management or supervision for what they consider weaknesses in the program to improve quality."[19]

The Budge study did have certain defects. It is unlikely that older

workers were as docile as the report claimed. Many of these same operatives had participated in the rash of wildcat strikes that had periodically
hobbled production in textile centers during the war years, and in talking
with them consultants doubtless mistook caution for submissiveness.
Yet the contrast drawn between older and younger employees was well
taken. In the previous section, we saw how various wartime and postwar
developments sharpened the lines of division between two clearly defined groups of manufacturers that we characterized as interregionalists
and persisters. During this period, similar groupings emerged among
wage earners in the neighborhoods and mills of regional textile centers.
Inside the typical Lawrence or New Bedford plant, one could find a band
of shop-floor persisters who had spent the better part of their lives in the
industry, and whose skill and experience provided employers with one of
their few competitive advantages. Many of them could scarcely conceive
of employment outside textiles. They were joined by groups of younger
workers, some of whom also hoped to make cloth production their life's
work. But the latter were a distinct minority. Most of these youths were
just passing through, and whether they stayed in the industry would
depend in great measure on what the industry was willing and able to do
for them. We begin our examination of these workers by looking at the
persisters.

In June 1945, a group of investigators from the Bureau of Labor Statistics (BLS) interviewed two hundred cotton-textile workers (97 men
and 103 women) in Fall River, New Bedford, and Lewiston, Maine. The
wage earners chosen were all experienced spinners, weavers, and loom
fixers; they had been selected because, rather than seek more remunerative employment elsewhere, they had remained at their jobs throughout
the war years. For that reason, they constitute as representative a sam-
pling of persisters as one could now hope to assemble. One of the
group's most striking characteristics was its age structure: 70 percent of
the men and 50 percent of the women were forty-five or over. The early
age at which they had entered the industry was equally notable. The
majority had begun work shortly after their fourteenth birthday, some
even younger. As a consequence, most had a limited formal education:
69 percent left school between the fifth and eighth grades, and only 5
percent had completed a year of high school. With this background,
it was little wonder that one fifty-seven-year-old weaver, when asked
if he had changed jobs during the war, "seemed to find the question
amusing."[20]

Some persisters, though they never left the mills for long, did occasionally venture into other fields of employment. One such worker was Raymond Dupont, a New Bedford slasher tender, who during the course of a 1947 arbitration case was asked to provide union representatives with an account of his work history. Complying with the request, Dupont recalled that his textile career had begun at New Bedford's Wamsutta Mills, where he learned to weave and worked as a spare hand until December 1926, when he quit to become a peg boy at the Nashawena Mills. Two decades and ten job changes later, he would be back at Nashawena. On two occasions, mill closings had forced him to seek new employment. On two other occasions, he left the mills altogether: in 1937, he worked in the construction industry for a year; and during the war, he worked at an East Hartford aircraft plant.[21]

That Dupont then returned to New Bedford and the textile industry was hardly surprising. The locational immobility of the textile workers interviewed by the BLS researchers was nearly as great as their occupational stability. Most of these men and women had grown up in ethnic enclaves amid a dense network of kin relationships that often extended onto the shop floor of local mills. It was a world where family and work were inextricably bound together in a seamless web of mutual interaction. Many features of this world still existed during the immediate postwar period. "Workers' attachments have not only been solidified by family traditions," the BLS study observed, "but also by the fact that community life has to a large extent centered on mill employment." Raymond Dupont was one of many wage earners influenced by such considerations. In the department where he worked in 1947, three of the other seven slasher tenders were his cousins and the overseer was his uncle.[22]

In their efforts to aid shop-floor persisters, textile unionists sought to reinforce the material bases of this traditional world. The seniority provisions contained in TWUA contracts gave older wage earners a measure of job security that they had never before known. BLS investigators believed that an unwillingness to sacrifice seniority rights was a major reason that the workers they interviewed did not change jobs during the war. The TWUA also sponsored a broad range of programs designed to make life more attractive in the region's textile centers. From the outset of the TWOC campaign, national leaders had reminded organizers that the educational and recreational needs of workers were just as important as their economic interests. In the months and years to come, innumerable dances, concerts, picnics, athletic contests, and workers' classes all testified to the seriousness with which local officials accepted this counsel. These activities had an impact on the lives of union members. According to the BLS study, unions "increased the attachment of workers to their jobs and homes, because they not only act as bargaining agents, but also as the focus of much of the workers' social life."[23]

In so doing, though, unions posed a subtle threat to the cultural bases of the textile worker's traditional world. A major purpose of union-sponsored programs was to give wage earners "a sense of unity and maintain their interest in the organization." Through them union leaders hoped to create new forms of group identification among workers. This did not make unions an inveterate foe of the ethnic and familial loyalties that continued to shape shop-floor relations in textile communities. Many local officials were products of this world, understood its workings, and preferred to accommodate rather than confront these older particularisms. There were occasions, though, when conflict could not be avoided. In 1947, for example, a dispute between Raymond Dupont and his uncle, who was overseer of the department in which he worked, had to be resolved by an arbitrator. It is unlikely that this was the first time that family members, working together in kin networks, were unable to get along with each other. What was new—indeed unthinkable a generation earlier—was that an outside authority should intervene in the matter. And it was the union presence on the shop floor that made such intervention possible.[24]

Where unions acted to transform the traditional world of the textile worker, other developments threatened to destroy it altogether. Apart from deindustrialization, the most important of these was generational discontinuity. Unlike the persisters, most of whom entered the mills at an early age and afterward came to view textiles as their life's work, their children were able to form a more expansive outlook. One reason they could do so was that they tended to be better educated than their parents. The enactment of child labor legislation was in part responsible. The Fair Labor Standards Act of 1938 barred the employment of children under sixteen years of age. A more important factor was the long textile depression of the 1920s and 1930s. With few jobs available in major cloth centers, children inevitably stayed in school longer.[25]

Many probably did so at their parents' urging. Here again we need to bear in mind the impact of the long Depression. It may be true, as apologists for the status quo never tire of reminding us, that adversity builds character. But the persisters scarcely needed such advice. In places like Fall River and New Bedford, no one could forget the awful uncertainties of the twenties and thirties. And no one wanted their children to have to raise families under similar conditions. What resulted was a general skepticism, in some cases a visceral antipathy, toward textile employment. Any program that broadened the economic opportunities available to one's offspring, be it formal schooling or any other type of training, could expect the support of mill parents.

World War II was another event that further weakened the attachment of these youths to both the textile industry and the locales in which they had grown up. Those who served in the armed forces gained firsthand exposure to that broader world outside the mill community. When they returned, the old hometown was not quite the same. It was certainly good to see family and friends again, and to reclaim one's seat at the neighborhood tavern. But for many, this was not enough. "Global conflict," John Hoerr has written, "seems to have a broadening effect on such people as it doesn't kill." Speaking of the Pennsylvania mill town of his youth, Hoerr adds, "When the war was over, McKeesport and the Mon Valley looked a lot smaller, dirtier, and less offering of opportunity to the men and women who came back, as well as those growing up. People began leaving, especially young people." A similar outmigration occurred in the textile centers of New England after the war. Meanwhile, other returning veterans who did not leave could use the educational benefits provided by the GI Bill to stay out of the mills. According to one Fall River priest, the GI Bill changed general attitudes toward schooling among that city's Portuguese workers. With higher education now a viable option for those who served in the military, he remarked, "Indifference toward education which had then been widespread was broken."[26]

The war also affected those who stayed at home. Given the opportunity to obtain higher earnings in war plants, many workers, both young and old, secured jobs outside the textile industry for the first time in their lives. At war's end, as these companies closed or cut back production, some wage earners resumed their former roles in regional textile factories. But others did not. One reason was that they had greater mobility. Wartime prosperity enabled many of these workers to purchase automobiles, a means of transportation that relatively few textile operatives could afford during the prewar period. Thus freed from local labor market constraints, and with memories of the higher wages paid in war industries still fresh in mind, they were able to seek more remunerative employment elsewhere.[27]

During the postwar period, the labor supply question became a matter of vital concern to New England textile manufacturers. Southern competition had forced them to concentrate on the production of high-quality goods, and they could not expect to maintain acceptable levels of output or product quality with a labor force comprised mainly of casual workers. Someone would have to be there when industrial artisans like Joseph Mercier, a Rhode Island loom fixer who at age seventy-five was still considered one of the most able craftsmen in the area, decided to retire. Experience also counted in less skilled positions. Machine tending might appear simple enough to outside observers, but industry veterans knew better. As we saw in Chapter One, the best weavers not only repaired broken threads but were able to detect loom malfunctions that were indiscernible to most eyes and ears. And as we noted there, such skills were not acquired overnight.[28]

Where these developments caused unmitigated alarm among manufacturers, they elicited a more mixed response from textile unionists. On one hand, TWUA officials were able to use mill owner fears of labor shortages to increase their leverage at the bargaining table, especially during periods of relative prosperity when product demand was steady. At the same time, though, union leaders could not entirely ignore the labor supply problem. If regional producers concluded that the situation was indeed hopeless, it could touch off a massive wave of liquidations and destroy everything that they had worked so hard to achieve. Although the union never engaged in labor recruitment activities, it did as part of its effort to develop capable plant-level leadership create programs that appealed to ambitious, younger wage earners. These included workers' forums, shop steward seminars, labor studies classes at local colleges, and summer institutes for the training of rank-and-file leaders.[29]

Many of the union's social and recreational activities were also directed at younger workers and their families. One was the Kiddies Christmas Party, a major annual event for nearly all joint boards that usually began with "good, loud community singing," followed by various skits, a motion picture, and the distribution of gifts. More than seven thousand children attended the 1949 Lawrence party. Other programs designed primarily for younger workers, but which sometimes stimulated the interest and enthusiasm of the entire membership, included the broad range of athletic activities sponsored by union locals. In 1948, the Lawrence joint board made and seconded a motion "to give the CIO softball team our moral and financial support." When the club went on to post a 29–5 record, the board voted to supply all team members, including the batboy, with jackets and to purchase a trophy cabinet.[30]

As important as these programs were, union leaders knew that they were hardly enough. In the end, worker loyalty to both the organization and the industry depended on the success of union efforts to provide adequate wages, job security, and good working conditions. In textiles, these three demands were tied together by the work assignment question. The degree to which workloads corresponded with what textile operatives considered a fair day's toil had an enormous influence on how they viewed their employers, their jobs, and the industry in general. It is equally significant that union leaders saw work assignment changes as part of a broader constellation of interests that included worker earnings and company investment policy. The ways in which these matters intersected formed the core of TWUA policy in postwar New England, and the remainder of this chapter will focus on union initiatives dealing with these concerns.

IN TRYING TO PIECE together union policy on wages, workloads, and investment, a good place to begin is the writings of TWUA research director Solomon Barkin. His observations on these matters are especially noteworthy because they not only state what TWUA policy was, but also reveal a number of the assumptions that undergirded it. According to Barkin, the TWUA approach to wage bargaining in the postwar period was based on the dynamic theory of wages, a term he had coined to pacify academic audiences that needed "a high faluting word to express the theories of the labor movement." At negotiating sessions with employers, Barkin elaborated, "I usually explain the Dynamic Theory of Wages something like this":

> There is no greater compliment a union leader pays to an employer [than] when he comes in asking for a wage increase. It means that we have such great confidence in your competence, in your managerial capacity that we are not only discounting the increases in productivity, in your competence in the past, but we are sort of mortgaging your future competency and discounting it ahead of time so that we can enjoy it and so that you will have more incentive to move ahead.

Barkin was aware that not everyone appreciated the logic of this formulation, yet he insisted that he was not being disingenuous, but simply stating a fact: "This is what the trade union movement is constantly saying."[31]

To make the industry a good place to work, Barkin recognized that higher wages alone were insufficient. Workers also required some measure of job security. In an article entitled "Labor's Code for a Free Enterprise Economy," he observed that unlike management, most wage earners were not enterprise oriented. Where mill owners looked to the success of individual firms for profit and gain, workers tended to subordinate such concerns to "the prosperity of the entire economic community." Labor needed this broader state of material well-being, Barkin explained, to "assure alternative job opportunities and provide the setting for effective bargaining with the great mass of enterprises." Unions thus expected manufacturers to make every effort to keep pace with their competitors: "the earnings of the enterprise must be used to maintain its modernity. Where earnings are dissipated by unusually liberal dividends and benefits to management and the company's physical, competitive, and financial position are neglected, no workers will approve of the management."[32]

As Barkin well understood, however, reconciling increased wages with plant stability was more easily stated than achieved. This was especially so in textiles. Although wartime contracts and the subsequent consumer boom had temporarily reversed a wave of mill closings begun in the mid-twenties, textiles remained an extremely unstable industry, with more than its share of marginal producers. This presented TWUA officials with problems then unknown to labor leaders in industries like steel and autos. "Very few other unions in our modern industrial set-up," Barkin remarked, "have to worry about whether the company will be resourceful enough to work out the higher labor costs." In its efforts to come to grips with the dilemma, the TWUA urged companies to modernize their plants, even though such programs invariably eliminated jobs. At the same time, union leaders demanded that workers be given a share of the benefits resulting from increased productivity. Aware that underinvestment often presaged liquidation, the TWUA sought to preserve a contracting number of high-paying positions by linking wages to investment policy. In this way it hoped to manage a process of industrial restructuring that it could not stop.[33]

To accomplish these aims, union leaders not only had to induce mill owners to make needed investments. They also had to convince both workers and local union officials that facilitating economic modernization was in their best interests. This was an unfamiliar role for labor organizations, and it carried real risks. A program designed to promote economic efficiency could easily be perceived as class collaboration, and if rank-and-filers came to embrace such views, TWUA leaders would lose all credibility.

These were not idle fears. TWUA officials knew that earlier instances of union-management cooperation had sometimes ended badly. At Salem's Pequot Mills, for example, United Textile Worker initiatives during the early thirties to help management increase productivity had resulted in a rank-and-file rebellion against union leaders. They also remembered how stretchout-engendered unrest had facilitated union development. During the 1934 strike, Horace Riviere declared that the abolition of "the vicious stretchout system transcends any demands of organized labor." And in 1937 a TWOC organizer told *The New York Times* that the "eventual aim" of New England unionism is "control of the machine load"; stretchouts not only exhausted workers, but were often "used to circumvent rises in pay." These experiences left a legacy of suspicion, a sense among wage earners that the more things changed, the more likely they were to get the short end of it.[34]

One step union leaders took to reassure workers was to create a formal policy on handling work assignment changes. Although willing to help regional mill owners boost productivity, they had no intention, as Mariano Bishop put it, of allowing them to "use the sweat and blood of human beings as a substitute for machinery." The TWUA thus distinguished between routine work assignment adjustments and adaptations that involved changes in the level of physical effort, work duty patterns, and methods of compensation. Whereas manufacturers were given wide latitude to make whatever routine adaptations they believed necessary, changes that altered the terms of employment required prior union consent. To ensure that routine adjustments were indeed just that, the research department assembled a team of industrial engineers to assess the level of work effort before and after any questionable changes.[35]

A third category of work assignment changes involved technological innovations. These too could be instituted without prior approval, though the union did insist that it be notified several weeks beforehand so it could arrange a trial period, which lasted until actual performance of the new device met proposed job specifications. Because technological adaptations reduced employment, the TWUA attempted to assist displaced workers by demanding that they be granted separation bonuses, preferential hiring rights, and training for new employment, whenever practicable. Lastly, to moderate the pace of workload adjustment, the union discouraged management from making too many changes at any one time. "Recurrent changes within a short period on the same job," Barkin warned, "stimulate uncertainty and engender suspicion." This made it difficult to develop that "atmosphere of persuasiveness" union leaders deemed essential for the successful implementation of workload changes.[36]

Education was another means TWUA officials used to acquaint workers with union policy on technological innovation and work assignment changes. Shortly after the war, an "On the Job" column prepared by the research department became a regular feature in *Textile Labor*. These articles described recent technological breakthroughs, explained why employers would need to implement them to remain competitive, and showed how their implementation would improve working conditions. They also discussed how union representatives might use the increased productivity resulting from these adjustments in bargaining sessions with employers. The main purpose of the column was thus twofold: to let workers know that change was likely to occur and to provide assurance that the union would be there to protect them when it did.[37]

On a day-to-day basis, the most important form of union protection available to workers was the grievance process. In an industry where job security had required unceasing attention to the whims of overseers, and where stretchouts and speedups had long been integral features of managerial policy, being able to contest adverse changes in shop-floor conditions was a cherished right. For some workers, filing a grievance was a matter of simple justice. "Whoever is right—there is no more fight," Lawrence operative Gabe LaDoux observed. "Sometime the boss was not right." For others, it meant much more. Rose Diamentina, a New Bedford weaver who began working in local mills during the 1910s, recalled that overseers "used to bawl you out for things that were not your fault and you had no control over." However unjustifiable such harassment might have been, "You kept your mouth shut, because if you didn't, out you'd go." Later, though, all this changed. "Now you can talk and send them where they came from."[38]

A reasonably full set of grievances for New Bedford mills during the 1940s has been preserved, and the discussion that follows is based primarily on these records. Before beginning, it should be noted that the New Bedford experience was not entirely representative. Before their affiliation with the TWUA, local unionists had created grievance procedures that went well beyond anything that could be found in most regional textile centers. Yet, because the earlier system did not protect all operatives, TWUA actions on this matter did make a difference. As Mary Pereira, a spooler at the Soule Mill, later stated, the United Textile Workers (UTW) "never gave us any service. That's why I helped to turn it out in 1943, and I voted against it in 1945, 1947, and 1951."[39]

Efforts to establish a more inclusive grievance system in New Bedford began shortly after the 1943 elections in which the TWUA displaced the AFL as bargaining agent in local mills. The first step was to obtain complete descriptions of all full-time jobs. The provision of this information was crucially important for the adjustment of work assignments. "No job routine should be worked out by management which has not had the workers' approval," Solomon Barkin observed. "They know the job and can furnish suggestions concerning the best way of performing the job." Operatives also knew that revised job routines often resulted in excessive performance requirements when they were not accompanied by appropriate changes in tools, machinery, and general working conditions. To protect workers from "management's deficiencies" and thus secure their cooperation, Barkin stated, it was absolutely necessary that they be able to insist upon the strict observance of a detailed set of job specifications.[40]

The TWUA's demand for this information took New Bedford mill owners by surprise. Unaccustomed to preparing such data, much less sharing it with union officials, they were uncertain what to do. Some furnished narrow descriptions that were plainly inadequate; most sent the demands on to the New Bedford Cotton Manufacturers Association (NBCMA), where they received attention from the group's president, Seabury Stanton. As the region's premier persister, Stanton both recognized the need to boost productivity and appreciated the constructive role that unions might assume in the process. He clearly played a major part in the association's decision to supply the requested job specifications. In one letter to Solomon Barkin, Stanton praised a union analysis of weave and picker room duties the research department had furnished him, noting that "no survey ever prepared by manufacturers, to our knowledge, has been as detailed as yours."[41]

Obtaining adequate job descriptions was only a beginning. If grievance systems were to function effectively within mills, workers had to be aware of their rights and ready to defend them. This often meant challenging the traditional prerogatives of shop-floor supervisory personnel. When overseers and second hands in New Bedford plants tried to dissuade newly hired workers from joining the union, posted their own seniority lists, and required the performance of tasks unrelated to accepted job specifications, they quickly learned that they had overstepped their authority. They also learned that customary forms of worker harassment were no longer acceptable. In a 1943 incident at the Naushon Mill, a second hand attempted to intimidate a group of winders by using a watch to time them while they ate. Responding to complaints from the infuriated winders, upper management not only told the second hand to put his watch away, but urged him to "get acquainted with workers, gain their confidence, and not be too militant."[42]

As it became clear to all concerned that the union could not be ignored, most grievances centered on some facet of the work assignment question. One source of discontent was management's failure to provide appropriate resources and working conditions for a given task, which resulted in work overloads that caused "undue fatigue" among workers. These expressions of dissatisfaction contained an implicit threat of decreased productivity that persuaded companies to take such actions as providing better warps for weavers, reducing the size of bobbins for winder tenders, replacing faulty spindles for twisters, and securing better grades of cotton for spinners. When promised improvements were not made, a union official invariably demanded to know why; and when management was unable to make needed changes, it sometimes agreed to reduce workloads or to assign additional operatives to the job.[43]

On at least one occasion, unionists acted unilaterally to redress a workload grievance. In 1947, worker complaints prompted a shop steward at Pierce Brothers to slash weaving assignments from twenty-four to sixteen looms on his own initiative. Alarmed that the action might signal the beginning of a union campaign to usurp managerial rights, the New Bedford Cotton Manufacturers Association (NBCMA) promptly arranged a conference with local TWUA leaders. Although the subsequent discussions allayed management's worst fears, they did not lead to an immediate resolution of the problem at Pierce Brothers. Union leaders insisted that they could not "sell" a twenty-four-loom job to the company's weavers. The deadlock was finally broken when both sides agreed to a new trial period.[44]

As the bargaining system evolved, labor acquired additional rights. Contracts required manufacturers to obtain union consent before making other than routine work assignment adjustments. When companies failed to do so, union leaders did not hesitate to file a grievance. Although these disputes sometimes ended in union threats to take the matter to arbitration, during the immediate postwar years mill executives were often able to resolve the problem by explaining their actions to union officials or providing previously withheld information. Whatever their disposition, the filing of such cases indicated that significant changes were taking place within textile mills. By having to respond to the grievances, management learned that older patterns of shop-floor relations were no longer tenable. Conversely, the fact that these adjustments could be contested at all was an important advance for textile workers. The battle against excessive workloads and unsatisfactory working conditions was now being fought on terms that at least gave wage earners a chance.[45]

Textile workers were especially sensitive to work assignment changes that threatened to reduce wages. Compensation for most textile jobs was governed by a bewildering assortment of piece rates. Operatives nevertheless had a keen sense of what they should be earning. In a 1943 incident at the Kilburn Mill, two winder tenders were given an uncommonly favorable rate for a new job assignment. When upper management learned just how favorable, the overseer "got hell," the rate was set at the same level as that of the previous position, and the two winders filed a grievance. According to the business agent who handled the case, they "realize[d] that the rate was too high," but felt they should earn more on the new assignment because the yarn was coarser and they had to "work harder on it to make their pay." In subsequent years, the union processed numerous piece-rate complaints. Most involved job changes that decreased average hourly earnings; more often than not companies agreed to pay back wages to the workers affected.[46]

Not all work assignment grievances pitted union against management. There were a number of cases in which wage earners complained that a maldistribution of work within departments had resulted in an overload for certain operatives; that workers on a previous shift were not doing their fair share; or that the faulty work of people in another department was making their jobs unnecessarily difficult. When notified of these problems, companies almost always made some effort to ensure that jobs were more evenly distributed or to relieve operatives of particularly burdensome workloads.[47]

Grievances of this sort could be troublesome for union officials, especially when they centered on an individual wage earner. Operatives like the spooler tender at Naushon Mill who hit one of her coworkers on the head with a spool plainly had to be disciplined, but most cases were not nearly so clear-cut. When workers agreed with management that a particular operative was inefficient or "laying down on the job," or urged that someone be demoted for going home sick because she did not like the job she had been given, shop stewards and business agents had to proceed with caution. These incidents remind us that union building involved more than winning a representation election, obtaining a contract, and making sure that management honored the agreement. It also meant trying to resolve the sometimes conflicting demands of people who did not always get along with each other. Speaking of how difficult it was to develop effective plant-level union leadership, Solomon Barkin once remarked, "I am convinced if you can't sense what the other person is saying through his eyes or pores, you can't rely on language." Disputes such as the above tested whether local leaders had that sixth sense of which Barkin spoke.[48]

These examples raise the larger question of the degree to which rank-and-filers embraced union policy on mill modernization and work assignments. According to Seabury Stanton, many workers retained an instinctual aversion to increased workloads. "The northern textile operative," he declared in a 1951 statement, "through habit and through the teachings of the old craft unions and his father before him, has become accustomed to thinking of his work assignments in terms of the number of machines he is required to operate, rather than in terms of the actual time and effort required." Were Stanton the only person who believed this, we could safely ignore his contentions. Other regional mill owners, using much the same language, had been issuing similar declarations since at least the 1910s. As it was, though, a number of union leaders agreed with Stanton. One was Fall River joint board manager Edward Doolan, who told a 1949 meeting of the TWUA executive council, "Some people behave as if they are married to the job and will not allow any increase."[49]

Another was Solomon Barkin, who a year earlier had informed Emil Rieve that "there is still strong resistance to change" in most northern areas. Barkin, too, attributed this opposition to the "strong craft tradition" of New England workers. He also believed local leaders were not doing enough to convince operatives of the need for change. Rather than viewing a given work assignment in terms of its practicability, Barkin claimed, many business agents and joint board managers "conceive of it as a political issue and treat it as a political problem rather than on its merits." Fearful of arousing rank-and-file opposition to their leadership, these officials tended to resist all requests for workload changes, even in instances where they knew management had taken the steps needed to justify an increase. As a consequence, Barkin added, "we have had to go to arbitration with the full knowledge that our case is not sound."[50]

In making these assertions, Barkin was not trying to blame local officials alone for the shortcomings of TWUA policy on mill modernization. As he knew better than anyone, they frequently had good reason to resist mill owner demands for increased machine assignments. To create that "atmosphere of persuasiveness" needed to induce worker cooperation, manufacturers had to do their part. But for reasons we will now examine, this was not happening, at lest not to the extent union leaders desired.

ALTHOUGH TWUA OFFICIALS spoke often of cooperation with management, what they were usually talking about was participation in management. They knew the industry faced a problematic future in New England, and that changes would have to be made. Whereas union leaders in core industries could allow industrialists to assume broad managerial prerogatives without endangering the material well-being of rank-and-filers, experience had taught textile unionists that they could not stand by and hope that management would do the right thing. To ensure that change was in the best interests of both its membership and the industry, the union had to be involved in the decision-making process. This distinction was perhaps best expressed by Solomon Barkin. "I frankly don't really mean 'cooperation with management,'" he later told the Columbia University Seminar on Labor. "It's not cooperation, because 'cooperation' is not the word for our role in management. We have to pinprick management; we have to disturb management; we can never be complacent in our relationship with management. And just cooperating isn't enough. We have to provide continually disturbing leadership; cooperation is too passive a role for unions to perform."[51]

The problem was that mill owners had other ideas about the appropriate role for unions. In their minds, the union's main function was to enforce managerial policies, not help make them. Union leaders had no illusions on this point; they realized just how deeply ingrained such beliefs were. And in 1944 Barkin attempted to arrange a series of meetings with New England manufacturers as part of an effort to break down this resistance. "Look, we fight enough in the mill," Barkin said. "Let's get together once a month in Boston to talk generalities." The topics to be discussed might range from such broad issues as "the future of the United States" to such industry-specific concerns as the labor supply question. The proposal went nowhere. "They didn't even want to talk about it," Barkin recalled.[52]

Despite this rebuff, Barkin did not give up, and in 1946 New Bedford manufacturers expressed interest in devising a citywide plan for adjusting work assignments. This was certainly a promising development. Because New Bedford was the regional wage leader in cottons, any program instituted there was likely to have broader implications. And because New England's leading persister, Seabury Stanton, headed the New Bedford Cotton Manufacturers Association (NBCMA), there was a better than average chance that a workable plan could be created. As Barkin later observed, Stanton stood apart from most regional employers in his willingness to deal constructively with the union.[53]

Yet, however much they wanted an agreement on work assignments, union leaders were not about to give away the store, and they found several disturbing emphases in the initial NBCMA proposal. One concerned the role engineers would play in developing the plan. "We are not impressed with the thought of turning over the negotiations and the relations between management and the union to engineers," a proposed union response commented. "They tend to be rigid and overburdensome." Even more upsetting was the NBCMA's almost exclusive focus on increasing machine assignments. "From our point of view," the union replied, "the work should start from [an] analysis of hazards on the jobs and the sources of back-breaking work." By addressing these problems first, "you can truly speak of improving the work place and the work environment." The result would be a workforce genuinely committed to increasing plant efficiency, a commitment that it would be impossible to obtain through a plan that centered on the "eternally controversial problem of whether the worker is doing enough on the job."[54]

In raising these objections, the union emphasized its willingness to continue talks on the question. Seabury Stanton remained interested, but he was alone. As his local counterparts viewed the matter, they had made their proposal and there was nothing further to discuss. "They didn't even have the imagination to harness the constructive impulses of the union," Barkin remarked. "They had to have it their way. 'I want a 62 percent increase in work assignment; that is all.'" Barkin believed the obstructionism of Barnes Textiles Associates, the region's leading mill consultants, was a major reason the discussions ended as they did. He may have been right. Yet, as his own comments suggest, the problem went much deeper than that. Like most industrial leaders in postwar America, the vast majority of textile manufacturers were deeply suspicious of any arrangement that threatened their right to manage. And when the TWUA appeared to be encroaching on that right, they simply stopped listening.[55]

There were, nevertheless, some notable instances of union-management cooperation during the period. Despite the failure of the New Bedford plan, Seabury Stanton maintained regular contact with the union, on several occasions allowing the research department to train newly hired engineers at his plant. And at Crown Manufacturing in Pawtucket, Rhode Island, TWUA Local 44 worked closely with owners Joseph and James Axelrod to modernize the company's operations. When the Axelrods later purchased New Bedford's Wamsutta Mills, union leaders again helped management to install new machinery. The owners were duly appreciative. Asked why he rejected manufacturer assertions that northern mills could not compete against southern workloads, Joseph Axelrod replied: "My answer is that work loads are only a part of the story. Of course they are an important part but in the manufacture of quality products the intelligence and skill of your employees are even more important." Moreover, he contended, "because of an enlightened union leadership no gross inequity in work loads will long be allowed to hang over this area to threaten the dislocation of an entire industry."[56]

This was the type of response union leaders had hoped to elicit when they formulated plans to balance workloads, wages, and investment. As we saw, though, Axelrod was by no means typical. Nor was it possible, as Barkin suggested, to use him as "leverage" to prompt other mill owners to develop "a rounded cooperative program" on machine assignments. Most would not even agree to Barkin's request that they furnish the union with quarterly lists of intended technological changes. Given these developments, it was little wonder that business agents and joint board managers tended to view the work assignment question as a "political" problem; or that workers continued to resist all such changes.[57]

So where did all this leave union policy on workloads, wages, and investments? The results were mixed. Mill owners did obtain modest increases in workloads, but as we will see in the next chapter the question would ultimately be resolved in arbitration. In terms of wages, these were nevertheless good years for textile workers, probably the best they had ever experienced. At an October 1945 meeting of the National Association of Wool Manufacturers, executive committee members concluded "that a wage increase is inevitable and that it might as well be accepted gracefully." This seemed to be the general attitude of nearly all major producers at the time, in cottons and rayons as well as woolens and worsteds. Following the 1945 strikes in Maine and Rhode Island, most cotton manufacturers automatically adjusted their pay scales to changes in the pattern-setting New Bedford–Fall River agreements. By the late forties, textile wages still lagged well behind those paid in industries such as autos, steel, and rubber. But important advances had been made. For example, in Nashua, New Hampshire, where textiles and shoes were the two main local industries, the relative status of textile workers changed dramatically. Interviewed at decade's end, one plant manager for a nontextile firm observed: "Before the war, no one who could get a job here would go over to the [textile] mill; we used to call them 'mill rats' over there. But after the war they were hiring away from us all the time." Even more important for the long-term health of the regional industry, the series of wage increases obtained by New England operatives during the period were matched by both union and nonunion southern manufacturers. In December 1947, the average hourly wage was $1.18 in New England cotton-rayon mills and $1.11 in the South. The differential was still there, but it was, as the NACM informed its members in 1948, "the lowest differential that has ever existed."[58]

News from the investment front, however, was much less comforting. In 1947, expenditures per employee for new plant and machinery by New England textile manufacturers were $261.90, compared with a southern average of $320.50. Because regional mill structures and operating equipment were generally older than those found in the South, an investment differential of this magnitude was indeed worrisome. And when it is further noted that this was a period of major retooling and unprecedented profits in the industry, what a committee of the Massachusetts legislature characterized as the "sluggish rate of new investment" in regional plants left real cause for alarm.[59]

Meanwhile, informed observers began asking: What would happen when the great postwar sellers' market ended? Everyone knew it could not go on forever, and during the course of 1948 there were increasing signs of leaner times ahead. The degree to which New England manufacturers were genuinely committed to regional production would soon be tested. How they and the men and women who worked in their mills responded to that test is the main focus of the next chapter.

5 CRISIS YEARS, 1949–1952

In May 1949, the TWUA celebrated its tenth anniversary. At the local level, joint boards arranged a variety of festivities to commemorate the event, and in a nationwide radio broadcast Eleanor Roosevelt, Gov. Chester Bowles of Connecticut, and Sen. Frank Graham of North Carolina paid tribute to the organization's achievements. With more than 400,000 members, a union publication later observed, the "TWUA could look back with pride and satisfaction at the progress it had made in raising the living standards of textile workers and breaking down the social and economic barriers which had separated them from richer and more meaningful lives." This was more than the inflated, self-congratulatory rhetoric that normally attends such occasions. During the previous decade, the union had accomplished much and had ample cause to be proud. But no one had any illusions about the problems that still lay ahead. As the union publication further noted, 1949 was not a good year for textile workers, and the TWUA "faced the future with justified apprehension."[1]

There were good reasons for such apprehension. Not only was the great postwar boom clearly over, but mounting pressure for increased work assignments resulted in a series of arbitration decisions that raised serious questions about whether the new industrial relations system offered adequate protection to workers in declining industries such as textiles. Worse, there was also a growing crisis in woolens and worsteds, and while the Korean War temporarily revived the regional industry, it also set off a chain of events that widened interregional wage differentials and forced a disastrous showdown with southern producers. In the meantime, an increasingly bitter dispute between Emil Rieve and TWUA vice president George Baldanzi hindered the union's ability to deal effectively with these problems. By 1952, both the TWUA and the New England textile industry faced a truly dark future. Our examination of these troubled years begins with the 1949 recession.

THROUGHOUT THE LATE forties, there had been warnings from both industry executives and union leaders that prices and profit margins were getting out of hand. In October 1947, Arthur Besse of the National Association of Wool Manufacturers (NAWM) told the organization's board of directors that should current profit margins be maintained, wages and raw material prices would continue to rise as well. Because these advances "would increase the altitude from which the succeeding fall would start," he urged board members to consider taking steps to reduce prices. Although union leaders did not share Besse's fear of increased wages, they too were concerned about industry pricing practices. Several months later, a research department economic report noted that wholesale prices for textile products had risen 48 percent in the previous two years. These price levels were not only unjustified, the report observed, but represented "a policy which can only depress the industry and eventually bring about an economic bust."[2]

The subsequent crash was just as severe as Besse and union analysts feared it would be. Beginning in late 1948, demand for textile goods declined sharply, and by mid-1949 about one of every five textile operatives was jobless, while many of those still on company payrolls were working part-time. The situation was especially bleak in New England, where 26 percent of the Lawrence labor force was unemployed and seven thousand out of eighteen thousand New Bedford textile workers were walking the streets. During a September visit to the latter city, a writer for *Textile Labor* found "an air of foreboding" among wage earners. Although local operatives knew better than most how to "roll with the punches," the reporter observed, "There's a feeling deep down inside most workers that this thing's different." The reporter was hard pressed to account for this anxiety. New Bedford wage earners had seen mills shut down before; moreover, most local plants were in relatively strong financial condition. Yet there seemed "to be no confidence, none of that drive that pulled New Bedford out of the hole before."[3]

There had, however, been three recent mill closings in New Bedford, one of which was mentioned in the article. The mere fact of these liquidations was, as the reporter suggested, not especially significant. But the nature of these shutdowns was an entirely different matter. The three

mills involved — Naushon, Nonquitt, and Pierce — had all been purchased within the previous decade by outsiders; they had all made substantial profits in recent years; and none of them had taken steps to
modernize plant and machinery. In one case — the 1938 acquisition of
Naushon by Philip See and Associates — the federal government, city of
New Bedford, and local operatives had worked together to help provide
the new owners with needed financing. During the next decade Naushon staged a remarkable comeback. In 1947 the company not only was
making money, but had ample working capital and few debts apart from
current bills. Despite all this, See was not satisfied, and in April 1948 he
closed the mill. To justify his action, See contended that, because of
persisting cost differentials between New Bedford and the South, Naushon would have serious problems operating successfully once the postwar boom ended. By liquidating now, he added, everyone concerned
would be able "to readjust more easily." See's explanation may have
fooled some observers, but the union was not among them. "In simple
English," a TWUA report on the shutdown declared, "this means that
the present owners bought control of this mill to collect the profits
resulting from a few years of war-time demand and prices, and then after
milking its assets they plan to sell the mill piece by piece while inflated
prices on all kinds of equipment, mill properties and real estate still offer
a quick speculative profit."[4]

The other two plant closings involved mills that had been acquired by
outside interests during the wartime merger movement. Of these, the
Nonquitt liquidation represented an especially serious blow. Purchased
in 1945 by William Whitman Company, a textile sales agency headed by
Albert A. List, Nonquitt enjoyed healthy returns through 1948. But at
the first sign of difficult times, List discontinued operations and began
selling the plant's machinery. What made the shutdown so disturbing
was that List also controlled such important regional concerns as New
Bedford's Nashawena Mills and Lawrence's Arlington Mills. And if a
solid property like Nonquitt could not meet List's criteria for continued
operations, it was not likely that these companies had much of a future
either. In fact, the union had already learned that Lawrence banks were
"sore as hell" at what they considered List's "milking" of that city's
Arlington Mills. In an equally alarming development, New Bedford
bankers refused to back a local group that had offered to purchase Nonquitt following List's liquidation announcement.[5]

As noted, no one initially knew what the wartime merger movement portended. Textile workers were just now finding out, and it was little wonder they felt "this thing's different." It is equally little wonder that TWUA initiatives to forge an agreement on workloads and mill modernization with the New Bedford Cotton Manufacturers Association (NBCMA) had failed. Concerned only about short-term gains, owners such as See and List wanted no part of an arrangement that would have required them to upgrade their New Bedford properties, however much they may have wished to increase work assignments.

While all this was taking place, unionists were not standing by and waiting for those market self-adjustments that economists assure us will inevitably occur. In New Bedford, joint board officials informed Washington of the city's plight in letters proposing ways to boost local employment. At the same time, the international was doing what it could to stem the tide of mill closings: by helping distressed concerns to obtain government loans, and by challenging the actions of liquidating owners. In this latter regard, the union's primary target was Textron's Royal Little, who had developed a reputation as the most ruthless of the new interregionalists. To maintain the cash flow needed to sustain his highly leveraged empire, Little set strict productivity and profit requirements for Textron mills. Those that did not measure up were singled out for liquidation. The union recognized, as an editorial in *Textile Labor* observed, that Little "was simply abiding by capitalist rules." But that did not make what he was doing right, the editorial added, and "[w]e can no longer allow innocent men and women to suffer because of the manipulations of a single man."[6]

One way in which the union hoped both to slow Little and help its members was by obtaining severance pay for displaced workers. This was the tactic pursued at Esmond Mills, a multiunit blanket concern with plants in Rhode Island, New Hampshire, and Virginia. In June 1948, less than a month after acquiring Esmond from a family that had operated the firm for three generations, Little sold the Rhode Island plant and equipment to a machinery dealer. When the TWUA demanded severance pay for the laid-off operatives, Little refused and the case went to arbitration, where union officials argued that long training in the industry gave Esmond workers "an equity in their jobs." Although the arbitrator felt that "on equitable grounds there is much merit to the Union's request," he ruled that he had no power under the contract to grant the demand. This was the first of many disappointments that union leaders would experience at the hands of regional arbitrators.[7]

In another case involving New Hampshire's Nashua Manufacturing Company, the TWUA looked to the federal government for assistance. Founded in 1823, Nashua was one of the oldest industrial enterprises in the country. Little acquired the company in 1945 and several years later announced that it would be shut down because of high production costs and inadequate returns. At the union's urging, Sen. Charles Tobey of New Hampshire initiated a congressional investigation of Textron, which took a probing look at a broad range of company policies. Appalled by the findings, Tobey stated his conviction that over time businesses acquired a social responsibility to the communities in which they operated and asked if it was fair for a corporation to say, "Unless we make a profit every year, unless we make a profit of 10 percent, we are going to close up and out you go[.]" Such questions, coupled with a host of equally embarrassing inquiries about Textron's manipulation of charitable trust funds, prompted Little to reconsider his plans for Nashua. Although he would later close the mills during the early fifties, the hearings did gain a brief reprieve for Nashua workers.[8]

Meanwhile, there were growing problems on the woolen and worsted front. Compared with cottons, woolens and worsteds had come through the interwar crisis in reasonably good shape. The main reason was that these firms had traditionally faced limited competition from southern concerns. Manufacturing processes in woolens were more varied than those in cottons, thus making it more difficult to develop a skilled labor force. As a result, few southern producers had entered the field. At the same time, neither woolen nor worsted manufacturers had any compelling reason to migrate south. The main product markets for woolen goods were located in the North, and because manufacturers produced few staples that sold in large quantities, nearness to market was a more important factor in their operations than was the case for cotton producers. For worsted owners, the fact that most of their mills were large concerns that had been built around the turn of the century made relocation an unattractive solution to whatever problems they faced during the interwar period. As late as 1948, woolen and worsted plants employed about 160,000 workers nationally, most of them in northern mills; in New England, they accounted for 40 percent of regular textile employment.[9]

By the late forties, though, there were indications that the industry was entering a major period of restructuring. The most significant development was the increased production of blended fabrics of synthetic yarn and wool, which could be produced more cheaply than products made entirely of wool; they could also be manufactured with cotton equipment, which opened up opportunities for the industry's expansion in the South. As consumer acceptance of the new fabrics undermined the market for traditional woolen and worsted products, northern producers faced unprecedented challenges for which many were not well prepared. It is true that some efforts were being made to identify new uses for wool fibers. But, as one industry analyst noted, little could be expected from such research: "the experimentation is just an unstructured trial and error process of substituting this for that."[10]

Even more worrisome was the multitude of operational problems that hindered production in the average northern plant. Woolens, a 1951 report by the Council of Economic Advisors observed, "has the doubtful distinction of being selected by many writers as the branch of the New England textile industry least likely to succeed in the future because of management lethargy. . . ." Perhaps no producer better exemplified these shortcomings than the Lawrence-based American Woolen Company. Although American Woolen made a profit in each of the thirteen years following 1939, it was by the late forties a deeply troubled concern. Industry observers could barely find the right words to describe the company's managerial failings. "Their cost control was thoroughly inadequate, simply astounding," said one analyst. "There was no organization, no chain of command, no coordination." "The first thing I would do if I were to take over American Woolen," another commentator remarked, "would be to give everybody a broom and start to clean up."[11]

Inept leadership was by no means the company's only failing. The woeful state of American Woolen's physical assets both reflected and magnified its managerial deficiencies. The company could take some comfort in that it was not alone in this regard. According to Sumner D. Charm, one-time personnel director at American Woolen, more than 90 percent of New England woolen and worsted factories were "as obsolete as the water clock." But this was small comfort indeed. To illustrate his point, Charm added a description of American Woolen's primary plants:

> The mills in Lawrence look like medieval castles complete with towers. For the most part they are of brick and stone construction. Without exception they are multi-story affairs. For the most part they have wooden floors; many, and leaky, windows; over-high ceilings; workrooms completely bro-

ken up by supporting posts and columns. They are hard to heat and hard to improve. Without exception they were built for the operation of machinery from master driveshafts. They contain few employee facilities and no economical room for more. They are full of hazards. They make a nightmare out of the industry's inherent problem of atmosphere control.

Because of their antiquated plant, Charm calculated, regional producers operated at a cost disadvantage of seven cents a yard compared to facilities housed in modern, single-story structures.[12]

Given these conditions, one can begin to appreciate why an industry analyst remarked that American Woolen's "manufacturing was not just inadequate — it was brutal." The observation becomes even more understandable when the company's technological shortcomings are taken into account. It was not that American Woolen failed to invest in new equipment. The problem was that it had no idea as to where among its twenty plants such investments could most effectively be made. The company also suffered from the consequences of short-sighted efforts to modernize on the cheap. When it belatedly installed automatic looms, for example, it do so by converting older hand-fed looms rather than purchasing newer, more efficient machines. The result was that, even though few woolen and worsted mills could be characterized as models of technological innovation, productivity at American Woolen generally lagged behind that of its competitors.[13]

Despite all its troubles, American Woolen remained the industry wage leader. This placed TWUA officials in an awkward position. They recognized that faltering productivity threatened future wage advances and, as the NAWM periodically reminded its members, were "receptive to proposals regarding increased efficiency." Yet, because the industry standard setter showed so little initiative, union officials were reluctant to adjust work assignments elsewhere. Emil Rieve had foreseen this problem nearly a decade earlier. At the time, though, he did know what to do about it. Because woolen manufacturers refused to deal with the union as a group, targeting American Woolen and then forcing other firms to grant comparable concessions seemed the only way to establish industrywide standards.[14]

Those standards were now in dire peril. During the immediate postwar years, such northern woolen and worsted producers as Pacific Mills, J. P. Stevens, Deering-Milliken, and Bachman-Uxbridge opened branch plants in the South. Compared with northern mills, these facilities were able to operate at a significant cost advantage. One reason was wages. In the North, woolen and worsted workers had traditionally been paid more than their counterparts in cottons. In the South, however, woolen wages were tied to prevailing cotton rates. A 1950 study found that wages in southern plants were 16 to 26 cents an hour lower than those paid in northern plants. Another reason was work assignments, which exceeded those in northern plants by substantial margins. Not only were most southern mills nonunion, but few of their workers had any experience in woolen and worsted manufacturing. As a result, managers encountered little resistance when they set workloads that were often twice as high as those in northern mills. The degree to which such machine assignments could be characterized as stretchouts is difficult to determine. Southern woolen and worsted concerns of this period had lower production standards than those in the North and tolerated a higher rate of seconds. More important, most were modern, single-story structures, equipped with the latest machinery. This enabled managers to establish machine loads that workers in the North's older plants would have been physically incapable of handling, even had they been willing to do so. For these and other reasons, it is now time to resume our examination of the workload question.[15]

UNSURPRISINGLY, GIVEN THE developments described in the preceding section, the number of jobs lost through plant liquidations rose sharply in all sectors of the New England textile industry during the late forties: from 7,700 in 1947 to 13,900 in 1948 and 15,800 in 1949. This in turn hindered TWUA initiatives on the wage front. In January 1949, the union took northern cotton manufacturers to arbitration in an effort to obtain a ten-cent hourly increase. Union officials contended that the raise was necessary to bring cotton wages in line with those paid in other industries, boost purchasing power, and provide operatives with their rightful share of the benefits of increased productivity. But the arbitrator was more impressed by the weakness of textile markets and rejected the union's demand; a month later another arbitrator ruled against a similar request on behalf of woolen and worsted workers. And as the recession deepened, New England locals voiced little dissent when Emil Rieve decided to bypass a scheduled wage reopening the following January. Many regional unionists shared the pessimistic outlook of New Bedford joint board manager George Carignan. "I feel if we do push for any-

thing that will make any material additional cost at this time," Carignan remarked, four of the five mills still operating in the city "will just
discontinue."[16]

For the most part, manufacturers were happy to let the wage question
rest. They knew that efforts to slash worker earnings would provoke
strong resistance. In July 1949, the National Association of Wool Manufacturers (NAWM) noted that several small nonunion concerns had
recently been organized after attempting to reduce wages. But the recession could still be used to cut costs elsewhere. "We believe it should be
possible," the association advised its members, "to negotiate a contract
that will enable the mills to operate to greater advantage on workloads,
seniority, and other administrative features."[17]

The NAWM was not alone in adopting this tack. Textron's Royal
Little had long been critical of worker resistance to workload increases.
In 1946, he purchased the Gossett Mills, an eleven-unit chain of cotton
and rayon factories in the Carolinas, and began making detailed cost
comparisons between these plants and the company's northern operations. The results, he claimed, showed that "our Carolina employees
produced from 25 percent to 100 percent more yards and pounds per
hour than many of our people in the North." Although most mill owners, not to mention union officials, put little faith in such comparisons,
claims that New England operatives refused to work as hard as their
southern counterparts became increasingly common during the late forties. This was especially so among regional persisters who believed increased productivity was the key to the industry's salvation. And while
these producers generally disapproved of Little and much that he stood
for, they did not hesitate to follow his lead on the work assignment
question. Citing the Textron experience in Nashua as an example, New
Bedford's Seabury Stanton declared it should be unnecessary "for any
New England mill to be obliged to resort to closing down and starting
to liquidate before it can induce its employees to give a fair day's work."[18]

The TWUA response to these accusations was not entirely dismissive.
Union leaders remained willing to adjust work assignments and cautioned workers, "let's be sure our resistance to change is based on something better than a fear of the unfamiliar." Yet, while the recession may
have weakened rank-and-file objections to increased workloads, it did
not eliminate them altogether, and the union had no intention of submitting passively to mill owner demands. Moreover, as various studies
of the work assignment question had shown, distinguishing legitimate

changes from stretchouts could be a maddeningly complex process under the best of circumstances. Yarn quality, upkeep of machinery, atmospheric changes, and a host of other factors all influenced the level of effort a given machine load required of operatives. Interplant comparisons, though frequently submitted as evidence in arbitration cases, were usually of dubious value. In a 1952 statement, New Bedford's Hathaway Manufacturing Company declared that work assignments must be based on existing conditions at each individual mill: "an assignment of 40 looms per weaver, for example, at Company X could constitute an overload, whereas an assignment of 80 looms at Company Y could be less than a full job." A union official later wrote "agree" in the margin of the New Bedford joint board's copy of the document. It turned out to be one of the few matters concerning workloads on which union and management did agree.[19]

For one thing, union leaders resented the vehemence of mill owner charges, as they knew how hard they had tried to reach an accord on work assignments. Cotton director Mariano Bishop spoke for many of his colleagues when he told Fall River workers that manufacturers had "invent[ed] the workload problem" to hide their failure to update plant and equipment. The union also had a number of practical reasons for digging in its heels. One was the refusal of manufacturers to grant workers technological severance pay. Another was the magnitude and nature of the changes demanded; many, in addition to requiring "unusually high effort levels" of operatives, went well beyond the gradual increases union officials were willing to concede. As Solomon Barkin later observed, management made little effort "to devise a system which would keep the worker aware of the fact that changes in work assignments were inevitable." And this was one of several occasions when the union leadership was "placed in a position where it realized change was necessary, but couldn't negotiate such changes with ease because of the way management presented the problem to the workers."[20]

Another obstacle was management's refusal to share the benefits of productivity increases with workers. Because manufacturers believed the practice would unbalance existing wage structures, they ignored union assertions that such a policy was necessary to enlist wage earner cooperation. Although the NAWM's Arthur Besse encouraged woolen and worsted producers to make such concessions, there is no evidence that any member mills followed his advice. Meanwhile, the NACM's William Sullivan was carefully scrutinizing union contracts to ensure that they contained no provisions that would undermine management's claims. When he found an objectionable clause, like the stipulation in the Dan River agreement that piece rates on new work assignments "should be so fixed as to reflect added productivity," Sullivan warned association members to guard against similar demands. Mill owners also continued to oppose any arrangement that threatened their managerial prerogatives. Their position on these matters was perhaps best summarized in a 1949 arbitration brief by the New Bedford Cotton Manufacturers Association (NBCMA) that recounted the history of textile unionism in local mills.[21]

Before the 1930s, the statement related, no single organization represented all workers in New Bedford. Efforts to introduce labor-saving innovations met stiff resistance from craft unionists, who equated technological change with job loss and "held up" manufacturers seeking to introduce new machinery until job rates were increased. "This, in turn, created inequities and dissatisfaction among other groups of workers." All this began to change in the late thirties when local mill owners granted the New Bedford Textile Council a preferential union shop "for the express purpose of giving to the Council the power to enforce the Agreement and discipline recalcitrant members." Since then, increasing productivity resulting from technological innovation had not been considered an appropriate basis for raising wages. To grant these premiums, the statement contended, would create conflict among different occupational groups and might even "foster the resurgence of independent 'craft' unionism in the mills." An industrial union could only resolve such disputes by obtaining a commensurate increase in earnings for all its members. But solutions of this sort "would be fatal" for everyone concerned, the statement concluded. "Money spent for modernization which results only in higher costs, wage inequities, and unrest, is money wasted."[22]

TWUA officials contested these assertions. A written reply declared that manufacturers had on many occasions "sweetened" piece rates in order to secure shop-floor acceptance of increased workloads. The result was not interoccupational conflict, but greater job satisfaction among wage earners affected by the change. However well taken, the union response did little to obscure the fact that manufacturers both rejected its position on technological change and refused to recognize its claims as an agent of industrial transition. Indeed, the real significance of the exchange was less what it said about the work assignment question than what it revealed about capital's perceptions of unionism. Where the

TWUA believed it had a mission to save the New England textile industry by promoting needed investment and at the same time making it an attractive place to work, mill owners assigned the union a much more circumscribed role: that of a policeman whose sole duty was to keep the rank and file in line.[23]

Given these differences, it was no surprise that the number of nonnegotiable work assignment changes rose sharply during the 1949 recession. In New Bedford, where most major cotton disputes originated, there were only two management-initiated workload adjustments requiring union consultation in 1948, and both were implemented through negotiation; during the next two years, there were fifty such adjustments, a dozen of which went to arbitration. In these cases, the TWUA compiled a decidedly mixed record. It did preserve certain basic protections for operatives. One was that new or revised piece rates must allow wage earners to maintain current hourly earnings. Another was union consent to nonroutine work assignment adjustments. Arbitrators consistently ruled against manufacturers who raised workloads without following established procedures. In one 1949 case, a New Bedford mill was ordered to reinstate twelve doffers who had staged a slowdown to protest an unauthorized increase in the number of sides they had to tend. Although critical of the doffers, the arbitrator decreed that management had violated contractual obligations by failing to consult union officials before making the change. Arbitrators also accepted union contentions that job assignments must provide workers a 15 percent fatigue allowance, sometimes expanding it for especially exhausting tasks.[24]

On other matters, though, the TWUA had less success. A March 1950 award that doubled loom assignments at New Bedford's Wamsutta Mills had troubling implications, given the city's position as a standard setter for the regional cotton industry. So did a Fall River case later in the year, which indicated that some arbitrators accepted employer characterizations of New England operatives. "It is clear that the fundamental difference here, as in all workload disputes," A. H. Myers observed in a ruling that significantly increased loom assignments at the Spindle City's Pepperell plant, "arises from the Company practice of considering effort and time utilization while the workers think in terms of number of machines."[25]

Woolen manufacturers also made major gains through arbitration. Although the union continued to hold the line at American Woolen, insisting that any workload changes "would have to be on a chain-wide basis," arbitrator John Hogan handed the TWUA a serious setback in a 1950 case involving Dorr Woolen. Speaking for the union, woolen director John Chupka had asserted, "I am going to tell you that I will never say that you can increase over four looms as long as other companies do not do it." Chupka feared that any increase in an industry where so few companies had installed modern machinery would have devastating consequences for workers. The problem in New England, he believed, was not simply equalizing interregional machine loads but adopting "some system whereby large capital investments are made." Although Hogan had some sympathy for the union's position, he felt the increase was justified. Brushing aside Chupka's concerns, he allowed the company to increase weavers' assignments from four to twelve looms; and in the succeeding months, fifty additional woolen mills sought to reopen the workload question.[26]

Equally unsettling were several decisions concerning the relationship between wages and productivity. Arbitrators did boost earnings when work assignment changes required operatives to expand greater physical effort on the job, but they refused to accept union claims that wage earners should share the benefits resulting from increased productivity. According to a March 1950 decision, "the prevailing tendency [in arbitration awards] is toward the establishment of rates related to the requirements of the job rather than the output from the job." The point was reiterated six months later in a ruling that endorsed company assertions that "increasing the output of a machine is not in itself sufficient reason to increase a rate of pay, since savings from lowered costs should be shared by others than the operator."[27]

The TWUA had approached the workload issue with an open mind. "The question," Solomon Barkin wrote in January 1949, "is whether we are to work out a complete program for handling [higher machine loads] in exchange for a wage concession and protection for the workers or await critical economic reverses when we may be forced to accept the increased assignment with no protection to the workers or no share in the gains." As it turned out, the worst did not happen—at least not at this juncture. But what did happen was nearly as bad. Although arbitrators upheld some union claims, their decisions more often undermined the TWUA's position. One reason the union did so poorly was the tendency of arbitrators to base their rulings on time-study data submitted by employers. The union was doubly disadvantaged in this regard. Not only did it lack the staff needed to undertake comparable investigations, but most such studies were inherently flawed because they provided an incomplete picture of the total work situation and invariably reflected a number of subjective judgments on the part of the engineers who prepared them. As a New Bedford union official later reported, one local executive "as much as admitted that top management has its own idea of how much it wants to save in labor cost when introducing changes and that time studies are made to fit into the scheme." Barkin tried to impress these facts on arbitrators, but few were willing to question the findings of company engineers.[28]

Even more troubling was the union's inability to develop the "complete program" on workloads of which Barkin spoke. In late 1949, he penned an evaluation of recent arbitration rulings and the people who made them. A major difficulty, Barkin observed, was that most New England arbitrators were influenced by Harvard and MIT, where academics promoted "an economic philosophy [that] is basically unsympathetic to a dynamic economic program." The union, he believed, would get a better hearing if regional lists of the American Arbitration Association were extended to include people from Yale and other institutions that "do not reflect the pessimism of the Boston Bourbon philosophy." Yet as Barkin went on, it became clear that he was less concerned about the background of particular arbitrators than about the nature of the arbitration process itself, and that he was seeking a way to break through its narrow legalism and create a forum in which broad questions of industrial policy could be discussed. This was especially necessary for the proper settlement of work assignment disputes, which arbitrators showed little ability to handle "maturely." "We believe," Barkin concluded, "that we might well consider tripartite panels, with union and employer representation to insure understanding of issue, clarification of differences, more direct bargaining, and sounder decision."[29]

The TWUA was never able to follow through on Barkin's suggestion. As a number of scholars have noted, this was not an auspicious time for unions to be seeking an expansion of their authority. Not only were manufacturers fiercely defensive of their right to manage, but government too was backing away from earlier commitments to organized labor. In June 1947, Congress passed the Taft-Hartley Act, which bolstered managerial rights and placed sharp restrictions on union activity. Although capital claimed the bill was needed to balance the prolabor provisions of the Wagner Act, its impact on unionism was a good deal more severe than such statements suggested. In protesting the measure,

Nelson Lichtenstein has written, "Union leaders correctly recognized that the act represented the definitive end of the brief era in which the state served as an arena in which the trade unions could bargain for the kind of tripartite accommodation with industry that had been so characteristic of the New Deal years." If TWUA officials had not realized this immediately, they certainly sensed as much by decade's end.[30]

On top of these setbacks, there was growing discord within the union itself. The main actors in the dispute were Emil Rieve and executive vice president George Baldanzi. According to education director Lawrence Rogin, the feud first surfaced at the 1948 convention when Baldanzi, acting against Rieve's wishes, attempted to have Roy Lawrence, a southern official, removed from his post. Although unsuccessful, the move aroused fears concerning Baldanzi's ambitions and the way in which he would run the union should he ever replace Rieve; and while Rieve afterward assured Baldanzi that he harbored "no grudges," other union officials began laying plans to oust Baldanzi. The members of this latter group were mainly New Englanders; they were also Rieve's staunchest supporters on the executive council. And when Fall River's Mariano Bishop challenged Baldanzi for the executive vice presidency at the 1950 convention, he did so with Rieve's backing. After Baldanzi defeated Bishop, Rieve again declared he would do all that he could to "see whether or not the team can be re-established." But even as he spoke, the hall still echoed with the personal vituperation so freely dispensed during the previous days' sessions, and it seemed unlikely that the matter would be so easily resolved.[31]

As convention delegates headed home that May, thoughts about what the future held in store for their union must have crossed more than a few minds. For those who did consider the question, recent developments held out little cause for optimism. With the end of the postwar boom, all indications were that the TWUA's northern base would continue to contract. If this were not enough, growing factionalism within the union had sown seeds of rancor and distrust that made concerted action on the part of the leadership increasingly problematic. And such action would soon be needed, for the organization was about to enter what would prove to be the most fateful period of its history.

ON JUNE 25, 1950, North Korean troops smashed across the thirty-eighth parallel and began moving south. Two days later, President Truman dispatched air and naval units to provide support for the rapidly disintegrating South Korean army. They were soon joined by American ground forces, and within a few months the North Koreans were in full retreat. But the war was far from over. Another two years of inconclusive though often savage fighting lay ahead before a final armistice was signed. Meanwhile, the economic effects of the conflict were being felt at home.

In New England, increased government orders created jobs and tightened labor markets throughout the region. With more remunerative employment now available elsewhere, workers in low-wage industries like textiles deserted their looms and spinning frames for higher-paying jobs in the durable goods sector. And as textile producers struggled to meet their labor needs, the TWUA made plans to turn the situation to its own advantage. Although the reopening date on major contracts had passed, union leaders knew they would be derelict in their duties if they let this opportunity slip by. They also knew they could expect inadvertent support from manufacturers, and the research department was immediately set to work assembling information on prices and profits. As anticipated, "The facts were sensational." Declaring the data indicated "profiteering pure and simple," Emil Rieve called for a congressional investigation and demanded that mill owners voluntarily raise wages.[32]

The first response came from an unexpected quarter. On the evening before union leaders were scheduled to meet with employer representatives from Fall River and New Bedford, Emil Rieve and Textron's Royal Little signed the most lucrative pact in TWUA history. Quickly dubbed "the Textron formula," the three-year agreement contained provisions for an immediate 10 percent wage boost, annual improvement increases of 5 percent during the second and third years, and cost-of-living adjustments based on changes in the Bureau of Labor Statistics consumer price index. By industry standards it was an extraordinary contract, and union officials could barely suppress their glee at this unanticipated windfall. "Underlying the new program," *Textile Labor* commented, "is TWUA's determination to close the present gulf between textile wages and those in industries such as auto and steel."[33]

Although some regional persisters like Crown Manufacturing adopted the Textron formula, the reactions of others ranged from dismay to outrage. The NACM's William Sullivan characterized annual improvement increases as a "piece of intellectual dishonesty and folderol . . . based on some vague over-all labor productivity figures [that have] no meaning for a particular mill, or even for a particular industry."

Sullivan was equally critical of cost-of-living adjustments, because "at the end of hostilities the Consumer Price Index rapidly rises to a peak and then falls off again almost as sharply," leaving employers "stuck at the highest point." The Fall River and New Bedford employer groups, with which Sullivan was closely associated, thus strongly resisted TWUA demands that they accept the Textron plan. In September 1950, they granted a 10 percent wage increase, but refused to go beyond that. The following spring they proved more accommodating. After New Bedford workers voted by a two-to-one margin in favor of a strike, the employer associations signed a pact that provided an additional 7.5 percent wage boost, together with a cost-of-living formula similar to that negotiated with Textron.[34]

TWUA dealings with New England woolen and worsted manufacturers were more conflict-ridden, but produced much the same results. In October 1950, American Woolen, the regional standard setter, granted its eighteen thousand operatives a 12.5-cents-an-hour wage increase in order to halt a slowdown in company mills. When union leaders later presented demands based on the Textron formula, however, the NAWM executive committee greeted the proposal "with amazement," and American Woolen decided to take a strike. The final settlement, signed in March 1951 following a four-week walkout, gave workers another 12.5-cent wage boost and contained a Textron-like cost-of-living clause.[35]

The TWUA would have little time to celebrate these advances, as there were increasingly ominous signs of trouble ahead. One was the reaction of certain interregionalists to recently negotiated contracts. During the woolen and worsted talks, J. P. Stevens not only refused to consider union demands, but insisted that steps be taken to increase work assignments and reduce current wage levels. Rather than follow American Woolen's lead and adopt the new regional standard, it began liquidating mills in Rockville, Connecticut, and Haverhill, Massachusetts. By late spring, all of the company's unionized plants in New England were either shut down or in the process of closing.[36]

Meanwhile, there was continuing pressure from other producers on the work assignment question. In January, Joseph Axelrod stated that he was planning to move south unless the union agreed to substantial workload changes at his Wamsutta and Crown plants. Coming from someone who had heretofore been one of the region's most outspoken persisters, this was an alarming declaration. It was made even more so by recent indications that workers were in no mood to accept further increases. New Hampshire operatives had criticized union leaders for granting increased loom assignments as part of the Textron settlement; stewards at New Bedford's Hathaway and Nashawena mills reported growing support for the United Textile Workers "as a result of dissatisfaction with the way in which the workload problem has been handled in arbitration"; and at the very moment Axelrod issued his demand, weavers at Fall River's Pepperell plant were on strike, protesting a recent arbitration ruling that had increased their machine loads from sixty to eighty looms on certain styles and from forty to eighty on others. Union officials were able to end the Fall River walkout by persuading the company to forego part of the arbitrator's award. As for Axelrod, they could only hope he was bluffing, and that an "upswing in business" would put them "over the hump."[37]

Most worrisome was the situation in the southern cotton industry. In October 1950, Dan River and other organized concerns signed contracts calling for an 8.3 percent wage increase. As this failed to match the 10 percent raise granted by northern producers, the latter complained of the widening differential and insisted that the TWUA close the gap. But that was only part of the problem. What truly complicated matters was that the consequences of the union's failure to extend its organizational base in the South were finally being felt. Departing from earlier practice, many nonunion southern mills had refused to accept the new regional standard. Thus when union officials later presented organized firms with demands for cost-of-living adjustments based on the Textron formula and an additional wage boost, the contending parties were unable to reach an agreement. The result was a southern strike that nobody really wanted. To understand why TWUA officials feared such an encounter, it will be necessary to leave New England for a while and examine the state of textile unionism in the postwar South.[38]

AT WAR'S END, TWUA leaders looked southward with real optimism. Having already established relations with some of the largest producers in Virginia and North Carolina, they fully expected to extend those achievements in the immediate postwar period. For a variety of reasons, those hopes were never realized. One was the failure of Operation Dixie, a much-publicized and well-financed CIO effort to bring industrial unionism to southern wage earners. Although *Textile Labor* and the *CIO News* continued to print inspiring accounts of southern organizational successes throughout the late forties, prospects were considerably less sanguine than these stories implied. During their first six months in the field, organizers made limited advances. Then at its 1946 convention, the CIO reduced funding for the campaign, which necessitated cuts in an organizational staff that was already spread too thin. These developments did little to diminish TWUA support for the project. Even during periods of financial stringency, New England joint boards gave generously to southern strikers and continued to raise funds for the "Southern Drive." But with each passing year, the situation deteriorated further, and by the late forties only the most congenitally optimistic unionists could still detect signs of progress.[39]

A major obstacle was the Taft-Hartley Act, which Congress passed in 1947 to give employers rights comparable to those provided wage earners by the Wagner Act. Apart from the encouragement it offered anti-union diehards, Taft-Hartley furnished several more tangible aids as well. One was a "free-speech" clause that allowed manufacturers to use "plant-closing prophecies" and other forms of intimidation during representation elections. Even more effective was the time-consuming chain of appeals it made possible once an election had been won. After listening to considerable TWUA testimony about the evasive tactics employed by southern mill owners to avoid collective bargaining, Sen. Wayne Morse remarked that the evidence appeared to confirm a prediction of his own. "I remember distinctly during the debate in 1947," Morse recalled, "I said . . . that as a lawyer for an employer, I would be perfectly willing under the Taft-Hartley bill to take a case and have my fee be entirely contingent on whether or not I could prevent a settlement of that case for five years." Morse was not that kind of lawyer, but other attorneys were only too eager to exploit the lucrative opportunities the act made possible.[40]

CIO efforts to organize the South were also hampered by labor's Cold War. In 1949, after several years of mounting tensions, the CIO convention voted to expel the United Electrical Workers (UE) and Farm Equipment Workers for Communist affiliation; similar charges were filed against ten more international unions, nine of which would subsequently be excluded. Although Operation Dixie was in serious trouble by that time — and had been for several years — a number of the expelled unions had made substantial contributions to the drive and were organizations that could be counted upon to stay the course. Their departure from the CIO further isolated textile unionists in the South.[41]

Apart from these problems, the TWUA was still seeking an effective means of appealing to a broad range of southern workers. "When we look at the southern situation we find an unorganized area that will require different tools than the other regions," George Baldanzi told a 1949 meeting of the executive council. "It has been proven in the last ten years that most of our old methods have not been successful." Simply promising to increase wages was not enough. "That is not the yardstick of measuring the determination of these people," Baldanzi added. "There is a tremendous feeling in the South about things that affect their dignity." The TWUA thus had to find ways of grounding its message in regional worker cultures and of making unionism an expression of that "dignity" so cherished by southern operatives.[42]

These were insightful observations that revealed a refreshing capacity for self-criticism on the part of union leaders. But these were also matters that should have been resolved earlier, and by 1949 time was running out. One reason the union decided not to reopen the northern contract in January 1950 was that Emil Rieve believed a wage advance could not be extended to southern mills. And that fall, when Seabury Stanton asked why TWUA leaders had accepted a smaller southern wage settlement than that obtained in the North without calling their members out, Mariano Bishop told him they "had no choice"; the union "did not have the strength to strike."[43]

The main problem was the breakdown of the postwar bargaining structure in the South. Throughout the late forties, TWUA wage negotiations had centered on a group of firms that union leaders referred to as the "big five"; Virginia's Dan River Mills and four North Carolina–based concerns, Cone, Erwin, Marshall Field, and Lowenstein. Contracts with these companies set the regional wage pattern, and other producers, both union and nonunion, fell into line afterward. New England manufacturers, though they maintained pressure on the TWUA to extend its southern base, were generally satisfied with the arrangement. As Seabury Stanton put it, they believed "wages should be removed from competition" and felt that "enlightened southern management is of the same opinion." This was not entirely wishful thinking. In a January 1951 conversation, Dan River vice president Basil D. Browder told William Sullivan that "the interests of Dan River are much closer to those of New England than [those of] the southern mills."[44]

As noted, however, this arrangement began to unravel during the fall of 1950, when nonunion firms refused to meet the new wage pattern established by the "big five" mills. And the following spring when union leaders sought an additional 7.5 percent advance, plus a cost-of-living clause, the major southern producers would not even consider the demands. At Dan River, Browder angrily complained that union officials had assured him that his company "would not be used as the 'guinea pig' in the next negotiations." He also criticized northern employers for accepting such a settlement: "We have no intention of committing suicide because the New England manufacturers have done so and we have no intention of contributing to the ego and arrogance of your national leaders who have conducted these negotiations with a gun at the head of management. They might intimidate New England people that way but when they move down South they will find we do not scare that easily." Despite the tough talk, Browder remained willing to negotiate and at one point thought Rieve would settle for the 6 percent increase that Dan River was offering. In the end, though, Rieve stood firm and insisted that Dan River match the New England agreement.[45]

Browder believed Rieve did so mainly because of pressure from New England unionists. Although there is some truth to Browder's observation, it misses the broader context in which Rieve acted. New Englanders certainly objected to any southern settlement that would widen interregional wage differentials. During recent negotiations, regional manufacturers had "served notice" that such an outcome could have dire consequences: "Okay, we are going through with the wage increase, but we are telling you now that we are not going to stay in existence up here unless the union is able to do something about the southern situation." Having lost more than twenty thousand members through mill liquidations over the past several years, union officials took the warning very seriously. These considerations no doubt influenced Rieve, but they were not the only reason why he decided to take a strike. Another factor was his ongoing feud with George Baldanzi, which created additional pressure for him to appear as a "man of action" and made it all the more important that he retain his base of support in New England. Under the circumstances, calling out southern workers became the easiest — if not necessarily the wisest — course of action.[46]

The strike began April 1 and involved forty thousand workers, about half of the union's total membership in the South. Union leaders recognized they would have to obtain a settlement at one or more of the "big five" firms to achieve their aim of establishing a new regional wage standard, but they believed it would be "unwise" to confine the conflict to these concerns. Instead they decided to strike "every mill whose contract permitted it, and where the morale of the workers was such that the plant could be shut down immediately." It soon became clear, however, that the struggle at Dan River would determine the strike's outcome, as manufacturers throughout the region were waiting to see what would happen there.[47]

It was also clear by the strike's second week that Dan River was a major weak spot. As was often the case in southern labor struggles, support from state and local authorities in the form of "police violence, mass arrests, and the inevitable court injunctions" gave management a formidable advantage. The union was prepared for this. What they did not anticipate was that Dan River would hire a New York publicity firm to mobilize community opinion against the strikers; and because as one strike leader put it, "This is the kind of warfare we're not accustomed to dealing with," the ensuing propaganda campaign proved extremely effective. Nor did union leaders foresee the degree of interfirm cooperation that would develop during the strike. From the outset, there was mounting evidence that other regional producers were helping Dan River keep its plants open by granting some of their own operatives temporary leave so that they could work in Danville.[48]

Even more serious was the state of textile unionism in Danville. Before the strike, Kenneth Kramer later informed Rieve, "the affairs of the locals were run by small cliques who operated as political units with little or no guidance from national staff people." As a result, no more than half of Dan River's 7,600 workers "could be termed union members in the sense that they were willing to go along with union decisions, including a strike." Given this weak foundation, it was not surprising that many operatives broke ranks when, in response to the company's public relations campaign, local merchants denied credit to strikers and local bankers threatened to foreclose on their homes. In an effort to prevent further defections, the union poured massive amounts of money into Danville. But it was to little avail. At an April 18 strike meeting, Boyd Paxton reported that for the past week each shift change had brought a "new crisis"; and Emanuel Boggs offered this advice: "if we can get anything to hang our hats on, we'd better get in out of the rain, because when it starts slipping, it may slip fast."[49]

Conditions were at least somewhat better elsewhere, and the strike continued for another two weeks, at which time Rieve sought to have the dispute arbitrated by the recently formed Wage Stabilization Board. But the initiative went nowhere. Southern manufacturers, knowing they had the union on the ropes, unanimously rejected the proposal; and after telling Rieve that he had "lost his strike," Cyrus Ching of the U.S. Conciliation Service said the best he could do was appoint a mediation panel to help bring the two sides together. Although one management observer described Ching's offer as a well-intentioned but ineffective "attempt to save Rieve's face," the TWUA president had few alternatives by that point. The strike was indeed lost, and that November a *Textile Labor* editorial entitled "Strike-Breaking by Mediation" reported that the panel, after doing nothing for six months, had recently closed the case.[50]

At staff meetings following the strike, union leaders tried to determine what had gone wrong at Dan River and other mills where operatives had returned to work. Jack Rubinstein believed the main fault was "ideological" rather than organizational. Over the years, the union had been too statesmanlike in its dealings with southern employers, and many workers were psychologically unprepared for a long struggle. "[W]e have to have a little more class struggle," Rubinstein contended, "not as a principle, not as something we desire, but as a recognition of what we have to have, because we do have it as far as southern management is concerned." There was certainly some basis for Rubinstein's comments. As John Chupka noted, workers at mills with long traditions of militancy had stood firm throughout the strike. But this was only part of the problem. The "Strike's Big Lesson," an editorial in *Textile Labor* stated, was that the union simply did not have enough members in the South, and "the tail can't wag the dog if the dog really plants his feet and resists." The strike also revealed the TWUA's relative isolation within the labor movement. Just as they had halfheartedly supported Operation Dixie after the war, other CIO unions provided little assistance during the conflict. To many organizations, the South was primarily a textile problem. They had yet to recognize that what happened there concerned all industrial unions and that, as dyers official William Gordon remarked, "the various Internationals must stick together or sink separately."[51]

The defeat was a grave setback for textile unionists. "The employers are playing it up as farethe[e]well in the North," Mariano Bishop told his colleagues that June. Pressure from interregionalists was especially acute. According to Bishop, they now contended that northern workers would have to take a pay cut in order to bring their wages down to the same levels paid in southern mills. Although most persisters were less gleeful about the strike's outcome, they too recognized that conditions had changed. In a letter to Seabury Stanton, written shortly after the strike ended, William Sullivan presented a survey of recent events that suggested a major turning point had been reached: "As I understand it, the labor policy of Fall River–New Bedford for the past eight years has been based on the premise that the Union, although numerically weak in the South, was nevertheless a strong factor in maintaining wage levels in that area. It was also based on the premise that the Union, through its 'Operation Dixie' would grow in numbers, or at least not be seriously weakened." But these assumptions were no longer tenable. "As things now stand," Sullivan added, "it now looks as if the Union [will] have little or no strength in the South, and that as a factor in preventing the widening of the differential it will not be important." What all this meant, Sullivan later concluded, was that wage leadership in the cotton industry had passed from New England to the South. "The anomaly of forces in one region setting wages while those in another determined prices," he told NACM members, was now at an end. "Like a ship in a convoy, New England mills can no longer dash ahead of the others without exposing themselves to destruction." For the TWUA, this was a decidedly unwelcome turn of events. With many of its southern locals still in disarray, the union had all it could do simply to maintain its existing membership; new organizational initiatives in the region were out of the question.[52]

To make matters worse, there were growing troubles in textile markets. By late spring of 1951, there was strong evidence that the Korean conflict was not providing sufficient stimulus to break the textile industry's traditional two-year cycle. Writing to Emil Rieve that June, Seabury Stanton acknowledged that textile manufacturers had made "satisfactory profits" during the previous six to seven months. But this performance could not be sustained because recent market activity had been based on false expectations. "Much of the buying," he explained, "has been in anticipation of shortages which have not materialized, and, as a result, all of the pipelines are choked with goods, customers have borrowed large sums to carry their inventories, and business is at a standstill and will remain so . . . until these inventories have been moved out." The situation had become so serious that Stanton believed the industry might be on "the threshhold of the worst depression it has faced since the early 1930's."[53]

Despite this gloomy prediction, Stanton did not despair. In succeeding months, he and William Sullivan embarked on what was in effect a two-man crusade to stiffen the spines of regional mill owners. Each sensed that the New England textile industry had reached a major crossroads, and that whatever future it had would depend in great part on how manufacturers responded to the present crisis. In a letter to Solomon Barkin, Stanton urged that labor also shoulder its part of the burden by helping to increase workloads. Barkin appreciated what Stanton was trying to do and characterized his efforts as a "constructive step forward." He too believed that work assignments could be increased, but to obtain worker cooperation manufacturers first had "to develop a more adequate concept of the meaning of collective bargaining." In addition to becoming more familiar with union publications on work duties, management needed to involve operatives in each step of the process. This apparently was not what Stanton had in mind. That December, in an open letter to employees of Hathaway's rayon division, he announced that it might soon be necessary to return to a three-day schedule if they did not accept enlarged workloads: "We have discussed the establishment of increased work assignments with the Union and the Shop Committee without success, and the whole matter will have to be taken to arbitration, unless you are willing to place us in a competitive cost position with other New England mills by your own voluntary action." As Stanton should have learned from his correspondence with Barkin, most workers felt that if a job change could not be negotiated, then it should go to arbitration; and in this case, that is exactly what happened.[54]

Continued pressure for increased work assignments was only one element in capital's campaign to stabilize the regional industry. Many manufacturers considered wages more important than workloads, and the deepening recession, coupled with the union's inability to narrow interregional labor-cost differentials, led to increased demands for action on the wage front. Textron formula mills, which were contractually obligated to grant workers a 5 percent advance before year's end, were especially hard pressed. These concerns, Walter Gallant of Lowell's Newmarket Manufacturing Company observed, had believed that "the national emergency would induce a tight labor market," and that product demand would remain steady. Because subsequent events had removed any basis for those assumptions, many producers were now "facing the stark question of survival." Equally upsetting was Textron's response to the crisis. In October 1951, it announced plans to terminate operations at

Nashua and build three new factories in the South; four additional New England plants would be closed in the coming year. As regional manufacturers watched these developments, they began referring to the Textron formula as "Roy Little's attempt to put all the New England mills out at the end of a gang plank."[55]

They also began calling for wage reductions. Without such relief, mill owners asserted, operatives could expect a marked increase in migrations or liquidations. To bolster their demands, some textile executives claimed they had worker support. According to Kenneth B. Cook, president of the Rhode Island Textile Association, "several manufacturers have reported to us that their employees have asked to take an immediate cut of ten cents an hour or more, provided they were guaranteed steady work." The TWUA was not impressed. "Let's face the facts," Mariano Bishop told New Bedford workers. "If any northern employer seriously intends to move, nothing our union can do will stop him, even if wages are cut to zero." Moreover, textile operatives were not getting their fair share as it was. "Can you conceive of an arbitrator awarding lower wages at a time like this," Bishop asked, "when prices are going up every day, and the wages of other workers are also climbing?"[56]

As it turned out, at least one concern did indeed believe arbitrators would look favorably on such a request. During the summer of 1952, Maine's Bates Manufacturing Company sought to have the 1951 wage pact annulled on the grounds that it had seriously undermined the firm's capacity to meet southern competition. As a result, the company claimed, between March 1951 and April 1952 employment at its five divisions had declined 28 percent, from 6,751 to 4,843 operatives. From the arbitrator's standpoint, these were compelling figures, as they indicated "employees are bearing the principal burden of the situation." He was also influenced by the TWUA's failure to extend the 1951 agreement to southern mills. "The basic fact in this case," the final decision stated, "is that Bates and the New England industry cannot continue to operate satisfactorily" at a wage disadvantage that is 11.5 cents per hour greater than it was before the 1951 contract. Nor was there any reason to believe the union would soon close the gap: "the time lag since the Bates increase of March 1951 is already fifteen months in contrast to a maximum of seven months on any prior occasion since 1945." Accordingly, the award eliminated the cost-of-living clause in the Bates contract and decreased wages 7.7 cents per hour. As soon as the ruling was announced,

Fall River–New Bedford manufacturers submitted a similar case to arbitration. Though unable to free themselves from the cost-of-living clause, they did obtain the 7.7-cent wage reduction.[57]

The Bates ruling enraged union leaders, but they were uncertain what to do about it. "The attitude that this must be accepted concerns me," Sol Stetin remarked. "It proves that we have lost some of our spirit." He recommended that a campaign of mass demonstrations, unauthorized work stoppages, and newspaper advertisements be mounted to protest the decision. But others believed there was little support for such a response. "You cannot demonstrate with people who are working 2 and 3 days a week," New England director J. William Belanger stated. Moreover, he added, a number of locals had indicated they were willing to accept a wage decrease. In the end, the executive council issued a resolution condemning the award and declaring its determination to redouble organizational efforts in the South, "so that artificial wage differentials, deliberately created by northern financial interests, can no longer be used as a club to beat down the standard of living of the workers in the north and south alike."[58]

Fulfilling this commitment would be no easy matter. In addition to the already formidable obstacles blocking southern organization, TWUA leaders also had to deal with the effects of a recent defection from their own ranks. A month earlier, the long-simmering Rieve-Baldanzi feud had finally come to a boil when Baldanzi challenged Rieve for the presidency at the union's biennial convention. Because the rivalry significantly affected union actions during this critical period, the affair merits more searching attention than we have thus far given it.

"WHAT A SAD STATE of affairs we are in," William Belanger remarked at a June 1951 session of the executive council. "One trying to outdo the other." As New England director, he knew as well as anyone the destructive effect the Rieve-Baldanzi rivalry was having on the union. Yet, despite this awareness, even he could not escape involvement in the dispute. Earlier in the meeting, after complaining that Baldanzi "refers to us as pork chops," Belanger had declared, "I want to say when it comes to name calling, those who live in glass houses should not throw stones."[59]

Belanger was not the only union leader who deeply regretted the feud but could do nothing about it. Other officials knew the dispute was largely responsible for the ill-conceived southern strike and recognized that employers were now exploiting the rivalry both at the bargaining table and in their efforts to hinder organizational campaigns. They also saw how it was hampering attempts to come to grips with the workload question. When John Chupka negotiated what he considered a "workable and fair" work assignment clause at American Woolen, pro-Baldanzi Lawrence business agents "went to the rank and file and started to make accusations that the administration is going to sell them out." This was the kind of "fake leadership" the union did not need, Michael Bothelo declared, given the uncertain future of New England woolen mills.[60]

To understand how affairs reached this impasse, the best place to begin is with the two principals in the dispute. Although there were no substantial ideological differences between Rieve and Baldanzi — "everyone was a Social Democrat," *Textile Labor* editor Kenneth Fiester recalled — they were very different kinds of people. Unlike the stolid Rieve, Baldanzi brimmed over with charisma. He had grown up in an Italian anarchist neighborhood in Paterson, New Jersey, and as one of the best orators in the labor movement, he had a remarkable ability to articulate the fiery enthusiasm of that militant culture. Concerned primarily with organizing, Baldanzi was an astute observer of rank-and-file needs who maintained close ties with the membership. At executive council meetings, his comments on grassroots developments were frequently insightful and stimulating. Yet, for all his talents, there was something missing in Baldanzi. Education director Lawrence Rogin, who initially looked forward to working with him, believed Baldanzi lacked "depth" and could not be trusted; susceptible to flattery, he sometimes "played favorites without regard to ability" and was reluctant to take public stands that might be unpopular with the membership, regardless of the actual merits of an issue.[61]

Where Baldanzi's limitations were less visible than his strengths, the opposite was true of Rieve. A stocky, "barrel-chested" man who tended to look "paunchy" in street clothes, Rieve spoke "as bluntly to workers as he [did] to employers." Oftentimes, though, Rieve's appearance was deceiving. While he sometimes derided union intellectuals, referring to them as "long hairs," he was "one of the best read men in the labor movement" whose interests included literature, music, and the arts. As head of the Hosiery Federation, he had established a pioneering education department; and as TWUA president, he tried to surround himself with the most talented advisers available. "[G]ruff in manner" and always ready to debate, Rieve frequently challenged the views of others at staff meetings. But he did so less to exhibit his authority than to force speakers to justify their position, and once persuaded of the wisdom of a particular course of action, he put his own objections aside. This was all part of what Sol Stetin called Rieve's "way of getting the best out of people." It was a leadership style some people may have found intimidating, but that provided considerable leeway for aggressive, self-confident individuals who were willing and able to assert themselves.[62]

Ironically, this was just the kind of environment in which someone of Baldanzi's personality and abilities might be expected to prosper, and for many years he did. On a related note, any discussion of the differences between Rieve and Baldanzi should recognize that each possessed strengths that complemented those of the other: though Rieve's steadfast practicality sometimes suggested a lack of imagination, he was an able administrator, capable negotiator, and good listener; while Baldanzi's novel ideas about organizing, keen powers of observation, and close rapport with rank-and-filers made him a valued second-in-command. In short, they formed a good team and functioned as such for more than a decade. This brings us to what was perhaps the most tragic aspect of the whole affair: had the dispute been confined to them alone, it might well have run its course without major incident.

But this was not to be. Both Rieve and Baldanzi were strongly influenced by their supporters. One reason the latter played so active a role in the feud was the embattled condition of the union. As William Gordon observed, a shrinking industry and contracting membership reduced the number of available staff positions and slowed the pace of advancement within the organization. Consequently, while matters of principle were never entirely absent from the dispute, many of the individuals involved were also seeking to further their own personal aims. This in part explains Rieve's decision to back Mariano Bishop's candidacy for vice president at the 1950 convention. Although Rieve clearly preferred Bishop to Baldanzi, a number of observers believe he would have stayed on the sidelines if Bishop and other ambitious New Englanders had not pressured him to make his preference known. Afterward, Baldanzi understandably viewed Rieve's intervention as a hostile act.[63]

Among Baldanzi partisans, personal ambition was inflamed by a belief that they comprised the union's best and brightest staffers. "In my opinion," Charles Hughes wrote Sam Baron, "we have a virtual monopoly on whatever ability and competence there may be in the Textile Workers

Union." Baldanzi, who had a lofty regard for his own talents, did his part to encourage such attitudes. When dealing with the young intellectuals who were his most ardent supporters, Lawrence Rogin recalled, Baldanzi often mocked Rieve's seeming lack of sophistication. As this arrogance spread and deepened, a conviction grew that the TWUA had no problems that a change of administration could not resolve.[64]

Of his various supporters, none had a greater influence on Baldanzi than Sam Baron. The son of Polish immigrants, Baron was a New York socialist who had pursued a wide variety of occupations — both within and outside the labor movement — before joining the TWUA staff in the early forties. He had once been a theater manager and still looked like one, with his neatly trimmed mustache, elegant attire, and ostentatious manners. To Rieve, he was a "long hair"; but so long as Baron did his job as Canadian director, Rieve left him alone. Baron's problems with Rieve began during the late forties when, after deciding to support Baldanzi, he told the TWUA president: "Loyalty is a personal thing you can't demand; you must earn it." Then, to demonstrate just how little loyalty he had to Rieve, Baron began publicly criticizing TWUA policy and initiated a series of structural reforms in Canada that Rieve feared would detach the Canadian division from the international. In June 1951 the executive council, at Rieve's urging, handed Baron his walking papers.[65]

Apart from whatever personal inconvenience his dismissal may have caused him, Baron was by nature and experience predisposed to view Rieve's action in the darkest possible light. As a reporter during the Spanish Civil War, he had exposed the activities of a secret Soviet police organization; and since that time he had sought every opportunity — including an appearance before the red-hunting Dies Committee — to portray himself as a resolute foe of all undemocratic institutions. At a final meeting with Rieve, he declared: "I shall use every forum to reply to any statement made in *Textile Labor* which I think is either a distortion or an outright lie. I will not stand by silently and watch, under the direction of the president, that individuals be destroyed, either their personality or their character, over any political cause that the president sees fit to fight in the manner he does." By now completely exasperated, Rieve replied, "Sam, why don't you go to a psychiatrist and get your mind examined."[66]

Baron's dismissal quickly became a rallying point for Baldanzi partisans. Although they sometimes attacked Rieve for the union's organizational failures in the South, the main issue was always "dictatorship" versus "democracy." In public, they maintained that the problem was structural rather than personal, and could be resolved through a decentralization of authority. Yet policy statements claiming their opponents used the same arguments that "fooled the German people into handing over all governmental power to Hitler" and "caused the Russian people to submit to the ruthless dictatorship of Stalin" indicated otherwise. And behind closed doors, all pretense of objectivity disappeared. Rieve's supporters on the executive council, Baldanzi told one group, "bowed three times in the direction of New York" after getting out of bed each morning.[67]

It is true, as Kenneth Fiester remarked, that Rieve sometimes "sounded like the dictator Baldanzi portrayed him as." On one occasion, for example, he stated that the editor of *Textile Labor* had no right to verify the truthfulness of any story the president submitted to the paper, and would be "fired immediately" if he ever did. At the same time, though, Rieve insisted that *Textile Labor* meet high journalistic standards and not be used as a propaganda organ. In 1942, when Horace Riviere questioned the paper's practice of publicizing TWUA losses — that was not how things had been done in the old UTW — Rieve responded, "Our paper should contain the facts." This policy continued throughout the dispute with Baldanzi. To be sure, some articles had a pro-Rieve slant, but the paper also presented a reasonably accurate version of Baldanzi's reform proposals.[68]

Even more important, the executive council made a serious effort to address Baldanzi's criticisms. In July 1951, at what *Textile Labor* characterized as a "turbulent session" of the council, a majority of the union leadership supported a constitutional amendment that would give rank-and-filers a means of expressing their disapproval of state and area directors. The council also agreed to hold a series of area conferences to gather recommendations for further changes in the union's structure. Despite these actions, Baldanzi was not satisfied. In addition to calling for a review of all recent staff changes, he described the proposed area conferences as "an insult to the intelligence of the membership" that indicated the administration's continued "intention to avoid discussion and democratization." This was demagogic nonsense, and in the end one must agree with William Gordon's assessment of the democracy issue: it was nothing more than a "political gimmick."[69]

Meanwhile, at the local level union members were growing increasingly weary of the leadership dispute. Although some New England unionists had initially voiced support for Baldanzi's reform proposals, the tide was now running against the executive vice president. In August 1951, the Lowell Joint Board voted to send a letter to Rieve stating its opposition to "the fight now going on." But after further discussion, the board instead decided to "condemn" Baldanzi's actions. In New Bedford, where rank-and-file irritation with the dispute had surfaced during the March negotiations, the joint board drafted a resolution that made clear its conception of union priorities:

> At a time when we are faced with reactionary forces that are working day and night to weaken and destroy labor unions, and

> At a time when our International Union is burdened with the job of rebuilding a very weak Southern organizational situation.

> It is certainly not for the best interests of our Union and its membership for Vice-President Baldanzi to be calling rump conferences in opposition to General President Rieve.[70]

These protests made little impression on Baldanzi, who believed that most New Englanders would be only too happy to see Mariano Bishop displace him. And in the following months, both sides marshaled their forces for the final showdown at the 1952 convention. It was, according to *Textile Labor*, one of the most raucous gatherings in TWUA history: "There were boos and cheers; whistles, cymbals, horns, and gongs. The vast, vaulted ceiling of Cleveland's Public Auditorium all but bulged under the pressure of the din. During the rival demonstrations the noise was almost a physical force; the hall was like a diver's compression chamber." The bedlam continued for four days, at which time the delegates cast their ballots and Rieve retained his position by a decisive 1,223 to 720 margin.[71]

Rieve afterward pledged that there would be "no reprisals" and asked the competing factions to submerge their differences "behind a revitalized drive to organize the unorganized, particularly in the south." Most delegates responded enthusiastically to Rieve's appeal, but Baldanzi was not among them. At this critical moment, when the organization he had served for fifteen years was literally fighting for its life, he once again let personal considerations dictate his course of action. Rather than second Rieve's call for unity, he instead gathered his remaining followers and led them into the AFL. At this, Rieve abandoned his promise to forget past differences and discharged the pro-Baldanzi staffers who had been willing to stay in the organization.[72]

The secession movement dealt a crushing blow to TWUA hopes for recovery. During the next year, the union lost bargaining rights to nearly 29,000 workers in fifty-two mills. Although *Textile Labor* tried to make light of these developments, insiders knew better. "I get a little weary of the attitude that some stroke of genius on the part of the publicity department will cause George Baldanzi to dry up and blow away," Kenneth Fiester wrote Solomon Barkin. "The facts are that in terms of *elections* they have been clobbering us." Losses were especially serious in the South, where 22,500 members deserted the TWUA. Included among Baldanzi's followers were Virginia's Dan River locals. Still disillusioned by the outcome of the 1951 strike, for which they blamed Rieve, Dan River operatives voted in November 1952 to join the United Textile Workers; and the following spring the UTW negotiated a contract that not only lacked a checkoff clause, but made no provision for dues collection within mills. In light of Dan River's reputation as a regional standard setter, the settlement had catastrophic implications. As Baldanzi himself had once remarked, any southern agreement that based union security on the good faith of employers was "suicidal."[73]

Baldanzi had considerably less success in New England, where fewer than a thousand workers responded to his call. But this was small consolation to union leaders. In cottons, the failure of the 1951 southern strike had seriously undermined their bargaining position with regional mill owners; and in woolens, the continued decline of American Woolen foretold an even gloomier future. What all this meant for New England workers is the subject of the next chapter, which examines the industry's final days as a major employer of regional labor.[74]

THE COLLAPSE, 1952–1960

6

The 1950s were lean times for the U.S. textile industry. During these peak years of the American Century, when other industries accumulated enormous profits and experienced extraordinary growth, textiles stagnated. Whereas total industrial production shot up 45 percent between 1947 and 1957, textiles registered a 2 percent decline. During this same period, per capita consumption of textile products fell from 44.5 to 36.2 pounds, as other commodities captured an increasing share of the consumer dollar. Equally damaging was the decreased industrial consumption of textile goods caused by the expanded use of paper and plastic substitutes. Meanwhile, textile producers were making little headway in creating new markets for their wares.[1]

These developments, which affected all textile manufacturers, had an especially devastating impact on the New England industry. Those mills that, in Steve Dunwell's words, had "bet *against* the inexorable advance of technology" and failed to replace aging machinery now had to contend with the consequences of underinvestment. In addition to stagnant markets, they also faced increased competitive pressures as a renewed wave of mergers swept the industry. The combinations of the fifties were in many respects an extension of the early postwar movement. A major feature was the acquisition of finishing plants and sales organizations to complete the integration process. The concerns involved were also seeking to spread risk by purchasing companies that would enable them to diversify their product lines. A further impetus was the federal tax code, especially its carryover provisions, which allowed corporations to use the losses incurred by unprofitable units to offset the tax bill of money-making operations. Nearly all of the largest enterprises initiating mergers were either southern-based firms or interregionalists with little interest in preserving their northern properties. More fully integrated, better equipped, and with deeper pockets than smaller companies, these new giants were better prepared for hard times.[2]

The merger movement hastened the demise of the New England textile industry in several ways. Many marginal mills, unable to operate profitably in this competitive environment, simply closed their doors. Other concerns, recognizing the struggle that lay before them, were only too happy to sell out to "financial speculators" like Royal Little and Albert A. List, who exploited special tax incentives to purchase the companies at prices favorable to both parties. Once in possession of a plant, these professional liquidators sometimes auctioned off its fixed assets after transferring the most modern machinery to their southern holdings. On other occasions, they ran a mill into the ground before shutting it down. In either case the result was liquidation, job loss, and a factory that no longer served any productive purpose.[3]

As more mills closed and a belief grew that textiles had no future in New England, manufacturers who intended to remain in the region found it increasingly difficult to finance modernization programs. Sometimes the obstacles were internal. When Collins and Aiken considered refurbishing its Bristol, Rhode Island, plant in 1953, one faction on the board of directors declared that only mill owners "with holes in their heads were putting money into New England." Although strong-willed persisters could overcome this kind of opposition, the attitude of regional banks was more problematic. Most bankers believed that capital invested in New England textile plants was capital wasted, and they urged loan-seeking mill owners to forget about their regional properties and begin operations in the South. Persisters received much the same message from machinery manufacturers: those who were willing to move south could have long-term credit and all the equipment they wanted; those who were planning to stay in New England had to pay cash. On a related matter, studies by the Federal Reserve Bank of Boston, predicting dramatic job growth in new industries, added to the persisters' problems. The bank "now proposes to siphon the remaining investment out of New England textiles under the 'guise' of diversification and on the grounds that there may be a greater return on capital in other ventures," the NACM's William Sullivan observed of one such report. "This represents a new low in defeatism."[4]

The hostile climate of opinion caused by the rising tide of liquidations extended well beyond bankers and machinery producers. "In the final analysis, it is people's attitudes that most affect our situation," William Sullivan once remarked. "It would probably amaze you to know how your employees and the public really feel about your plant." In

1951, when Sullivan penned these comments, some manufacturers may indeed have been surprised; by mid-decade, all such illusions were gone. Indeed, Sullivan believed a point had been reached where decline was creating the conditions for further decline in ways that might be irreversible. Mill liquidations, he said in a 1955 address,

> [have] had a depressing effect upon morale, and coupled with the seniority system (which in itself is an outgrowth of insecurity) [have] resulted in a very great shortage of young people seeking employment in the mills. The low morale, the insecurity which has led to the attitude of opposition to larger work assignments and change has been an additional discouragement to the investment of money and new machinery in New England. The whole complex makes a cycle which feeds upon itself like an atomic reactor which in operation makes fuel for continued operation.

As Sullivan's remarks suggest, and the observations of others confirm, there were many people in New England — workers as well as community leaders — who felt the region would be better off without a textile industry. This was increasingly so as the crisis of the fifties deepened and the insecurity about which Sullivan spoke spread.[5]

Needless to say, this was not a happy time for textile workers. Increased mill closings both north and south, coupled with furious efforts to boost productivity on the part of manufacturers, eliminated more than one of every three textile jobs during the fifties and early sixties. Between 1947 and 1957, New England witnessed a 50 percent decline in textile employment, as the number of wage earners in regional mills plummeted from 288,500 to 144,100 operatives. While many displaced workers would never again earn what they had in the past, those still employed saw earlier advances negated. Where textile earnings averaged 84 percent of the amount received by all manufacturing workers in 1947, the figure had dropped to 72 percent a decade later — this during a period when annual average increase in output per man-hour for textiles topped that of manufacturing in general by a substantial margin.[6]

Meanwhile, the mood at TWUA headquarters was equally grim. Urged to make *Textile Labor* more of a "morale-builder," the paper's editor Kenneth Fiester replied, "all that's needed is the raw material." But as he and other union leaders knew, the material did not exist, and there was no response when Fiester asked: "What can we promise? What hope — what new, inspiring hope — can we offer? What bright new world are we building?" Rather than creating new worlds, the organization had all it could do to survive during these dark years. As

Solomon Barkin bluntly put it at a 1952 staff meeting: "There is no question but that the union will continue to contract and we will have to adjust to that."[7]

As it turned out, the union would find small opportunity for adjustment in its dealings with New England mill owners. With some concerns, the rot ran too deep. Elsewhere, there was no will to take the steps needed to stay in business, while those manufacturers who remained committed to continuing production in New England often issued demands that left little room for compromise. In relating this dreary story, the first two sections of this chapter look at the problems union leaders faced in woolens and cottons. A final section examines the response of regional textile workers.

IN 1947, WHEN A group of cotton producers proposed forming a Textile Industry-Wide Committee on Public Relations, the National Association of Wool Manufacturers (NAWM) passed a resolution objecting to the use of the term "industry-wide." Because they had traditionally paid higher wages than cotton employers, woolen owners believed any association with other branches of the industry would diminish their own reputation. Even though the new organization did not claim to represent woolen and worsted employers, the NAWM observed, "the wool textile industry has certain property rights which should not be usurped by such an 'Industry-Wide' Committee." Woolen manufacturers had a hard time letting go of this deeply ingrained arrogance. As late as 1951, a proposal by E. F. Walker of the Rhode Island Textile Association to form a group that would examine developments threatening to accelerate mill liquidations in New England met much the same response. The following year, however, the NAWM agreed to urge members to appear before the New England Textile Committee. This new attitude toward industrywide initiatives reflected a dawning recognition that something had changed. Unfortunately, for many regional woolen workers and their communities, it came too late.[8]

By the early fifties, the New England woolen and worsted industry was in serious trouble. In 1952, producers experienced their worst year since the 1938 recession and prospects were bleak. New, lower-priced fabrics, better adapted to consumer preferences for lightweight clothing and casual wear, were driving woolen and worsted goods from traditional markets. Although some firms responded to the challenge, they were most often companies like Deering-Milliken, a Maine-based concern then in the process of transferring its operations to the South, where it would establish a reputation for antiunionism fully equal to that of such industry troglodytes as Cannon Mills and J. P. Stevens. For their part, most regional producers seemed intent on confirming the perspicacity of a *Boston Herald* reporter who wrote: "The great woolen and worsted industry in New England is physically obsolete, mentally archaic, technologically bankrupt and at least 40 years behind the times."[9]

The situation was most serious in worsteds. Where the majority of regional woolen producers were small concerns with a few hundred workers, most worsted production took place in massive structures like American Woolen's Wood Mill in Lawrence. With their lower fixed costs, woolen producers had greater flexibility and were better able to adjust to changing consumer demand for well-styled, novelty lines. A number of these firms managed to survive the crisis of the fifties by carving out relatively safe niches in specialty markets, where competitive pressures were not nearly so intense as they were in worsteds.[10]

This was especially bad news for Lawrence, which remained the worsted capital of the nation and where more than 40 percent of the labor force depended on textiles for employment. By mid-1952, the number of operatives at work in local mills had dropped to 7,000 from an October 1950 peak of 35,000; during World War II, the Wood Mill alone had employed 7,800 workers. It was equally bad news for American Woolen. When the Korean War prompted an increase in government orders for worsted goods, the company set aside whatever plans it might have had for adjusting to the new market environment. On two prior occasions, during World War I and World War II, international conflict had saved American Woolen from disaster, and company leaders apparently believed it would do so again. Totally preoccupied with winning and servicing military contracts, they allowed their staff of stylists and designers to disband, cut back research on new synthetic blends, and permitted their already inadequate sales promotion program to deteriorate. When the war boom ended much sooner than anticipated, American Woolen was less prepared than ever to compete in commercial markets.[11]

Had the company been sound, it might easily have overcome this setback. But it was not. Since 1948, the depreciation of fixed assets at American Woolen had outpaced investment in new plant and equipment; and this, as the TWUA put it, "apparent preference for old fixed assets over more efficient new ones" even extended to expansion policy. When the company established plants in North Carolina and Georgia during the early fifties, it did not build or acquire modern factories but purchased aging structures that required extensive renovation: in one case, a two-story cotton mill that had been built around 1890; in the other, a tobacco warehouse ill designed for wool manufacturing. It sometimes seemed that American Woolen could not do anything right. After permanently closing five plants in 1952, it made little effort to liquidate its investment in the properties, thus canceling out whatever benefits the company might have gained from the action. Meanwhile, company leaders were still seeking, with little evident success, to devise a management structure that would both decentralize authority within the corporation and coordinate operations among its numerous plants.[12]

Yet, for all its woes, American Woolen remained the industry standard setter on labor matters. And in 1953, when the company demanded a 20 percent wage reduction, union leaders resisted, and the case ultimately went to arbitration. Noting that it had lost $13 million in 1952, American Woolen contended that interregional wage and workload differentials prevented it from competing effectively. The arbitrator was not persuaded. Not only was the current national trend toward increased wages, but the 1952 deficit was the company's first loss in thirteen years. Moreover, he observed, the problems then facing woolen and worsted manufacturers went well beyond what they were required to pay their workers, and "even the granting of the entire thirty one cent reduction would not cure the ills of this sick industry."[13]

Although gratified by the ruling, union leaders knew the industry's prospects were every bit as dismal as the arbitrator had suggested. In January 1954, the TWUA proposed a five-point program designed to preserve what was left of the New England woolen and worsted industry. The plan called for the elimination of import duties on raw wool, higher tariffs on foreign goods, an increase in the minimum wage for federal contracts, and the creation of an industrywide research and development organization. The union also pledged to cooperate with manufacturers on the workload question, but asked that current wages and fringes be maintained.[14]

Although woolen manufacturers were always ready to accept union assistance on the tariff and workload issues, they had other ideas about wages. Less than two weeks after the TWUA announced its program, the Forstmann Woolen Company of Passaic, New Jersey, opened negotiations on the coming year's contract by demanding an 11.5 percent reduction. Just as troubling as the demand itself was the company's rationale for making it. Forstmann claimed that UTW-AFL firms had failed to match the nine-cent increase granted TWUA members in 1951, thus raising another problem the union did not need at this juncture. Where the UTW had made little progress in the northern cotton industry, its pacts with such Lawrence-area concerns as Pacific, Arlington, and M. T. Stevens had given it a solid foothold in woolens. Like their CIO counterparts, these companies had followed American Woolen's lead on labor matters throughout the late forties. As early as 1950, though, there were indications that the UTW was undermining TWUA workload policy by using plant-closing threats to force Lawrence-area members to accept increased assignments. Then, as Forstmann contended, UTW mills broke with the 1951 wage pattern. Emil Rieve strongly suspected that UTW leaders were now offering American Woolen the earlier wage cut "as well as a deal on workloads."[15]

Subsequent events suggest that Rieve's suspicions were well founded. After the TWUA trounced the UTW by a decisive 4–1 margin in a March election at Forstmann, the company joined thirty other woolen firms in extending their current pacts with the union. But American Woolen was not among them. Rather than go along with the settlement, the company locked out its workers that May after announcing a 21.5-cent wage reduction. In the meantime, other mills that were also seeking a wage cut decided to take the case to arbitration; and a June ruling, based largely on the differential among union concerns created by the 1951 UTW agreements, ordered a 9.5-cent decrease. Soon afterward, the TWUA came to terms with American Woolen and grudgingly accepted a contract that reduced wages 10.5 cents, cut back fringe benefits, eliminated technological severance pay and the cost-of-living clause, and eased restrictions on the installation of new work assignments.[16]

As union leaders knew, it was one of the worst contracts they had ever negotiated. But they believed they had little choice. Apart from the pressures created by UTW competition and the June arbitration decision, there was limited rank-and-file support for an extended struggle. Unemployment remained high in Lawrence and had begun to take its toll on local unionists. Several months before the American Woolen lockout, joint board manager Arthur Brown had reported: "Our people are frightened and accepting jobs paying, in many instances, less than one-half of what they formerly received and are afraid of participating in organizational work for fear that they may lose whatever job they may hold." To have prolonged the dispute under these circumstances would have been folly.[17]

Union leaders were also troubled by the desperate financial condition of American Woolen. "There appears to be considerable confusion and lack of decisioning," Solomon Barkin wrote John Chupka in June 1953. "There is much pressure for abandoning the Wood Mill." The situation did not improve, and by early 1954 the company was losing a million dollars a month. To prevent complete collapse, the directors first considered a reorganization plan that would eliminate the corporation's least efficient plants. Sumner D. Charm, one-time personnel director at American Woolen and now vice chairman of a stockholders' fact-finding committee, believed the company still had a future in New England. He further believed its main problem was not labor costs but "inefficient selling and outmoded production methods," which could be corrected through an intensive two-year rebuilding program. Implementing such a plan, Charm argued, would place American Woolen in a position where it deserved "the highest degree of labor cooperation," at which point company and union could work together to restore some measure of the firm's former greatness.[18]

TWUA leaders heartily endorsed Charm's observations and pledged to do whatever they could to rescue the ailing concern. It soon became clear, however, that Charm represented a minority position. And as various financial vultures eyed American Woolen's $19 million in cash reserves and $30 million in tax-loss credits, union officials looked to Washington for assistance. In a letter to New England senators, the union contended that this was not a private transaction but a public matter whose resolution would affect the economic future of numerous regional communities. Financial resources that had been "accumulated over many years through the hard labor of the workers and the sacrifices of the community" were in imminent danger of being "perverted for the personal interests of outsiders intruding themselves into the operations of the company." Congress thus had a duty to revise the tax laws that permitted such "parasitic enrichment."[19]

It was an intelligent response to a bad situation, but like Sumner Charm's modernization proposal, the union's protest was ignored. Reluctant to do anything that would impede the free movement of capital, Congress refused to act, and American Woolen was eventually acquired by Textron's Royal Little, who had no intention of reviving the nearly moribund concern. What he did want was its cash and tax-loss credits. In fact, Little subsequently remarked, "If [American Woolen] hadn't been such a God-awful mess I couldn't have picked it up." Unsurprisingly, he did not keep it for long. Within the next two years, his newly created Amerotron Corporation had shut down all of its New England properties. "As a result of this merger and the use of their surplus cash, loss carry-forward, and losses of millions of dollars on the sale of fixed assets that were later liquidated," Little observed in his autobiography, "Textron was able to continue its unrelated diversification program. Without the American Woolen merger, Textron would never have amounted to anything."[20]

The death of American Woolen marked the end of pattern bargaining in woolens. Since the company's formation at the turn of the century, both unions and other manufacturers had recognized American Woolen's role as a standard setter. "It is true we had to browbeat the mills in Maine and New Hampshire," Solomon Barkin observed, "but eventually everyone knew that prices and wages set by American Woolen provided a pattern." Those days were now gone. The "confused" situation that resulted was perhaps best described in an NAWM memo to member mills: "The financial standing of the company seems to dominate [negotiations] in some cases, while with others, operating mills both north and south, there is a feeling that [interregional wage] differentials cannot be increased. Still others feel some adjustment must be made to hold and attract help." To the extent that anyone now established industry-wide standards, it was such southern-based giants as Burlington, J. P. Stevens, and Deering-Milliken; and these companies were among the most virulently antiunion firms in American manufacturing.[21]

The events surrounding American Woolen's demise also ended Lawrence's days as a center of textile unionism. Between 1947 and 1954, woolen and worsted employment in New England declined more than 50 percent, from 105,000 to 40,000 operatives. With 12,000 workers still unemployed in February 1955, Lawrence was especially hard hit. In addition to the liquidation of such local landmarks as the Wood, Ayer, Shawsheen, and Arlington mills, other companies of varying sizes sharply reduced their payrolls, requiring the joint board to make "drastic curtailments" in its activities. Among the events discontinued were the annual Kiddies Christmas party and Labor Day picnic, while staff cuts left the board without an education director and with one fewer business agent.

Continued mill closings forced the departure of other union personnel such as Joseph D'autiel, who in September 1956 "gave his verbal resignation as Vice-President of the Joint Board because the Patchogue Plymouth Company has been liquidated, thus dissolving Local 572."[22]

Even more disheartening was the effect these developments had on worker morale. "There are very few [woolen] plants in New England where the workers take a 'damn them' attitude," Solomon Barkin remarked at a 1955 meeting. "This is in sharp contrast to the attitude in the Middle Atlantic states where workers are prepared to see the plant close since many other job opportunities are available." Barkin's observations certainly applied to Lawrence. When joint board manager Arthur Brown attempted to organize a small wool combing plant in 1955, he was barely able to collect enough signed cards to petition for an election. The response of most former union members was "very discouraging," Brown reported. "These people have become frightened and having exhausted their unemployment benefits are fearful of losing their jobs again through liquidation."[23]

"The only thing that will save any of the textile industry for Lawrence will be when the textile manufacturers screw up the courage to say, 'This is the wage. This is the machine load. Take it or leave it.'" So wrote Howard Bennett, the reactionary editor of *America's Textile Reporter*, in a 1953 article. News of Arthur Brown's travails would have pleased Bennett, as would the observations of a local manufacturer who told Seabury Stanton that many Lawrence operatives were leaving union plants where they had been working part-time to take full-time jobs in non-union mills at reduced wages. Yet, as TWUA leaders knew and Bennett apparently did not, any realistic program to save the New England woolen industry required much more than a savaging of regional labor standards. The changed market environment of the postwar era demanded an unaccustomed flexibility and readiness to innovate on the part of woolen and worsted producers, if they were to remain in business. This is not to say that the union's response to the woolen debacle was faultless. Efforts to preserve American Woolen's role as a pattern setter, long after it had become clear that the company was among the least innovative firms in the industry, obstructed the implementation of potentially worthwhile initiatives elsewhere. Nevertheless, union officials did understand the need for change. Too often, though, capital's reluctance to make needed investments and rigid insistence on its right to manage placed sharp limitations on what they could do; too few people shared Sumner Charm's insight that the union was part of the solution rather than the source of the problem.[24]

ALTHOUGH THE NEW England cotton industry lost approximately the same number of jobs as woolens during the postwar years, the cotton experience differed from that of woolens in several important ways. One was the pace of deindustrialization. More than 50 percent of the jobs lost in woolens between 1945 and 1957 disappeared during a brief three-year span beginning in 1952, which in part explains the extreme demoralization of Lawrence workers that Arthur Brown described. By contrast, cotton shutdowns were more evenly spaced across the entire period. This was by no means a cheerful time for these operatives. In Fall River and New Bedford, whose mills employed more than 25 percent of the regional cotton workforce, unemployment rates were substantially higher than the national average throughout the fifties. Yet, compared with their counterparts in places like Lawrence, most cotton workers had a little more time to adjust. Even more important, this was not their first encounter with economic disaster. Where woolen communities had escaped the worst ravages of the interwar crisis, it had struck cotton centers with full force. And workers there developed a certain toughness and cynicism that reduced their psychological dependence on textiles.[25]

This did not make cotton workers thoroughgoing militants, ready to take to the streets at the first sign of managerial aggression. They knew the industry faced serious problems and did not wish to hasten its decline. At the same time, though, they believed they had done their part. For many, the regionwide wage reductions prompted by the Bates decision were the last giveback. When, during the 1953 Fall River–New Bedford negotiations, William Pollock declared, "If the only hope of saving the northern cotton-rayon industry is substandard wages and working conditions, I don't think the people want to save it," a roomful of rank-and-filers seconded the assertion with shouts of "Right!" By the following year, there were indications of dissatisfaction with union leaders. "The membership," Solomon Barkin observed in a memo describing the situation among New England cotton workers, "is disturbed they have followed the union's officers in a conservative wage policy and are dismayed by the change in course and effect."[26]

Meanwhile, regional mill owners were not certain what to do. The persisters who dominated the pattern-setting Fall River–New Bedford Manufacturers Association expressed frequent complaints about the interregional wage differential and insisted that some action had to be taken to close it. Yet, sensing the increased restiveness among workers and worried that a wage reduction would complicate efforts to secure skilled labor, they decided against a wage reopening in 1954. When the Pepperell Manufacturing Company, a major interregionalist with plants in Maine, Fall River, and various locations in the South, sought a 10 percent decrease through arbitration, an arbitrator ruled that there was insufficient reason for the concern to depart from "its long established adherence to the New England 'pattern' in the middle of a two year agreement."[27]

By 1955, the years of indecision had ended. This at least was the case at Hathaway Manufacturing, where Seabury Stanton was in the process of implementing a long-term strategy for the company's survival. His first move was to engineer a merger with Berkshire Fine Spinning. Concerned about increased competitive pressures from such southern-based giants as Burlington and J. P. Stevens, Stanton believed the merger would permit greater product diversification and higher-volume production. Another attraction was Berkshire's large cash reserves, which could be used to finance an ongoing program of plant modernization.[28]

This accomplished, Stanton next turned his attention to labor matters and demanded that the union accept wage and fringe reductions that would eliminate interregional differentials. He was particularly upset by the agreements TWUA leaders were accepting in the South. "Our labor costs continue to be far above those of union Southern mills," he wrote Emil Rieve. "By signing contracts with Southern mills and refusing to sign with us on similar terms, you are by your own action making it virtually impossible for us in New England to operate our mills competitively." For four years, regional cotton producers had waited patiently for the union to correct these discrepancies, and they were unwilling to wait any longer. "Gentlemen," a statement issued by the Fall River–New Bedford Manufacturers Association declared, "the hour of decision is at hand."[29]

TWUA leaders lost little time deciding what they would do. Because as Rieve acknowledged, "We cannot equalize wages between the north and the south," they either had to submit or take a strike; and they had no intention of submitting. Among other reasons, they believed manufacturers were willfully ignoring the broader picture. Regional cotton operatives had made numerous concessions on workloads over the years, nowhere more so than at Hathaway, where worker cooperation had enabled the company to save $2.5 million after a September 1954 hurricane had destroyed the main plant. They also knew employers were not of one mind concerning the givebacks: a New Bedford mill superintendent expressed "surprise" at the owners' demands, while thirty-four smaller concerns renewed the existing contract. Last, and perhaps most important, rank-and-filers were in no mood to take a wage cut. After discussing the matter with New Bedford workers, joint board manager George Carignan reported "that there was a strong feeling against any reductions whatsoever."[30]

The strike began at midnight, April 15, and involved about twenty-five thousand workers from six of the region's largest cotton producers: Berkshire-Hathaway, Pepperell, Bates, Continental, Luther, and Wamsutta. It was the last major textile strike in New England, and compared with earlier struggles, it was a relatively tame affair. In some locales like North Adams, where strikers received broad community support, morale was high, but elsewhere the worker response was much more subdued. During a tour of Rhode Island and southeastern Massachusetts, an official from the Northern Textile Association found "[c]omplete laxity on both sides": "It's the most unpopular and friendliest strike ever." He also believed that many operatives wanted to return to work. Although these observations doubtless overstate worker opposition to the walkout, they do capture a certain ambivalence that many strikers must have felt: on one hand, a quiet determination to defend standards they had struggled so long to achieve; on the other, a fear that if they pressed too hard, mill owners would carry out the plant-closing threats issued during the strike. Yet, whatever misgivings some might have had, no one broke ranks.[31]

The same cannot be said of the mill owners. Aware that Bates president Herman D. Ruhm Jr. had long resented Stanton's self-designated role as primary spokesman for regional cotton producers, TWUA officials attempted to detach Bates from the other striking concerns by offering to grant the company any concessions contained in a final settlement. Not only did Ruhm go along with the deal, but Wamsutta and Continental later accepted similar proposals that provided a slight saving on fringes and eased restrictions on work assignment changes. Meanwhile, Stanton tried to maintain a bold front, publicly declaring that the Wamsutta and Continental agreements did practically nothing to make regional mills competitive with southern producers. Privately, though, he was bitterly disappointed that these firms would "so abjectly capitulate." In early June, as other executives began to question the wisdom of continuing the strike, the president of Fall River's Luther Manufacturing Company urged union leaders to find "some face-saving device for Stanton, who at this point feels he must have a few cents."[32]

Despite these overtures, the strike continued for another month, at which point the manufacturers dropped their demand for a 10 percent wage reduction. The two sides then reached an agreement that included the Wamsutta and Continental concessions and eliminated the cost-of-living clause. Stanton claimed to be happy with the settlement, writing Brackett Parsons of Pepperell, "I feel no regrets for having maintained our position throughout the strike, and hope that your decision to stand shoulder to shoulder with us turned out to be as advantageous for you as I feel it was for Berkshire Hathaway." Although these sentiments were no doubt genuine — in that Stanton relished a good fight — there was much about the strike's outcome to give cause for dissatisfaction. For one thing, any thoughts he might have had about leading a regionwide revival of the cotton industry were now gone. The strike revealed that not even the New Bedford and Fall River manufacturers' organizations could be counted upon for support. The defection of Wamsutta, which was now controlled by the southern-based Lowenstein corporation, showed that the New Bedford association was but a "shell" of its former self; while the inability of Spindle City mills to obtain revised workload language indicated "the unreliability of any assumption that the Fall River Group will present a united front in a difficult situation."[33]

The strike also exacerbated an ongoing labor supply problem. As we saw in Chapter Four, the postwar textile workforce comprised two broad groupings of operatives: a group of aging persisters who had spent much or all of their working lives in textile mills and felt they had nowhere else to go; and a group of younger workers who had no real commitment to textile employment and were skeptical about what the industry could do for them. Unsurprisingly, each group reacted differently to the reemergence of hard times following the postwar boom. Because of seniority, the persisters were less affected by layoffs, and when a mill closed they most often sought textile work elsewhere. Displaced younger workers, on the other hand, tended to look for jobs outside the industry, and when they found them they did not look back. One such operative, a thirty-two-year-old Fall River wage earner interviewed during the early fifties, spoke for many of his peers when he told William Miernyk: "It is a pity that I gave so much of my time to a firm that left me empty handed in the end." Another worker put it even more simply: "Let them all get out of here."[34]

These divisions among rank-and-filers sometimes complicated union policy. Worker response to the pension question provides the best example. In 1950, after the steelworkers' union obtained pension rights for its members, the TWUA put the issue before New England operatives. From the outset, Rieve doubted whether any consensus could be reached. "What inducement," he asked a meeting of the executive council, "is there for a younger person to go out on strike and fight for a pension system which he might not receive after all?" It was a good question, for apparently there was very little incentive. At one New England firm with three plants, operatives at one mill were willing to fight for pensions; at another, they were not. "They wanted it in the pay," Herbert Payne explained, "primarily because they were young people." Similar differences no doubt surfaced at what William Sullivan characterized as a "stormy session" of two Maine locals, where workers instructed Mariano Bishop to focus on increased wages because they had "no assurance that the mills would be around to pay pensions at a later date." In the end, union leaders dropped the pension issue and sought to negotiate retirement severance plans that provided stated amounts of money for each year worked.[35]

However troublesome, these problems were relatively small compared to the difficulties worker retention created for manufacturers. In a 1952 conversation, Herman Ruhm of Bates told Solomon Barkin that "moving south was becoming vital because the irregular operations in the north are influencing the younger people not to come into the industry." Each layoff prompted these operatives to seek employment elsewhere, and many "were unwilling to come back to Bates" if they had found "regular jobs in some other areas or industries." This produced the higher than average age structure in regional plants. According to Royal Little, "in all the mills that [Textron] started from scratch in the South, the average age of the employees when we began was about twenty-three." But in New England, where young people "were too smart to go to work in textile mills," the average age "was over fifty-five years." Although a study conducted by the Northern Textile Association in the mid-fifties suggests that Little was exaggerating, its findings provided small comfort to regional mill owners: 60 percent of the cotton workforce was forty years old or over, and more than one of every three operatives had passed their fiftieth birthday. Even more alarming was the growing shortage of skilled workers, which was especially evident in weave rooms, where mill owners were finding it increasingly difficult to secure adequate supplies of weavers, loom fixers, and drawing-in hands.[36]

Job insecurity was the primary but by no means the only cause of these developments. Another factor was the industry's substandard wages. And the 1955 strike, which was prompted by employer efforts to reduce worker compensation even further, increased wage earner discontent and gave younger people additional reason to flee textile employment. Afterward, when Biddeford-Saco owners asked 1,200 operatives to work overtime, only a dozen accepted, much to the consternation of local manufacturers. Confident that after a thirteen-week strike workers would be more than eager to restore lost wages, manufacturers failed to recognize the sense of injustice many operatives felt. As joint board manager Michael Schoonjans explained, "During the strike we operated a good food kitchen—now they refuse to work for starvation wages." What happened in Biddeford-Saco was not unique; reports from other cotton centers echoed the same themes. In New Bedford, local mills lost 150 skilled workers during the strike, and both Wamsutta and Berkshire-Hathaway couldn't find enough labor with appropriate training to operate their weave rooms at full capacity. George Carignan believed the day was fast approaching when mill owners would not be able to "get people to man the jobs because of low wages."[37]

In normal times this would have been good news for union leaders, an indication that they were well positioned to obtain a wage increase. But the mid-fifties were not normal times. The 1951 southern strike had demonstrated that New England mills no longer set industry wage patterns; and as Herman Ruhm observed, firms unable to secure sufficient workers were more likely to discontinue operations or move south than to offer financial inducements to prospective employees. What all this meant was that something had to be done in the South. Manufacturers there had not raised wages since 1951, and until they did, pressuring New England owners would only accelerate the pace of regional decline. The first move took place during the summer of 1955, when southern dyers sought an increase at unionized concerns; at the same time, they began an agitational campaign to organize the dye shops at Burlington, a longtime bastion of antiunionism and the nation's largest textile employer. Worried that promises of higher wages would prove irresistible to their employees, Burlington granted its workers a five-cent advance that established a new regional pattern; it also put southern wage scales, exclusive of fringe benefits, on approximately the same level as those of New England.[38]

Over the next decade, the TWUA made limited organizational gains in the South. But on five separate occasions — in 1956, 1959, 1960, 1962, and 1964 — it did mount successful agitational campaigns that prompted southern mill owners to advance wages. The typical drive began with a massive leafleting effort centered on such nonunion giants as Burlington, J. P. Stevens, Deering-Milliken, and Cannon. The union then sent open letters justifying an advance to industry managers, in the form of advertisements placed in *The Wall Street Journal* and various trade papers. As such pressure mounted and was sustained over a period of months, nonunion manufacturers became increasingly concerned about the effect this activity was having on their workers. In 1959, for example, Cannon Mills was the first to give way because, as a company executive explained, management feared that if a wage increase "started [at] a union operated plant, there was no telling what kind of twist it might take."[39]

The agitational campaigns were a creative response to a bad situation. Yet, while rank-and-filers doubtless appreciated the wage advances, union leaders could not hide the fact that they were bargaining from weakness. As Barkin observed, "we cannot initiate a wage increase movement from our organized mills but must always tease the unorganized mills into getting a wage increase." Moreover, interregional distinctions between union and nonunion mills — at least so far as they concerned wages and working conditions — were rapidly fading. Even industry leaders acknowledged as much. Commenting on a 1959 Barkin article justifying a southern wage increase, William Sullivan wrote Seabury Stanton that many of Barkin's contentions were "equally valid" or "even stronger when applied to Northern mills."[40]

We can best understand why this was so by examining TWUA relations with New England's two leading cotton firms during the late fifties, Bates and Berkshire-Hathaway. At Bates, Herman Ruhm had long sought to establish intraregional wage differentials that undercut the Fall River–New Bedford pattern. Even though a change of ownership in 1955 displaced Ruhm, Bates continued efforts to depress worker earnings. In April 1956, the company followed other New England mills in granting its operatives an eight-cent increase. The following year, though, Bates sought to withdraw the advance, despite the fact that southern mills had raised wages ten cents the previous fall. Union leaders were outraged by the demand and the matter ultimately went to arbitration. Although the TWUA won the case, its victory was more attributable to past failures than current initiatives. In denying the company's request, the arbitration board noted that the "money wages [of Bates workers] are much the same as in 1951; their real wages are substantially lower." Meanwhile, citing decreased demand, Bates had closed its Biddeford-Saco mill. Local workers felt the real reason was to induce operatives at other plants to cooperate with company wage-cutting efforts. Although there is no evidence to support the charge, the fact that workers believed the story reduced union leverage in its dealings with the company.[41]

Berkshire-Hathaway also reduced operations during the late fifties, closing four of its least efficient plants and transferring their best machinery to other company mills. Even with this reorganization, Berkshire-Hathaway still had serious financial problems. At a time when the company was coming under increasing pressure from corporate raiders, regional bankers not only refused to lend it money at prime rates, but placed rigid limitations on its credit line as well. Union leaders could not ignore these developments. Not only did Berkshire-Hathaway's six thousand workers make it the largest cotton employer in New England, but Royal Little was among the people seeking to acquire the company; and nobody had to explain what a Textron takeover would mean. In an effort to help save the concern, TWUA president William Pollock agreed to bypass a wage reopening and local unionists supported management initiatives to improve operating conditions. With this assistance, Berkshire-Hathaway survived the crisis without a change of ownership, and its New Bedford plant would continue operations into the 1980s, decades after most regional cotton producers had closed their doors.[42]

Union leaders had acted wisely under the circumstances. But they did so at a price. In addition to foregoing a wage advance, they had assented to another round in what by then must have seemed an endless series of work assignment changes. Yet, as they knew all too well, they lacked the strength needed to pursue more aggressive alternatives. "We now do what we have to because there isn't any choice," cotton director Victor Canzano told a 1958 meeting of the executive council. "If we were dealing for 200,000 organized workers in the south we wouldn't bother about all the workload changes requested by Berkshire Hathaway which covers only 6,000 workers. However," Canzano added, "that is not the situation."[43]

There was also little rank-and-file pressure for a more militant policy. Workers did occasionally rebel at work assignment changes, as when battery hands at the Chicopee Manufacturing Company responded to an increase in the number of bobbins they had to plug by conducting a sit-down. But such resistance was rare. As noted, many participants in the 1955 strike had mixed feelings about the struggle — a sense of injustice tempered by fear. By the late fifties, fear had won out. Union leaders did not press harder for wage advances in 1957 and 1958 because joint board managers were reporting that most workers would be "happy to renew" existing agreements "in the hope that they can work 40 hours a week. ..." And in one 1959 incident, Willimantic workers voted to accept a contract that TWUA president William Pollock had turned down. By the mid-sixties, this "lack of pressure and militancy" on the part of New England operatives, coupled with the success of the southern agitational campaigns, had placed the union in what Pollock called "an embarrassing position." "With the south giving wage increases so rapidly," Pollock explained, "it is going to result in the average hourly earnings being higher in the south than we are getting in our contract plants. We are faced with the dilemma of plants like American Thread and Pepperell granting wage increases in their non-union [southern] plants but not voluntarily offering the same in the plants we have under contract in the north." The remainder of this chapter takes a closer look at the changing attitudes of New England textile workers that were in part responsible for this extraordinary turnabout.[44]

WHEN GOODALL-SANFORD liquidated its Maine plant in late 1954, many of its three thousand employees afterward went to neighboring Biddeford to work at the local Pepperell plant — so many in fact as to attract the attention of Biddeford workers. "Look at all the pep and ginger of those young fellows from Sanford," one veteran operative remarked to joint board manager Michael Schoonjans. "In the old days they would have been hired on the spot. Thank God for TWUA and the seniority clause you people won for us — it means our jobs are safe." It was, for several reasons, a revealing comment. On one hand, it explains much about the industry's age structure. Whatever their general opinion of textile employment — and by all accounts it was often negative —

younger workers recognized that the seniority system sharply reduced their job security in an industry that offered precious little to begin with. They did not need a course in labor economics to know they would be better off somewhere else.[45]

The remarks also provide perspective on the changing perceptions of those aging persisters who increasingly dominated the cotton workforce. Although it is unlikely that anyone really felt "safe" by the mid-fifties, older operatives were least affected by the initial wave of postwar shutdowns. For a time, they endorsed the dissatisfaction voiced by younger coworkers. But whatever sense of security they may have felt was fleeting at best. As mill closing followed mill closing, fear spread and thoughts of resistance died. More so than others, the persisters had good reason to be scared. Because they had the fewest alternatives, they would bear the heaviest costs of deindustrialization in the New England textile industry.

This is not to say that displaced younger people most often prospered after leaving textile employment. One study found that few former mill operatives of any age were "able to move into the relatively good jobs in growth sectors such as high-technology." Yet, compared with their more youthful coworkers, the persisters confronted special disadvantages. One was their greater immobility. Family responsibilities, homeownership, and other considerations made relocation a much less viable option for older workers. At the same time, many had worked in textile mills all their lives and were uncertain what else they could do. As one Nashua worker put it, "Winding is the only thing I know—I wouldn't be good at anything else. I'd look silly doing something I don't know anything about." Such feelings were widespread. Speaking of the persisters with whom he had worked, a forty-one-year-old former textile operative who had managed to obtain employment at an electronics firm told economist William Miernyk: "They don't know any other trade that would help them get a job."[46]

Not surprisingly, persisters tried desperately to stay in the industry. Unlike displaced younger workers, who were more apt to declare they were "through with textiles," their first response was to seek employment at another textile mill. Because employers both valued their experience and were having so little success recruiting younger operatives, skilled persisters could, for a while at least, find suitable jobs. During the course of the 1950s, though, such options contracted and in most areas eventually disappeared. It happened at different times in different locales—

quite early in places like Lawrence, somewhat later in many cotton centers — but nearly everywhere the day arrived when displaced persisters had to admit that they would never again work in textiles. "Textiles are gone, and neither you nor anyone else can bring them back, although I wish you could," a sixty-year-old Providence weaver remarked. "[T]he only things running in Rhode Island today are the race tracks!"[47]

This bleak outlook was no doubt shared by many persisters. If nothing else, the age discrimination they invariably confronted when attempting to obtain nontextile employment was a constant source of discouragement. "Everywhere I went they laughed at me," said a fifty-nine-year-old woman from a largely nontextile area of her efforts to find work. A slightly older worker spoke of similar rebuffs: "They ask your age before your name and when you tell them they say they aren't hiring." And when persisters were not queried about their age, employers wanted to know if they had any experience, to which they could only respond: "Of course we don't if we always worked in textile mills." Over time, as the rejections multiplied, more than a few must have asked the question that a fifty-five-year-old Fall River worker put to William Miernyk: "What is a man supposed to do, go out and shoot himself?"[48]

Some persisters did find work, but in nearly all cases they had to accept reduced earnings. Many of the new companies that set up shop in abandoned plants were fly-by-night enterprises attracted by the inducements of local development commissions and the desperation of displaced textile workers. "A lot of cheap factories are coming into Lawrence," one former operative observed. "I'll say what every other person will say, they're nothing but sweatshops paying 75 cents an hour. They are not good for anyone who has a family." Even some members of the Greater Lawrence Citizens' Committee for Industrial Development agreed with this assessment. Giving voice to the family living wage doctrine so cherished by Catholic progressives, Father McQuade of Merrimack College told a 1954 meeting that the city needed more "hard-core industries." There were already enough garment firms, he added, and "if we bring in many more we are going to have men walking the streets and women working." All too often, though, this was the only kind of work available, and displaced textile workers ultimately had little choice in the matter. "We thought the shoe shops were beneath us. We thought only the people without any education went to the shoe shops," Blanche Sciacca of Lawrence recalled. "But, once the mills closed we gladly went to the shoe shops!"[49]

Although most other textile centers did not experience the same degree of devastation as Lawrence, what happened there was hardly unique. The result was a situation in which union leaders found it increasingly difficult to promote rank-and-file resistance to managerial intransigence. "I know how many strikes we would have liked to have called in many places where the people told us to go fly a kite," Solomon Barkin told a 1960 meeting of the Columbia University labor seminar. "They weren't sure that the circumstances were such that they would sacrifice the job for higher wages." This is not to say that workers held capital blameless for their condition. In some instances, criticism focused on specific companies that had plainly failed to replace aging equipment. In other cases, workers accused mill owners in general of taking actions that blocked economic diversification. "The textile mills had a monopoly in Fall River," one former operative observed. "They would not allow other industries in for fear of paying higher wages." Yet, while similar observations could be heard in Lawrence and other textile centers, no one had any idea how to change matters. Nor was there much inclination to do so, as most wage earners were more concerned about meeting current exigencies than redressing past injustices.[50]

Moreover, some workers believed unions were primarily responsible for the industry's demise. "Unions are all right up to a point," a Lawrence worker told William Miernyk, "but they asked for raises, raises, raises, and then raised us right out the door." Although Miernyk noted that this was a minority view among the people whom he interviewed during the 1950s, it became increasingly popular with the passage of time. In an analysis of oral history interviews, John Bodnar has observed that "historical participants, like historians, place conceptual frameworks on past events." In the decaying textile centers of New England, unions emerged as major culprits in the dominant interpretation of industrial decline. "Oh, yes," said a former Lawrence operative interviewed during the 1980s, when asked if unions had gone too far in their demands. "That's what made them close down over here. They moved completely down South." "Once the unions came in," another interviewee remarked, "I think that's when they started looking for cheaper places to go, like down South."[51]

The diffusion of such beliefs had disastrous consequences for regional unions. Between 1953 and the mid-1970s, the proportion of the non-agricultural workforce in unions fell from 30 to 24 percent; and where New England labor organizations had won 70 percent of elections in

1950, this figure had been reduced by half two decades later. All too typical was the experience of TWUA organizer Ralph Corderre, who lost a 1974 election at a Webster, Massachusetts, mill when "company letters to the employees used the unemployment gag" to influence worker votes. "Although we answered the accusations," Corderre explained, "they had this fear instilled in them."[52]

The TWUA deserved much better. Even some mill owners acknowledged as much. When Solomon Barkin retired in 1963, among those wishing him well was Seabury Stanton, who wrote: "speaking as a manufacturer, I will miss the effect of your wise counsel to those who at times appear to be so blind they do not wish to see." That Stanton was the region's premier persister was certainly no coincidence. Despite their many disagreements over the years, he recognized that he and Barkin had at least one common aim: to save the New England textile industry. And unlike the revival-at-any cost entrepreneurs who would come to dominate local development commissions during the era of decline, he had learned that unions could play a positive role in economic affairs. It was unfortunate that others did not share this insight. For, as we will see in the next chapter, no organization worked harder than the TWUA to reduce the social costs of change for regional wage earners during those bleak years.[53]

7 THE POLITICS OF DEINDUSTRIALIZATION

Writing in 1963, Paul Jacobs observed that "unions have too little power of the proper kind." Labor's aims, he believed, were "too narrowly economic at a time when economic power is relatively useless and when a much wider spectrum of political goals is called for." More so than most unions, the TWUA understood all too well what Jacobs was trying to say. Although textile leaders, like their counterparts in other industries, looked first to organization and negotiation, they had learned that unions could not rely on collective bargaining alone. One source of this understanding was the fierce resistance of antiunion employers in the South. The union's most impressive advances in the region had been achieved during World War II with the aid of War Labor Board rulings. Afterward, the Taft-Hartley Act had placed nearly insurmountable barriers in the way of further gains. It was with this history in mind that Emil Rieve told the 1950 convention, "Political action for our union is like breathing: If we stop, we're finished."[1]

Another source was industry instability. No one who had lived through the devastation and suffering of the interwar crisis could seriously believe in the self-regulating economic world envisioned by conservative economists, and the reappearance of hard times during the fifties raised further doubts about the system. A third source was ideological. With few exceptions, TWUA leaders were thoroughgoing social democrats. As young men, Emil Rieve, George Baldanzi, Lawrence Rogin, and others had engaged in socialist politics, and in varying degrees the experience left its mark on them. They now accepted capitalism and no longer sought government ownership of the means of production; in fact, many had become outspoken anti-Communists. At the same time, though, they continued to question conventional economic pieties and to support initiatives that would increase state oversight of economic affairs.[2]

The person most responsible for many of these initiatives was Solomon Barkin. As he viewed it, part of his job as research director was to identify future trends and devise policies that would enable the union to deal with the social costs of change. He further believed that what he sought to do for textile workers the government should attempt to do for the economy as a whole. This perspective was perhaps best expressed in a 1947 address that asked, "Can We Maintain the Democratic Middle Course in the United States?" Nations that desired a "wholesome balance between economic progress and individual liberty," Barkin declared, "can no longer rely upon an atomistic concept. It must be built upon solid national planning. The national economic objectives must be spelt out and direct economic controls instituted. In this framework ownership becomes less important than the controls over ownership." Barkin recognized that establishing such a system could easily lead to new forms of tyranny; to prevent such an outcome, "the cooperation and constant representation of the trade-union movement" would be vital.[3]

It was a bold vision, but for several reasons there was little likelihood of its realization in postwar America. One was the nature of the two-party system. In a 1952 letter to Sen. Wayne Morse, the liberal Republican from Oregon, Emil Rieve asked, "how many years of Old Guard triumphs in the GOP and Dixiecrat triumphs in the Democratic party must we suffer before we all do something to bring about a sensible realignment of the parties?" It was a good question. Yet, as Rieve himself doubtless knew, organized labor was the last group to initiate such a realignment. During the 1930s, CIO support for the New Deal had generated substantial political gains for labor, and despite the long era of diminishing returns that followed, union leaders remained firmly attached to the Democrats. To be sure, there was much grumbling and occasional talk of a third party. But that's all it was. When election season rolled around, labor officials unfailingly lined up behind the party of Roosevelt.[4]

A second reason that people like Barkin found themselves swimming against the tide was the transformation of liberalism that occurred during the war years. Where many liberals embraced a regulatory philosophy that called for extensive state intervention in economic affairs during the Great Depression, they afterward retreated from this outlook. On one hand, the demonstrated ability of capital to turn the regulatory process to its own advantage undermined their faith in government planning. At the same time, returning prosperity, stimulated by wartime spending, suggested that economic stabilization could be maintained with minimal federal oversight. By war's end, Alan Brinkley has written, most liberals had become convinced that New Deal reforms had brought capitalism's most debilitating tendencies under control "by committing themselves to the belief that economic growth was the surest route to social progress; and by defining a role for the state that would, they believed, permit it to compensate for capitalism's inevitable flaws and omissions without interfering with its internal workings." Though supportive of special programs for society's most disadvantaged groups, they abandoned their former commitment to national planning and became advocates of a narrow, technocratic, demand-management form of Keynesianism that relied primarily on the manipulation of fiscal and monetary policy to promote economic stability.[5]

CIO leaders initially resisted this trend. At a 1943 conference of union research directors, Barkin urged "the need for direct planning and control of capital investment together with provision for stimulating technological discovery and aiding new industrial enterprise." The following year, the CIO issued its "People's Program of 1944," which called for the establishment of a national planning board, in addition to proposing a broad range of social welfare measures. But it was to little avail. Although some of the proposals would in one form or another ultimately be enacted into law, Democratic conservatives ensured that such successes, for the next two decades at least, were few and far between. And while the "People's Program" would in large part remain labor's political platform into the 1970s, even many CIO unions lost their initial enthusiasm for both planning and an expanded welfare state as they achieved ever-greater gains at the bargaining table. Meanwhile, the emergence of the Cold War reinforced the rightward shift in national politics.[6]

The TWUA could not escape the consequences of these developments. In this new, more conservative political climate, it had to moderate its demands on government if it was to be heard at all. But as it retreated, it did so slowly and never very far. Because they represented workers in an industry that the American Century had passed by, textile leaders could not share the complacency so prevalent among their counterparts in other, more prosperous industries. As Solomon Barkin remarked in 1956, the TWUA faced difficulties of "a very different order" from those confronting other unions: "The reason substantially is that we are a declining, shrinking union whose economic power is petering out and whose problems arouse very little sympathy and interest in the trade union movement." As a result, where other unions believed they could set aside the social democratic visions of an earlier period, the TWUA could not. In a 1955 appearance before the Joint Committee on the Economic Report, Barkin told legislators that government had greater responsibilities than simply devising countercyclical policies during hard times: "namely, of inducing the proper degree of stabilization and economic growth and equity within our society, which will assure us the long-term end goals which we have set for ourselves." In a world of constant economic change, he added, government "cannot sit back prayerfully and hope that these ends will be realized. It must determine whether the state of well-being conforms to these purposes."[7]

This chapter examines some of the ways in which the TWUA sought to use government to control the pace and nature of economic change and to shield workers from its more destructive consequences. Union leaders recognized that change was inevitable in a capitalist economy. But experience had taught them that when capital alone directed the process, wage earners bore a disproportionate share of the accompanying social costs. The first section thus looks at union efforts on behalf of tax law reform and other measures designed to regulate capital mobility and spread the costs of change.

As it turned out, nothing the union did could halt the demise of the New England textile industry. During the 1950s, New Bedford, Fall River, Lawrence, and other declining textile centers began to appear annually on government lists of distressed areas. Yet, as capital fled, the TWUA continued to seek assistance for those left behind by pursuing initiatives that ultimately resulted in the passage of the Area Redevelopment Act of 1961. The chapter's final section examines the struggle for this landmark piece of legislation against the backdrop of the union's long-standing interest in regional and industrial planning.

"THE INDUSTRIAL MAP of the United States has been undergoing vast changes," Solomon Barkin observed in a 1958 address, "and the future is likely to see the continuance, at the least, of the current rate of industrial mobility." Barkin was not opposed to capital mobility per se. He knew that as economies matured some areas lost locational advantages, while other locales gained them. What disturbed him was the callous nature of the process and the lack of any legislative safeguards that would require capital to bear the "social and human costs" of industrial migration: "Our price system has not yet invented a way to integrate all public costs into the prices of industrial goods. We have kept our national purposes and ethical principles separate and apart from our industrial system. We have continued to permit a section of industry to act at variance with decent behavior. We have not made it costly to be inhumane and socially wasteful." Barkin was as well qualified as anyone to speak on this topic. The TWUA, often at his instigation, had for at least a decade been seeking ways to deal with both the causes and consequences of capital flight.[8]

The union's first major initiative resulted in the Textron investigation of 1948. As we saw in Chapter 5, Royal Little's announcement that he intended to liquidate New Hampshire's Nashua Manufacturing Company, only three years after acquiring the concern, prompted the union to call for a congressional probe of Textron's operations. In the hearings that followed, the TWUA offered a broad-ranging analysis of the startling array of financial stratagems Little had employed to construct his empire. Many of these practices, supplemented by even more ingenious ruses, would remain characteristic features of corporate merger activity for decades to come. It would therefore be worth our while to take a closer look at the presentation Barkin's research department put together for the hearings.

In preparing the union's case, Barkin made no effort to disguise its purpose. The intent of exhibits titled "The Mining and Stripping of the Nashua Manufacturing Co.," "The Milking and Closing of Manville Jenckes Corp.," "The Purchase and Burial of Esmond Mills, Inc.," and "The Sale, Leasing, Bleeding, and Resale of Lonsdale Co." was immediately evident. Because Textron used a number of the same financial manipulations in various takeovers, this examination will be confined to only two of them: the Lonsdale and Nashua acquisitions.

The Lonsdale Company was a Rhode Island–based concern that could trace its history back to the very beginnings of the Industrial Revolution in America and had at one time operated seven plants in New England. Although the company spent considerable sums during the mid-thirties to maintain its competitiveness, the 1937 recession dealt Lonsdale a severe blow. By decade's end, it had liquidated its least efficient northern properties while continuing production at three Rhode Island sites and a South Carolina firm the company had recently acquired. The reorganization was apparently successful, as all of these mills turned a profit during the early war years. Despite this showing,

Lonsdale stockholders were looking for a way to get out of the industry, and in 1944 they offered to sell the company to Royal Little for $7 million. Because Textron had just borrowed $4.5 million to acquire Manville-Jencks, its credit line was then stretched to the limit. To overcome this obstacle, Little used his position as sole trustee of the Rhode Island Charities Trust to borrow another $4.5 million from Boston's First National Bank; and by adding $2.5 million in notes to the loan, he was able to complete the purchase, which gave him possession of 99 percent of Lonsdale stock.[9]

It was then that the games really began. Upon securing control of the company, Little sold Lonsdale's mill properties to two other charitable trusts he had established; the foundations leased them back to Lonsdale, and the company paid Little a $4.6 million dividend as head of the Rhode Island Trust, which he used to cover the cash portion of the original Lonsdale purchase price. It got even worse. After squeezing another $1 million in dividends from Lonsdale, Little afterward resigned his position at the Rhode Island Trust; and in late 1945 his designated successors sold the company to Textron for $1,654,000 — a transaction of dubious propriety that piqued the investigating senators' curiosity. Asked at the hearings why they let go of the concern so cheaply, the new trustees claimed that inadequate working capital and an inability to replace aging machinery had seriously impaired Lonsdale's long-term prospects. This was no doubt so, but committee members did not believe they were getting the whole story. "Needless to say," their final report observed with the kind of understatement that only a U.S. senator could muster, "the subcommittee was not impressed by the ostensible reasons presented by these trustees of the Rhode Island Charities Trust for their willingness to cooperate with Textron in selling Lonsdale at such a price."

Nor was this the end of the Lonsdale saga. In 1948, following a series of additional financial maneuvers, the company was sold to yet another Little-controlled enterprise for $3.5 million, thus enabling Textron to retrieve whatever money it still had tied up in Lonsdale. Responding several months later to union claims that he had been deliberately "bleeding" the company for years, Little maintained that Lonsdale was "very much alive and thriving." Alive it may have been, but thriving it surely was not. As noted, the immediate postwar period was a time of major retooling in the textile industry. Firms that did not use the extraordinary profits of these flush years to modernize plant and equipment were destined for the scrapheap. That of course was the whole point of the TWUA indictment; and that is exactly what happened to two of Lonsdale's three Rhode Island mills during the early to mid-fifties.

Like Lonsdale, Nashua Manufacturing was one of the nation's oldest textile concerns. Long considered a leading cotton producer, the company earned $5.5 million in after-tax profits during the war years, approximately 20 percent of which was used to purchase new machinery; and at war's end, a TWUA brief noted, "The condition of plant and equipment compared favorably with its competitors." Although Nashua's product lines bore almost no relation to Textron's cloth needs, Little learned that he could obtain control of the company at a bargain price. Engaging in what one Textron official described as "a bit of what you might call opportunism," he began buying Nashua shares in December 1945 and installed his own management team shortly thereafter; by the following winter, Textron owned 97.3 percent of the company's outstanding common stock.[10]

From the outset, Nashua's new managers played fast and loose with company assets. During the first half of 1946, they used the firm's substantial inventory of raw cotton for speculative purposes at the cost of maintaining regular production in the cotton-blanket division. And in December of that year, Little engineered a series of sales between Nashua and other Textron entities that resulted in the transfer of $9.5 million in cash and notes to the parent company, where it was needed to reduce the $11 million debt Textron had accumulated during the course of its highly leveraged operations. By mid-1947, several warehouses and mills in Nashua had been sold and an undetermined amount of machinery was on its way to South America. Little then announced that Nashua would require a major reorganization if it was to remain in business! He also demanded a number of concessions. His proposal, which became known as the "New Nashua Plan," called for the elimination of 1,500 of the company's 4,000 local jobs, reduced taxes and power costs, and increased work assignments. If union leaders, city officials, and power suppliers would agree to these conditions, Little promised to invest $1.2 million in plant and machinery over the next five years.

Although Little's proposal represented the worst form of corporate blackmail, the TWUA immediately began negotiations to hammer out a new workload pact. The resulting accord, which Little hailed as an "epic-making agreement," was signed a month later in August 1947, and over the next year, though modified on several occasions, it appeared to be working reasonably well. The problem was that Little had ignored his end of the bargain, as almost nothing was being done to modernize plant and equipment in Nashua mills. Then, in September 1948, he announced that Textron's remaining Nashua properties would be liquidated by year's end.[11]

It was this action that led union leaders to seek a congressional investigation of Textron's business practices. Coming at a time when workloads were emerging as a major issue in regional negotiations, Little's betrayal seriously undermined the union's ability to deal effectively with the question. If the TWUA could not link workload changes to job security, operatives had no reason to moderate their resistance to increased assignments. As arbitrator John Hogan observed, "The evidence is overwhelming that the basic cause of opposition to work assignment changes is fear of losing jobs." Unfortunately, this would not be the last time Textron placed such obstacles in the union's way. When the company later terminated operations in Suncook, New Hampshire, where operatives had a regionwide reputation for cooperating with management, Solomon Barkin asked, "Is there any wonder that northern textile workers continue to look askance at the constant plea that the workers make sacrifices so the industry will make profits?" The question, as Barkin knew, answered itself: none at all.[12]

As for the hearings, their outcome was for the most part disappointing. Though the committee recommended changes in federal tax laws that would prevent corporate exploitation of charitable trusts, this did little to restrain the activities of Textron and other liquidators. Nevertheless, the investigation was not a total bust. If nothing else, the city of Nashua benefited from the publicity, which not only energized local leaders but also prompted an embarrassed Royal Little both to support their efforts to find new occupants for abandoned mill buildings and to continue operating local plants several years longer than he had planned. As a result, while the process of economic transition was by no means painless, Nashua managed to make the shift to a more diversified economy without enduring the widespread suffering and dislocation experienced by other decaying textile centers.[13]

Union leaders recognized that the Textron hearings were only a beginning. Even before they had concluded, Solomon Barkin was urging Emil

Rieve to seek legislation mandating public access to corporate financial reports so the union could maintain its oversight of liquidating concerns. Afterward, the TWUA closely monitored the business practices of these firms. On a few occasions, the research department attempted to influence corporate policy by preparing financial analyses for presentation at stockholders' meetings. More often, though, union officials continued to look to government, which was sometimes the source of the problem. During the Korean War, for example, one program provided accelerated depreciation for new investment in defense-related plant and machinery, and the Reconstruction Finance Corporation furnished low-cost loans to participating companies. When the union learned that Textron was using the program to expand its southern base, Emil Rieve wrote Defense Production Administrator Manly Fleischmann that "construction of this plant will produce further unemployment in already distressed areas such as Nashua"; and Lawrence congressman Thomas Lane called for an investigation "to find out why the government was granting tax concessions and other benefits to build textile factories in the South while northern mills remained idle."[14]

Of the union's later initiatives on the tax front, the most spirited began as a response to Textron's 1954 takeover of American Woolen. As soon as it became clear that Royal Little was likely to secure control of the company, Barkin urged a congressional probe to "prevent a crude raid on the company's resources." He believed Textron had no interest in salvaging the ailing firm's still-viable plants, and that Little only wanted American Woolen to obtain its cash reserves and to exploit the carry-back provision of the federal tax code. The latter, originally intended to allow businessmen to spread operating losses over a period of years, had become a plaything for corporations engaged in the merger-and-acquisitions game. As *Textile Labor* explained, in perhaps the best description we have of its manipulation:

> Here's how the trick works. Suppose you control a very profitable company, or one which you think will make a lot of money in the next few years. If you're really a slick character you will look around for another company in your field, with antiquated buildings and equipment, that has lost a bundle of cash lately. Then you'll pay a good price for it (after all, you have to sweeten up the deal for the other boys, too); and then you'll liquidate it.
>
> All the losses of the broken down [company], suffered long before you bought it, can be charged off against your fat taxes for years to come. You can be rolling in dough and not give a cent to Uncle Sam.

And this was just what Little had in mind; as he later admitted, Textron could not have acquired American Woolen if it had been financially healthy.[15]

Although union leaders could not prevent the American Woolen debacle, Barkin continued to press for an investigation of the ways in which concerns like Textron manipulated corporate tax laws. In 1955, he finally got his wish when Congress held hearings to study the administration of federal antitrust policies. In his appearance before the committee, Barkin both described the financial stratagems of corporate liquidators and proposed a number of reforms that extended well beyond union concerns about the tax code. In addition to recommending legislation that would prevent merging corporations from exploiting various tax loopholes, he called for federal incorporation of large businesses to permit "uniform regulation and to develop a more appropriate code of managerial responsibility"; the creation of a government agency to assess the effects of mergers "on competition, industrial progress, and worker and community interests"; and the imposition of a special tax "on the financial gains of large organizations which abandon plants, the revenue from which should be used for the reconstruction and development of local communities."[16]

Barkin's recommendations looked much farther down the road of industrial reform than Congress was willing to travel. This was the heyday of the American Century, and U.S. corporations ruled the world. Any legislative initiatives that either threatened their mobility or sought to interfere with their internal operations had small chance of enactment. That these demands came from a union representing workers in an industry that many considered a relic of the first Industrial Revolution made them even less compelling. Not even Barkin's tax proposals received serious consideration. At decade's end, he was still trying to show congressional committees how the federal tax code abetted corporate decimation of northern textile communities.[17]

Any assessment of these efforts needs to assume a broader perspective than that possessed by the typical postwar congressperson. To begin, it should be noted that the union did not oppose liquidation per se; what most troubled Barkin and other TWUA officials was the nature of the process. No informed observer seriously believed the mid-century New England textile industry could be preserved intact. Plant obsolescence alone dictated that some mills would be closed. In testimony before the New England Governors' Committee on the Textile Industry, Royal

Little presented data showing that 40 percent of the production cost differential between one of Textron's four-story factories in New Hampshire and a one-story southern mill could be attributed solely to plant structure. Though one might question the representativeness of Little's figures, the problem was undeniably real. Nevertheless, there were numerous northern plants that could still be operated at a profit. And as Steve Dunwell observed in his fine survey of the industry, liquidation "can be used to prune and revitalize a company, nourishing its reduced assets with a proportionately larger working capital, or it can be used to kill it off." When Seabury Stanton shut down several of Berkshire-Hathaway's least efficient plants during the late fifties, he was acting in the positive fashion described by Dunwell; and while union leaders hated to see any mill closed, they understood what Stanton was attempting to do. Trying to convey such subtleties to the average legislator proved to be another matter entirely. This was truly unfortunate. During the 1980s, an even more ruthless band of speculators and leveraged-buyout artists would lay waste to broad areas of the nation's manufacturing base, using variations on many of the same tactics that the TWUA had exposed three decades earlier.[18]

In developing its critique, the union also raised broader questions about corporate responsibility. Where capital insisted on its rights, union leaders wanted to know what duties it was willing to assume. For Barkin especially, this was a matter of vital importance. Decades later, in the conclusion to a 1981 article on the rise and fall of the New England textile industry, he returned to the issue and asked:

> In what manner shall we revise our codes of rights and stewardship of private capital? What responsibilities have [employers] for the promotion of their industries to assure continuing growth and progressive development? What guides are there respecting the liquidation of established enterprises to preserve the positive nuclei for further growth? Is it enough to rely upon the short-term interest of a one-time management and controlling groups? What responsibilities have they for the worker and community well-being?

These are the kinds of questions labor must always be asking in an economic system where the only thing that has made capital responsible is responsible government. And in asking them, the TWUA came to recognize that proposals to reform corporate tax laws were not enough. Placing restrictions on capital mobility was plainly inadequate once a community's economic base had already been destroyed. Something more was needed, and the union was again in the forefront of efforts to provide it.[19]

ON MAY 20, 1961, President John F. Kennedy signed the Area Redevelopment Act. The bill, which provided various forms of federal assistance to distressed areas, had been introduced six years earlier by Sen. Paul Douglas of Illinois, and from the outset Kennedy had backed the measure as a means of reviving the depressed textile communities of his native state. During the recent presidential campaign, he had promised to give the bill top legislative priority and was now fulfilling that promise. The work of politicians like Kennedy and Douglas was certainly crucial to the act's passage. Yet, as much as anyone, the person most responsible for initiating and keeping the measure alive was TWUA research director Solomon Barkin. On five occasions during the mid-fifties Barkin had urged Douglas to submit such legislation, before convincing the senator that it was necessary; afterward, he helped form the Area Employment Expansion Committee to mobilize public support for the proposal. When the bill finally became law, Douglas graciously acknowledged Barkin's role, calling him "the most vigorous proponent of and worker for this measure."[20]

The road to the Area Redevelopment Act was a long one. Barkin's own interest in the subject began nearly two decades earlier, and it was not New England but the South that prompted his initial concern. In a 1944 memo to CIO president Philip Murray, Barkin and J. Raymond Walsh noted that recent developments in southern agriculture had forced scores of marginal farmers from the land, thus flooding regional labor markets and placing serious obstacles in the way of union organizing drives. To deal with the problem, TWUA representatives had on several occasions attempted to organize conferences within the region to promote industrialization. But these proposals had gone nowhere. Southern cotton manufacturers, fearing that a broad-based development effort would drive up regional wage levels, were "opposed to new industries other than apparel." This lack of initiative among southern industrialists, the memo continued, presented the CIO with an opportunity to "assume a place of leadership unparalleled in any other region of this country." By formulating its own economic program, the federation could both "gather support for this movement among very divergent interests in the area and help to improve our whole national economy."[21]

In advancing this proposal, Barkin was of course most concerned about the interests of his own union. As he wrote Emil Rieve later that year, "I am increasingly impressed with the fact that the ultimate salvation of the textile worker is bound up with an industrial program for the South." This was probably one reason why the federation did not act on the recommendation. Many CIO leaders believed the South was primarily a textile problem and had little enthusiasm for a program that might make it theirs as well. It would be wrong, however, to impose so narrow an interpretation on Barkin's actions. One of Barkin's greatest strengths as a labor intellectual was that he viewed unions as political institutions in the broadest sense of the term; and he believed that, to function effectively as such, unions had to be constantly seeking to identify labor's interest with the public interest, which they could best accomplish by becoming "the agents of economic progress." "The challenge," he later told a meeting of the Columbia University labor seminar, "is to propose a more advanced program than that contemplated by the business people in the industry, proving that they aren't doing enough to expand the industry, to expand employment, to expand opportunities. Our job is to get on the aggressive and indict American businessmen for their shortcomings."[22]

Promoting area development was one way in which Barkin took up this challenge. That he saw these efforts in broad political terms explains why the memo to Murray noted the "many divergent interests" that might be attracted to a program for southern economic development and stressed the national implications of southern industrialization. Similar considerations prompted Barkin's initial proposals for New England. As early as 1947, during the midst of the postwar textile boom, he saw that the union would soon face serious problems in the region. "The situation is growing worse," he wrote Rieve that August. "There will be many mills closing. There will be many charges directed against us. . . ." To "take some of the heat off labor," he recommended that the TWUA assume the lead in creating a regional planning program to prepare for the hard times that almost certainly lay ahead. Such an initiative, he believed, "could be a significant factor in building up union prestige" and "corraling many important civic groups."[23]

Although Barkin's observations were both shrewd and prescient, few others then shared his sense of urgency and nothing immediately came of his suggestions. It was not until 1950 that the six New England state CIO councils formed a planning committee and issued a program. Among other features, the plan recommended that steps be taken to develop hydroelectric resources, construct modern factory buildings in locales injured by deindustrialization, broaden unemployment compensation benefits, and create a regional agency to "gather and analyze economic data for use in aggressive expansion policies." Council members also urged legislators to form "a New England bloc" in Congress so that they could give concerted attention to regional economic needs. These actions, which led Connecticut senator Brien McMahon to remark that it was "significant that the move to bolster New England industry came from labor leaders rather than the Chamber of Commerce and businessmen," must certainly have pleased Barkin. In the end, though, little was accomplished. The state CIO councils periodically revived these proposals throughout the fifties, but they made no sustained effort to identify labor with economic development. New England legislators did even less. Harvard economist Seymour Harris's 1952 contention that, when it came to advancing regional interests, they had much to learn from their southern counterparts remained valid at decade's end.[24]

These developments in part explain why several other Barkin initiatives produced equally disappointing results. During the late forties, he persuaded both the Council of Economic Advisors and the National Planning Association to undertake analyses of the New England economy. The completed reports provided a broad-ranging inventory of regional resources and contained numerous suggestions on how they might be employed to negotiate the perils of economic transition. As such, the studies constituted a modest but necessary starting point for a regional planning program. Unfortunately, they never became anything more than that. "The effort for regional planning," Barkin later observed, "has died and now resides peacefully in the economic research section of the Federal Reserve System in Boston."[25]

During these years, Barkin also devised several industry-specific plans that called for state involvement. In early 1949, as increased mill liquidations confirmed his earlier predictions, he proposed that regional governors form a New England textile commission to investigate recent developments. Declaring that the industry's prospects were "no longer a private interest" but "a public concern," Barkin recommended that the commission be tripartite in character, with representatives from labor, management, and community groups. Its main task would be to assess the need for a permanent body to assist ailing firms that still had a future. To provide a sound basis for its conclusions, the commission might examine such questions as: "Are New England textile plants suffering from specific regional cost disadvantages?" "How enterprising is the ownership of New England mills?" "What is the policy of textile trade-unions toward progressive management?" "What facilities are needed for aiding individual plants and companies or groups of companies in meeting their problems?"[26]

Barkin first submitted the plan to Rieve, who had some reservations about it. Though he did not reject the idea, he cautioned Barkin to "bear in mind that we are a National union and that we cannot allow ourselves to be seen solely on [a] sectional basis." Despite Rieve's leeriness, Barkin pressed ahead and in October 1949 presented a state-level version of the proposal to the Massachusetts Special Commission on the Textile Industry. But that was as far as the initiative went. When he later sought Seabury Stanton's backing, the New Bedford manufacturer said he "could not conscientiously support the establishment of such a Commission for the purpose outlined in your brief." This was a major setback. In addition to being the region's leading persister and head of the pattern-setting New Bedford Cotton Manufacturers Association, Stanton was also one of the few mill owners who had shown interest in Barkin's earlier efforts to forge a joint union-management response to industry problems. If he was unwilling to endorse the program, there was little likelihood that other regional employers would even consider it. As Barkin later wrote Seymour Harris in a letter recounting various union proposals for cooperation: "Management continues to look upon unions as a grievance organization, rather than as a positive coordinate agency in the administration of the industry." Moreover, Barkin added, most mill owners "remained plant oriented" and preferred "to proceed on an individual basis," despite their complaints about regional problems.[27]

As it turned out, Harris initiated several projects of his own, working along lines first suggested by Barkin. One was a committee appointed by the New England governors to study the textile industry, whose 1952 report provided a detailed analysis of industry problems and the place of textiles in the regional economy. Harris also formed a successor organization, the New England Governors Textile Committee, with assistance from both the TWUA and Northern Textile Association (NTA). Although Harris's committee lacked the planning capability of the commission envisioned by Barkin — which was no doubt the main reason for Stanton's opposition to the earlier plan — it did perform a number of useful functions. In addition to preparing annual reports on industry conditions, the group closely monitored the interregional distribution of federal aid as part of an effort to "increase understanding of the relation of the Federal government to the region's economy."[28]

By the early 1950s, Barkin was also looking to Washington. When Fall River joint board manager Edward Doolan ran for Congress in 1952, Barkin urged him to make area redevelopment a major theme of his campaign. And at a union staff meeting that October, he introduced a resolution proposing federal assistance to depressed areas and industries. "We do not have the mechanism to handle the kind of situations that have arisen in Lawrence, Lowell," and other northern textile centers, he told the gathering. "The people are stranded in this economy which is making rapid changes." Everyone agreed, and the only question was whether the resolution would focus on textiles alone or include all industries. William Pollock believed that any TWUA initiative should deal only with textiles: "General problems should be handled by the CIO." That would not do, Barkin replied, as "we are trying to interest the other unions in this problem because what we are proposing will eventually happen to them too." It was a significant observation, not only for its prescience, but also for what it suggests about the unique difficulties textile unionists then confronted. Because they spoke for a declining industry in a booming economy, they could never assume that other unions would be concerned about, or even understand, their position; what they considered innovative thinking was often viewed by others as special pleading. It was thus unsurprising that the depressed areas resolution was a nonstarter. After being drafted according to Barkin's wishes, it was presented to the 1952 CIO convention and quickly forgotten.[29]

Unfortunately, the problems that had given rise to the proposal did not go away. Rather, as the textile crisis of the 1950s deepened, they became even more serious. By 1954, unemployment in Lawrence and other New England woolen centers was running at levels not seen since the worst years of the Great Depression; and if the situation in regional cotton centers was better, it was so only by comparison. Deeply troubled by these developments and concerned about the union's prestige, Barkin asked: "Where is our responsibility? What can we do for our people?" The union was continuing efforts, begun during the late forties, to aid displaced older workers by seeking a liberalization of social security laws. But was this enough? As Barkin pondered these questions, his thoughts returned increasingly to area development legislation, and by 1955 he was trying to enlist Paul Douglas's support. Again, though, the problem was demonstrating that the measure addressed the needs of wage earners in communities throughout the nation, and not simply those of northern textile workers. This proved more difficult than Barkin had anticipated. As he later told the story, "We had to club Senator Douglas into accepting it, but then when he saw its relationship to [the depressed coal towns] of southern Illinois, he took it on and now we have it in the platforms of both parties."[30]

Barkin soon learned that getting a legislative proposal into a party platform was much easier than turning it into law. The initial bill, which contained provisions for technical assistance, worker retraining, and the construction of both public and commercial facilities in distressed areas, was introduced in 1956. Although the measure sailed through the House and Senate banking committees, it never reached the floor of either chamber. The main obstacle was the House Rules Committee, whose reactionary chairman, Virginia congressman Howard Smith, killed the initiative. This gave opponents of the bill time to marshal their forces and mount what became a two-pronged counteroffensive: on one hand, the Eisenhower administration patched together a watered-down alternative to Douglas's plan, while on the other hand a variety of business groups, led by the U.S. Chamber of Commerce, sought to demonstrate that the legislation was unnecessary.[31]

These attacks could not prevent the act's passage, but they did delay it for another five years. During this period, Barkin emerged as one of the bill's most active proponents. Besides helping to organize political support, he played a major part in developing a rationale for the measure that placed the plight of distressed areas in a broader economic context. Aware that simply reciting the woes of places like Lawrence and Lowell would command little attention in Congress, he stressed that what was then happening in these locales could occur anywhere. "Economic and technological changes are continuing," he warned, and people who believed their communities had nothing to fear from these developments were living in a fool's paradise: "No group is protected from the ravages of this highly turbulent and dynamic economy. The prosperous ones of today may tomorrow be flat on their backs."[32]

Barkin also emphasized that the economic problems confronting distressed areas were structural rather than cyclical. Joblessness in these communities had become a chronic condition that could not be cured through standard remedies designed to raise the overall level of employment. "General monetary and fiscal measures will help the structurally sound community with a cluster of functioning industries," he explained. "But they will not help or assist the communities which have lost their factories and in which empty mill structures exist." Unfortunately, the message sank in slowly, to the degree that it was understood at all. Despite Barkin's testimony, most legislators viewed area redevelopment as just another antirecession measure, which in part explains why it was not enacted sooner. Congressional enthusiasm for the bill rose markedly during the 1957–58 recession, but fell off just as quickly as the economy afterward recovered.[33]

That Congress resisted analyses that went beyond the reigning economic orthodoxies of the period was regrettable but not surprising. More troubling was the AFL-CIO's response. Although the federation provided funding for Barkin's Area Employment Expansion Committee, these contributions were modest and the bill never ranked high on its legislative priority list. Among major unions, only the United Automobile Workers strongly supported the measure. It did so largely because of the same conjunction of circumstance and ideology that impelled TWUA efforts. Worried about the precarious position of Studebaker and what its collapse would mean for the people of South Bend, Indiana, the UAW's social democratic leadership had no trouble understanding the significance of area redevelopment legislation. Other unions, however, refused to look ahead. In 1960, when Barkin tried to tell steel unionists that foreign competition would soon be causing them serious problems, they flatly denied it. Their vision clouded by the myopic arrogance that was one of the American Century's most baneful products, these unions saw little need to look beyond the bargaining table.[34]

Whereas the labor movement offered tepid support to the area redevelopment initiative, other groups withheld their backing altogether. "This smacks too much of the welfare state for me," NTA lobbyist Joseph Miller said of the measure. "I believe our membership would concur, and that we do nothing." Though Miller did not know it, NTA president William Sullivan was willing to endorse the bill. Accustomed to assessing industry conditions from a regional rather than a plant perspective, Sullivan evaluated proposals that would expand federal involvement in the economy with an open mind; and in a 1957 letter to economist William Miernyk, he agreed that the depressed areas problem was "not just 'local,' but one in which the Federal government has a peculiar responsibility." Yet, as Miller had assumed in making his recommendation, most New England mill owners did not share this viewpoint. Although manufacturers like Seabury Stanton continued to press for increases in the minimum wage as a way of narrowing interregional labor cost differentials, they remained Yankee Republicans at heart, and these actions were only opportunistic exceptions to a political philosophy that sought to limit the role of government. Knowing this all too well from his correspondence with Stanton, Sullivan never took a public stand on the area redevelopment bill.[35]

Considerably more problematic, and at first glance rather dismaying, was the refusal of certain groups engaged in development activities to support the measure. At a 1956 session, the New England Council, a business organization concerned about promoting regional economic growth, declared its opposition to federal assistance, as did a number of New England representatives at that year's meeting of the Association of State Planning and Development Agencies. Of such resistance, the most widely publicized came from the Greater Lawrence Citizens' Committee on Industrial Development. Not only did it oppose area redevelopment legislation, but when William Miernyk prepared an NPA-sponsored study advocating the bill, committee member Kurtz M. Hanson, whose Champion International Company produced paper goods, appended this ringing dissent to the pamphlet: "It can be said without fear of equivocation that Lawrence has demonstrated that a program of Federal aid is wrong and needless. Lawrence today is facing an acute labor shortage."[36]

Something was obviously wrong here. Between 1948 and 1960, the U.S. Bureau of Employment Security listed Lawrence as a "very substantial labor surplus area" for the entire twelve-year period; and in 1957, when Hanson issued his dissent, the city's average unemployment rate was 8.9 percent. To be sure, local conditions had improved markedly since 1954, when nearly one of every four wage earners was jobless, but Lawrence was hardly experiencing "an acute labor shortage." Moreover, many workers expressed disapproval of the low-wage industries that were being recruited by the GLCCID. These discrepancies did not go unnoticed by proponents of area redevelopment legislation. One labor spokesman characterized the local promotional campaign as "a conspiracy of silence," led by narrow-minded civic leaders unwilling to embrace the broad range of remedial measures that was so clearly needed to put the city back on its feet; and Barkin linked the obstructionism of Lawrence and other such communities to Chamber of Commerce efforts to use the plight of depressed areas "to create what it calls a 'better climate for business and jobs everywhere'"—a climate in which concerns about local economic recovery could be utilized "to attack labor legislation, reduce business taxes, and promote other chamber policies."[37]

There was some truth to these accusations. Certain employers in declining areas welcomed increased joblessness as a salutary form of labor discipline. In their study of Nashua during the late 1940s, Charles A. Myers and George P. Shultz found that managers of firms with troubled labor relations, poor personnel policies, and substandard hiring rates seemed to believe that "a little unemployment is a good thing." There is evidence that similar views influenced the Lawrence response to industrial decline. In a 1955 letter to Seabury Stanton describing the beleaguered state of textile unionism in the Immigrant City, Kurtz Hanson noted with evident satisfaction that "a new and different situation now exists in Lawrence and the people *want to work.*" Unsurprisingly, Hanson joined local textile employer Russell Knight in defending the recruitment of low-wage garment and shoe shops at GLCCID meetings. Not all committee members, however, were happy with the kinds of firms coming into the city. At a stormy 1954 session, one local entrepreneur characterized these businesses as "trash" and stated that most wage earners felt "the majority of new companies are second-rate firms, paying second-rate wages and employing second-rate labor practices." Other members criticized the practice of misrepresenting Lawrence as a labor shortage area. "[T]here is still an abundant supply of unskilled and skilled workers," John O'Malley told a 1956 meeting, and not letting prospective employers know this only slowed the pace of economic recovery.[38]

If this was the actual state of affairs in Lawrence—and the best evidence indicates that it was—why did the GLCCID refuse to support area redevelopment legislation? That question can best be answered by taking a closer look at how local development agencies functioned. For the most part, these committees were loosely structured organizations with no clear mandate, whose members had little or no experience in promoting industrial development. Under the circumstances anyone with a well-defined ideological perspective—as Kurtz Hanson appears to have had—could exert more than ordinary influence on committee proceedings. This was especially so with regard to an issue like area redevelopment, where it required little ingenuity to persuade a board comprising largely local entrepreneurs that federal assistance to depressed areas actually constituted federal intrusion in local affairs.

As it was, a number of local development agencies did exemplary work during these years. The early and aggressive actions of Nashua civic leaders helped that community avoid the worst consequences of economic transition. Similar successes were achieved by local committees in Rockville, Connecticut, and Utica, New York, where redevelopment efforts focused on aptitude testing and worker retraining. In general, though, such responses were the exception rather than the rule. This was not altogether surprising, as most communities faced unprecedented difficulties of enormous scope. In Lawrence, for example, GLCCID members regularly noted how the obsolescent structure of the city's numerous multistoried mills inhibited the recruitment of new firms; and for a problem of this sort — which required that nineteenth-century industrial plant be transformed to meet the needs of twentieth-century producers — there was no easy solution. That most local development agencies did not accomplish more was, given their limited resources, understandable; that some opposed initiatives designed to augment those resources is unforgivable.[39]

Despite this opposition, the Area Redevelopment Act slowly moved forward and in May 1961 became one of the first measures signed by President Kennedy. The final bill provided nearly $400 million in assistance to depressed areas. Of this sum, $200 million went to commercial and industrial loans, $100 million to loans for public facilities, and $75 million to grants for public facilities; another $14.5 million was authorized for vocational training programs and subsistence payments to the displaced workers enrolled in them. At Barkin's urging, the bill also included a planning provision that furnished technical assistance to aid communities in realizing their economic potential and promoted long-range study of the area redevelopment problem.[40]

Barkin afterward viewed the passage of area redevelopment legislation as a major personal accomplishment — and justifiably so. Without his unrelenting advocacy, the bill would never have been proposed, much less enacted. Yet, as he soon recognized, pushing a measure through Congress was one thing; realizing its intended aims was quite another. And for a variety of reasons, the Area Redevelopment Act never met his expectations. One limitation was funding. Given the enormous problems many depressed areas faced, the $400 million Congress grudgingly appropriated was woefully inadequate. This shortcoming was compounded by the manner in which the act was administered. As Barkin later remarked, the Area Redevelopment Administration (ARA) quickly became a "log-rolling agency," more concerned about mending its political fences than developing an effective long-range approach to area redevelopment. By attempting to assist too many communities, the ARA spread its meager resources so thin that few if any areas truly benefited from the program.[41]

Given these defects, the Area Redevelopment Act was doomed from the start. Yet, even had the program been more adequately funded and more competently administered, there doubtless would have been problems. Barkin had always seen area redevelopment as a way of merging federal resources with local initiative to promote community responsibility for the labor market. As he noted, however, many localities did not understand their duties. Confronted with structural unemployment, they all too often responded by adopting what he called a "realtor approach" to economic development that focused almost exclusively on filling empty mill space, which resulted in the recruitment of fly-by-night "loft" industries, operated by industrial vultures who preyed on the misery of displaced workers in declining areas. Barkin also criticized the localistic orientation of many community development agencies, which not only caused needless competition among neighboring locales but prevented balanced economic growth. To achieve the latter, he stressed, the boundaries of development efforts "must be broad enough to encompass a true economic region." Unfortunately, this sound advice went largely unheeded in New England. "Probably to a greater extent than elsewhere," William Miernyk observed, "the problem of rehabilitating depressed areas in New England has been narrowly conceived and efforts to solve the problem have been largely confined to local activities."[42]

What such criticisms indicated was that, to be effective, federal legislation needed to be accompanied by vigorous local activity on the part of labor organizations. But this was one area in which TWUA efforts came up short. In some instances, local leaders did not pay sufficient attention to the redevelopment question. This appears to have been the case in Lawrence, where joint board manager Arthur Brown was a charter member of the GLCCID but rarely attended meetings and let his membership lapse. More serious were the strains industrial decline put on worker-union relations. Some New England officials, Barkin observed in a 1954 memo, "have been somewhat formal with their membership" and it was starting to become a real problem: "In the past, economic success has sufficed as a means of communication, but it is no longer adequate. There must be a more direct communication." Although Barkin was speaking about the need to enlist worker support for programs to assist troubled mills when he made these remarks, they are equally relevant to union initiatives on the redevelopment front. Where this "direct communication" did not exist, local officials lost touch with the evolving concerns and needs of rank-and-filers; and without the latter's solid backing, they had limited leverage in their dealings with local development agencies.[43]

Despite these failings, TWUA actions to promote area redevelopment remain significant. This becomes especially evident when one contrasts what it tried to do during the 1950s with the part unions have played in recent redevelopment efforts. Where the TWUA, acting as an institution, generated some of the most creative responses to the problems caused by deindustrialization during the earlier period, that role has now been assumed by aggressive local unionists; and where the TWUA had trouble linking its national initiatives to what was happening at the local level, a number of the most innovative community-based programs of recent years elicited more scorn than aid from union headquarters. The best examples of this curious turnabout come from the decaying steel towns of the nation's industrial heartland. When, for instance, rank-and-file activists mobilized a broad coalition on behalf of an alternative ownership plan to save Youngstown Sheet & Tube during the late 1970s, leaders of the United Steelworkers of America (USWA) initially withheld their backing; and by the time they did get on board, it was too late. During that same period, the Homestead unionists who formed the Tri-State Conference on Steel to prevent further mill closings in the Monongahela Valley struggled for years without assistance from the international.[44]

That the USWA did not respond more positively to these early campaigns was largely a consequence of union politics. Many of the most prominent local activists were also supporters of Edward Sadlowski's insurgency movement, which sought to replace the union's old-line leadership with officials more attentive to rank-and-file concerns. And since that time, the international has been considerably more supportive of community-based redevelopment programs. Nevertheless, we still need to ask: Why, given its vast resources and the earlier example set by the TWUA, has the union done so little to initiate these efforts? Barkin provided a good part of the answer three decades ago. "Once the union gets organized," he told a 1960 meeting of the Columbia University labor seminar, "the administrative process of collective bargaining overpowers the thinking of the leadership and this consequently drains it of interest in the broader purposes which originally created the unions." This was especially so in an industry like steel, where the impressive gains achieved through bargaining became an important source of institutional prestige. The TWUA, on the other hand, had to look elsewhere for prestige. As it did so, it was able to move beyond the postwar cult of bargaining and fashion a broader view of labor's role in society. "Our union," Barkin remarked, has been one of the few "to combine collective bargaining pressure with innovative legislation, and while our laurels have remained unsung, nevertheless I think it's well to keep in mind this combination." Indeed it is, today more so than ever.[45]

In closing, it should be noted that TWUA political activities did not stop at corporate tax law reform and area redevelopment legislation. In its efforts to regulate capital mobility, for example, the union's various tax reform initiatives were supplemented by calls for an international labor code to govern foreign investment. Similarly, demands for area redevelopment legislation were often coupled with proposals for a tripartite federal textile agency that would develop a comprehensive plan for industry growth, prepare annual surveys of industry problems, and promote basic research through the establishment of design centers and a fabric library. In these and other actions, the union's primary aims were twofold: to impose real responsibilities on capital; and to reduce the social costs of change for wage earners. In the end, TWUA leaders achieved considerably less than they had hoped. The community devastation and individual suffering that has accompanied recent economic changes is bitter testimony to that fact. Nevertheless, their efforts remain noteworthy. They may have lost their struggle to save the New England textile industry, but they were anything but losers.[46]

CONCLUSION

By the 1970s, the great postwar boom had ended, as had U.S. dominance of the world economy. The revival of Japanese and European productive capacity, the increased bargaining power of Third World raw materials producers, and the continuing diversion of funds to military spending that might have been used for productive capital formation had all taken their toll. One result was a falling rate of profit at a time when years of low unemployment, coupled with the benefits provided by New Deal social programs, had reduced capital's ability to discipline wage earners. Although corporate America could not do much to alter the new international economic environment, it could and did take steps to deal with labor. On the domestic front, corporations in core industries stepped up existing decentralization programs that shifted production from union plants under pattern agreements to small facilities located in semirural areas with no tradition of organization. These moves were accompanied by a dramatic increase in foreign investment. Between 1960 and 1980, U.S. private assets abroad rose to $579 billion from $49.2 billion. At the same time, major employers intensified efforts to introduce new technology designed to eliminate even more jobs. For organized labor, the consequences of these developments were disastrous. Declining membership and the fear of further employment losses sapped the bargaining strength of industrial unions and resulted in a series of givebacks that reduced wages and fringe benefits for those still working. As Nelson Lichtenstein has written, an era was over: "With the union movement at its lowest ebb since the early years of the Great Depression, the whole shape of the political economy and the structure of postwar labor relations have been brought into question."[1]

Although the TWUA was a product of the labor upsurge that created the postwar structure of industrial relations, it was never fully a part of that system. During the 1930s and World War II in New England, CIO textile unionists forged an organization that promised to transcend the parochialism of the Fall River Textile Council and improve upon the stumbling efforts of the United Textile Workers. Like their counterparts in the nation's core industries, TWUA leaders looked forward to a world in which workers obtained their fair share of the country's expanding economic surplus. But this was not to be. As a majority of the populace joined in celebrating the prosperity of the American Century, textile operatives often wondered what all the cheering was about. Unlike industries such as autos and steel, where unions provided wage earners with unprecedented benefits, TWUA officials had all they could do simply to maintain existing levels of employment. And as they struggled to furnish their members with some measure of job security, they learned early that the postwar structure of industrial relations did not work nearly as well as advertised—at least not in industries where market forces constrained profit margins.

This was not immediately evident to textile unionists, who initially tried to establish a framework that would balance wages, workloads, and investment. In so doing, they hoped to create conditions that provided both operational stability for employers and increased earnings for workers. As it turned out, it was these efforts that taught TWUA leaders just how little they could expect from the system of industrial jurisprudence that undergirded the postwar structure of industrial relations. Given employer unwillingness to make commitments that linked increased workloads to plans for mill modernization or to share the benefits of productivity gains, disputes over work assignments inevitably arose. When union leaders took such cases to arbitration, the resulting decisions were rarely satisfactory. The problem was not individual arbitrators but the process itself. As Solomon Barkin later wrote:

> Worker rights were sharply limited and their expansion obstructed by management claims on all residual rights; issues not specifically covered in an agreement remained within management's jurisdiction. Differences arising between the parties during the administration of an agreement were converted into legal bouts on the meaning of contract language. Only grievances—complaints charging violation of contract terms—could be processed. Arbitrators were restrained from viewing issues from perspectives other than the terms set down in the contracts, however costly that slant may prove to be to the state of industrial relations.[2]

These observations contain a deeper meaning that is central to any analysis of the postwar structure of industrial relations: the system of industrial jurisprudence that held it together was a reflection of power relations within a given industry. No arbitrator could give labor leaders what they could not extract from management at the bargaining table. Where capital flight, deindustrialization, and the insecurity they engendered among workers stripped unions of much of their leverage, the system simply confirmed and reinforced their weakness. Worse, these organizations usually had nowhere else to turn, as other unions offered little aid. "The American trade union movement is decentralized," Barkin observed in 1956, "and the smugness of each part is [so] pervasive that it is very difficult to carry on and maintain anyone's interest under adverse conditions." Unwilling to believe that what was happening to textile workers would one day happen to them and unable to recognize that the labor movement is no stronger than its weakest link, most of these unions gave only halfhearted support to TWUA initiatives that might have helped prepare them for their own future.[3]

So where does all this leave the contemporary labor movement? How should it respond to the current crisis? In recent years, we have heard much talk of the need for a new social partnership between capital and labor. Troubled by the faltering performance of American producers in an increasingly integrated world economy, and recognizing that the postwar bargaining system is obsolete, these commentators feel a less adversarial approach is needed to restore national competitiveness. Some analysts, believing that innovations such as Quality of Working Life (QWL) programs and the team concept are harbingers of a new era of industrial relations, have gone as far as to suggest that unions become involved in making strategic business decisions. The most ambitious of these proposals comes from economist Barry Bluestone and his father, Irving Bluestone, a former vice president of the United Auto Workers. In their study, *Negotiating the Future*, they urge that the traditional workplace contract be replaced by what they call an "enterprise contract." Whereas the traditional contract, with its management-rights clause, limited bargaining to wages, hours, and working conditions, the enterprise contract would create an entirely new industrial relations framework in which unions function as comanagers of the firm. In addition to participating in decisions concerning investments, pricing, and other strategic matters, they would also share responsibility for boosting productivity, ensuring quality production, and promoting product innovation. The result, the Bluestones contend, would benefit all concerned: by increasing the value of shareholders' investments, and by providing wage earners with added job security and an improved work environment.[4]

This is a marvelous vision. Unfortunately, the Bluestones say little about how labor is to muster the bargaining power needed to exact such concessions from capital. Instead, they assume that union promises to help companies improve their competitive position offer sufficient inducement for the negotiation of enterprise contracts. The TWUA experience casts serious doubt on this assumption. Seeking objectives considerably less grandiose than an enterprise contract, textile officials demonstrated that they were not only willing but able to play a positive role in modernizing textile production. During the crisis of the 1950s, they consistently proposed some of the most innovative responses to industry problems. "Union research departments," Robert Blauner said of these efforts, "have gathered more facts on the industry and have a considerably more sophisticated program for its revival than have the companies and their associations." For the most part, though, these initiatives went nowhere. A few employers such as Seabury Stanton, who were committed to maintaining operations in New England and appreciated what unions could do to increase productive efficiency, did express interest; and in a world of Seabury Stantons there might have been some hope for establishing a new bargaining relationship that expanded labor's functions and provided additional job security to workers. But mill owners like Stanton were exceptions in the 1950s; there is no evidence that they are any more prevalent in today's economy. If anything, contemporary firms that find themselves confronted with new competitive pressures and shrinking profit margins are even more likely to shift capital to other ventures than to seek ways of reclaiming lost markets. All of which is to say that power relations will be no less central to any future structure of industrial relations than they were to the postwar system.[5]

This omission on the Bluestones' part explains what is perhaps the most troubling aspect of their work. By ignoring questions of power, they were able to avoid addressing the many criticisms that have been lodged against QWL programs and the team concept. According to Mike Parker, applications of the team concept in the U.S. auto industry have not only done little to upgrade worker skills but also constitute a system of "management-by-stress." Others contend that QWL programs are part of a new management control strategy intended to diminish rather than enhance union power on the shop floor. Still others claim that these and related programs facilitate "whipsawing," a tactic corporations use to induce their various plants to compete with each other and that invariably results in the "management-by-stress" of which Parker writes.[6]

My purpose in reviewing these criticisms is not to suggest that all forms of union-management cooperation are to be condemned. The TWUA doubtless saved jobs through its efforts to promote mill modernization in the New England textile industry, as similar initiatives by garment unions continue to do in that long-beleaguered industry. Moreover, as David Brody has observed, because "the 'adversarial' work-rules system now so roundly condemned was adopted not in opposition to, but directly in conformity with the logic of the mass-production regime" created by capital, it would be perfectly consistent for labor to support employee involvement programs designed to meet current demands for flexible manufacturing. But, Brody adds, this does not mean that unions should scrap "them and us" as a basic approach to industrial relations: "The labor movement will not prevail by trying to persuade nonunion employers. It is their employees who have to be persuaded, and, if and when that time comes, what will persuade them will be the only kind of appeal that has worked with American workers since the days of Samuel Gompers: namely, the identification of the union with their demand for industrial justice." This is sound advice. The observations of Mike Parker and other critics of the team concept show that the new systems have not eliminated worker discontent. And the TWUA experience in New England testifies to the wisdom of basing worker organization on calls for industrial justice. Interviewed decades after they had left the mills, textile operatives who had little else to say about unions — either positive or negative — recalled the satisfaction that being able to file a grievance gave them.[7]

As the labor movement begins to regroup, it would also do well to adopt a more imaginative approach to politics. "The alternative" to the present industrial relations system in which "each dispute is framed in an individuated, minute, economistic form," Katherine Van Wetzel Stone has written, "is to define labor issues as a matter of public concern, and to submit resolution of these issues to the political process." Once again the TWUA experience is instructive. Not only was it one of the few postwar unions to combine negotiating pressure with novel legislative proposals, but its political initiatives are even more relevant today than they were four decades ago: corporate tax law reform remains one of the most effective means of curbing corporate flight and imposing real responsibilities on capital; and area redevelopment legislation should have a place in any campaign hoping to merge labor and public concerns. In an economy where fearful insecurity has replaced the buoyant optimism of the American Century, the odds that labor might mobilize extensive support for such reforms are much better than they ever were for the Textile Workers Union of America.[8]

In so doing, the labor movement can also begin to address another of its current shortcomings: the sometimes troubled relationship between unions as bureaucratic institutions, the wage earners they are supposed to represent, and the communities in which those workers live. "[W]hen you look at the trade union scene today," Solomon Barkin remarked during the mid-1950s, "you see that the workers have rejected the union in all areas except the shop. In other local activity the union is not the agent of the worker." Matters have not improved since Barkin uttered that observation; if anything, the problem is now much worse. Unfortunately, this is an area where most historical scholarship comes up short. In the past several decades, we have learned much about the social and cultural worlds of American working people and their struggles to form organizations that would protect them against the indignities and insecurities of a heartless economic system. Yet, when union-worker relations are viewed against the backdrop of a union's institutional development, the discussion most often focuses on the ways unions have restrained or alienated their members. A good example is Elizabeth Faue's recent study of Minneapolis working people. In it, Faue employs a community-bureaucracy dualism to explain the declining role of women in the local labor movement, which she does with some success. Moreover, her approach might usefully be adapted for other purposes. There are tensions between the community-based interests of workers — men as well as women — and the institutional concerns of unions; and a conceptual framework that allows us to analyze those tensions has much to recommend it. The problem is that Faue's application of the community-bureaucracy dualism borders on the Manichean: community good, bureaucracy evil. That the latter might conceivably serve some useful purpose is never considered.[9]

The limitations of this perspective become especially evident when dealing with the difficulties caused by deindustrialization. Because capital is far more mobile than labor, any response that eschews bureaucracy and relies on community alone is likely to make limited headway. This is hardly to say that community is unimportant. As noted, the most innovative programs for dealing with the current crisis in the nation's industrial heartland have come from community-based movements. We also saw that union support for these plans has sometimes left much to be desired. Yet, this does not mean that union bureaucracies are incapable of providing such assistance. The TWUA demonstrated otherwise during the 1950s and 1960s, when it was consistently in the forefront of efforts to revive New England's declining textile communities. We might further note that, whatever differences may arise, community interests and the bureaucratic concerns of unions are hardly antithetical. Indeed, as Barkin contended, unions can add to their institutional prestige by playing a conspicuous role in campaigns to aid distressed locales.[10]

The main point of the foregoing is not to discourage criticism of union bureaucracies. Like other institutions, unions are in frequent need of prodding, if they are to remain useful. Rather, it is to urge labor historians to avoid conceptual approaches that preclude recognition of the ways bureaucracy can be employed to further the interests of working people. To be effective, institutional reform requires some vision of the positive functions institutions can and should perform. Those who expect nothing good from bureaucracy will rarely be disappointed. All of which is to say that the relationship between community and bureaucracy is not dichotomous but dialectical; and that is how the community-bureaucracy framework and other such dualisms must be applied.

Such adaptations are important because, in David Brody's words, "labor's past is deeply and irrevocably implicated in whatever future it has." That belief was a major impetus for this study. Although the TWUA response to industrial decline does not provide a blueprint for today's troubled labor movement, it does speak to many of the problems unions now confront. By assessing other such efforts, unions may well find that they merit more than the "enormous condescension of posterity" that E. P. Thompson described as the customary lot of history's losers.[11]

NOTES

INTRODUCTION

1 Caroline F. Ware, *The Early New England Cotton Manufacture: A Study in Industrial Beginnings* (Boston: Houghton Mifflin Company, 1931), p. 3.
2 Seymour Louis Wolfbein, *The Decline of a Cotton Textile City: A Study of New Bedford* (rpt.; New York: AMS Press, 1968); Thomas Russell Smith, *The Cotton Textile Industry of Fall River, Massachusetts: A Case Study of Industrial Localization* (New York: King's Crown Press, 1944); Alice Galenson, *The Migration of the Cotton Textile Industry from New England to the South* (New York: Garland Publishing, Inc., 1985); Nancy Frances Kane, *Textiles in Transition: Technology, Wages, and Industry Relocation in the U.S. Textile Industry, 1880–1930* (Westport, Conn.: Greenwood Press, 1988); Mary H. Blewett, *The Last Generation: Work and Life in the Textile Mills of Lowell, Massachusetts, 1910–1960* (Amherst: University of Massachusetts Press, 1990); Laurence F. Gross, *The Course of Industrial Decline: The Boott Cotton Mills of Lowell, Massachusetts, 1835–1955* (Baltimore: The Johns Hopkins University Press, 1993); William F. Hartford, *Working People of Holyoke: Class and Ethnicity in a Massachusetts Mill Town, 1850–1960* (New Brunswick, N.J.: Rutgers University Press, 1990).
3 Leon Fink and Brian Greenberg, *Upheaval in the Quiet Zones: A History of Hospital Workers' Union, Local 1199* (Urbana: University of Illinois Press, 1989), p. xv; David Brody, "Labor History, Industrial Relations, and the Crisis of American Labor," *Industrial and Labor Relations Review* 43 (Oct. 1989): 15–16.

ONE. THE FALL RIVER SYSTEM OF UNIONISM

1 U.S. Congress, Senate, *Report of the Committee of the Senate upon the Relations between Capital and Labor*, 48th Cong., 2d sess., Senate Report 1262, 5 vols. (Washington, D.C.: Government Printing Office, 1885), 3:39; Massachusetts Bureau of Statistics of Labor (MBSL), *Thirteenth Annual Report* (1882), p. 195. The numerous citywide strikes that occurred in Fall River between 1870 and 1904 have been thoroughly examined elsewhere and will not receive extensive treatment here. Readers seeking further information on these struggles should consult Philip Thomas Silvia, Jr., "The Spindle

City: Labor, Politics, and Religion in Fall River, Massachusetts, 1870–1905" (Ph.D. diss., Fordham University, 1973); and John T. Cumbler, *Working-Class Community in Industrial America: Work, Leisure, and Struggle in Two Industrial Cities, 1880–1930* (Westport, Conn.: Greenwood Press, 1979).

2 MBSL, *Thirteenth Annual Report* (1882), pp. 220–21, 265–66, 341, 412; Silvia, "Spindle City," pp. 325–26.

3 Silvia, "Spindle City," pp. 241–43; Cumbler, *Working-Class Community*, p. 113; Thomas Russell Smith, *The Cotton Textile Industry of Fall River, Massachusetts: A Case Study of Industrial Localization* (New York: King's Crown Press, 1944), pp. 45, 54–57.

4 Smith, *Fall River*, pp. 57–63; T. M. Young, *The American Cotton Industry: A Study of Work and Workers* (New York: Charles Scribner's Sons, 1903), p. 2; Caroline F. Ware, *The Early New England Cotton Manufacture: A Study in Industrial Beginnings* (Boston: Houghton Mifflin Company, 1931), p. 85.

5 MBSL, *Eleventh Annual Report* (1880), pp. 57–58; Isaac Cohen, *American Management and British Labor: A Comparative Study of the Cotton Spinning Industry* (Westport, Conn.: Greenwood Press, 1990), pp. 121–23; Smith, *Fall River*, pp. 77–79.

6 Silvia, "Spindle City," pp. 249–51; MBSL, *Eleventh Annual Report* (1880), pp. 57–58.

7 Cohen, *American Management and British Labor*, pp. 121–23; Silvia, "Spindle City," pp. 268–69; Lillian B. Chace Wyman, "Studies of Factory Life: Black-Listing in Fall River," *Atlantic Monthly* 62 (Nov. 1888): 605–12; quotation in MBSL, *Thirteenth Annual Report* (1882), p. 341.

8 First and second quotations in MBSL, *Thirteenth Annual Report* (1882), pp. 242–43, 353–54; third quotation in U.S. Senate, *Relations between Capital and Labor*, 3:61–62; final quotation in MBSL, *Thirteenth Annual Report* (1882), p. 342.

9 Robert F. Dalzell, Jr., *Enterprising Elite: The Boston Associates and the World They Made* (Cambridge: Harvard University Press, 1987), pp. 54–55; U.S. Senate, *Relations between Capital and Labor*, 1:651–52; 3:499; MBSL, *Thirteenth Annual Report* (1882), p. 217; Henry A. Miles, *Lowell, As It Was and As It Is* (rpt.; New York: Arno Press, 1972), pp. 133–34; Ware, *Early New England Cotton Manufacture*, pp. 255–56; MBSL, *Thirteenth Annual Report* (1882), p. 363; U.S. Senate, *Relations between Capital and Labor* 1:632.

10 MBSL, *Eleventh Annual Report* (1880), p. 62; Rowland Tappan Berthoff, *British Immigrants in Industrial America, 1790–1950* (Cambridge: Harvard University Press, 1953), p. 32; Cumbler, *Working-Class Community*, pp. 148–53; first quotation in U.S. Senate, *Relations between Capital and Labor*, 3:61; second and third quotations in MBSL, *Thirteenth Annual Report* (1882), pp. 207, 201, 412; final quotation in MBSL, *Eleventh Annual Report* (1880), p. 59.

11 Berthoff, *British Immigrants*, pp. 88–89, 96; Cumbler, *Working-Class Com-

munity, pp. 147–53; U.S. Senate, *Relations between Capital and Labor*, 3: 487.

12 MBSL, *Thirteenth Annual Report* (1882), p. 313; David Montgomery, *The Fall of the House of Labor: The Workplace, the State, and American Labor Activism, 1865–1925* (Cambridge, Eng.: Cambridge University Press, 1987), pp. 155–56; Mary H. Blewett, "Manhood and the Market: The Politics of Gender and Class among the Textile Workers of Fall River, Massachusetts, 1870–1880," in *Work Engendered: Toward a New History of American Labor*, ed. Ava Baron (Ithaca, N.Y.: Cornell University Press, 1991), pp. 92–113; Cohen, *American Management and British Labor*, pp. 116–17. Fall River weavers will receive their due in a later section of the chapter.

13 Cohen, *American Management and British Labor*, pp. 31–35, 64–65.

14 Ibid., pp. 75–89; William Lazonick, *Competitive Advantage on the Shop Floor* (Cambridge: Harvard University Press, 1990), pp. 93–103. Although Cohen's thesis is more pertinent to my present concerns, I hope this and subsequent citations make clear my indebtedness to Lazonick. It should also be noted that not all scholars believe the introduction of the self-acting mule resulted in the extensive deskilling that Cohen and Lazonick describe. For an alternative view, see Mary Freifeld, "Technological Change and the 'Self-Acting' Mule: A Study of Skill and the Sexual Division of Labor," *Social History* 11 (October 1986): 319–43. Freifeld's argument is in turn critiqued by Lazonick in *Competitive Advantage*, pp. 88–93.

15 Cohen, *American Management and British Labor*, pp. 78–89, 124–25; Lazonick, *Competitive Advantage on the Shop Floor*, pp. 98–100, 109–10, 118–28.

16 MBSL, *Second Annual Report* (1871), p. 55; Cohen, *American Management and British Labor*, pp. 121–23; Silvia, "Spindle City," pp. 268–69.

17 Cohen, *American Management and British Labor*, pp. 109–12; Lazonick, *Competitive Advantage on the Shop Floor*, pp. 124–27; U.S. Senate, *Relations between Capital and Labor*, 1:631; quotations in MBSL, *Thirteenth Annual Report* (1882), pp. 308, 338.

18 MBSL, *Eleventh Annual Report* (1880), p. 62; Cohen, *American Management and British Labor*, p. 157.

19 MBSL, *Thirteenth Annual Report* (1882), p. 341.

20 First quotation in Berthoff, *British Immigrants*, p. 97; second quotation in *Labor Leader*, Jan. 15, 1887; final quotation in U.S. Senate, *Relations between Capital and Labor*, 1:498.

21 *Labor Leader*, Jan. 15, 1887; Berthoff, *British Immigrants*, p. 97; quotation in Silvia, "Spindle City," pp. 187–91.

22 Quotation in Fall River newspaper, June 7, 1880, in *Victorian Vistas: Fall River, 1865–1885*, ed. Philip T. Silvia, Jr. (Fall River, Mass.: R. E. Smith Printing Company, 1987), p. 379; Montgomery, *Fall of the House of Labor*, pp. 157–59; Melton Alonza McLaurin, *Paternalism and Protest: Southern Cotton Mill Workers and Organized Labor, 1875–1905* (Westport, Conn.: Greenwood Publishing Corporation, 1971), pp. 129, 132, 139.

23 *Labor Leader*, Feb. 19, 1887.

24 E. J. Hobsbawm, "Custom, Wages and Work-Load in Nineteenth Century Industry," in *Labouring Men: Studies in the History of Labour* (pbk. ed.; Garden City, N.Y.: Anchor Books, 1967), pp. 405–35.

25 MBSL, *Second Annual Report* (1871), pp. 77–78; Berthoff, *British Immigrants*, p. 101; quotation in MBSL, *Thirteenth Annual Report* (1882), p. 239.

26 *Detroit Advance*, in *Labor Leader*, Jan. 28, 1888; Fall River newspaper, Mar. 1, 1881, in *Victorian Vistas*, p. 386; MBSL, *Thirteenth Annual Report* (1882), pp. 329–31; Silvia, "Spindle City," pp. 176–79, 264–65; U.S. Senate, *Relations between Capital and Labor*, 1:633–40.

27 Silvia, "Spindle City," pp. 456–57; Lazonick, *Competitive Advantage on the Shop Floor*, pp. 117–18; Montgomery, *Fall of the House of Labor*, p. 163.

28 Lazonick, *Competitive Advantage on the Shop Floor*, pp. 117–18; Silvia, "Spindle City," pp. 461–64; Montgomery, *Fall of the House of Labor*, p. 163; quotation in Silvia, "Spindle City," p. 504.

29 MBSL, *Thirteenth Annual Report* (1882), pp. 313–14; U.S. Senate, *Relations between Capital and Labor*, 3:451; T. W. Uttley, *Cotton Spinning and Manufacturing in the United States of America* (Manchester, Eng.: The University Press, 1905), p. 4; Cohen, *American Management and British Labor*, pp. 132–33.

30 Walter Whipple to Russell T. Fisher, Nov. 25, 1938, box 11, folder 125, National Association of Cotton Manufacturers/Northern Textile Association Records (NACM/NTA Rcds.), Museum of American Textile History, North Andover–Lowell, Massachusetts (MATH).

31 William N. Mass, "Technological Change and Industrial Relations: The Diffusion of Automatic Weaving in the United States and Britain" (Ph.D. diss., Boston College, 1984), pp. 275–79; Laurence F. Gross, *The Course of Industrial Decline: The Boott Cotton Mills of Lowell, Massachusetts, 1835–1955* (Baltimore: The Johns Hopkins University Press, 1993), pp. 130, 184–85; first quotation in Mary H. Blewett, *The Last Generation: Work and Life in the Textile Mills of Lowell, Massachusetts, 1910–1960* (Amherst: University of Massachusetts Press, 1990), pp. 85–86; second quotation in Steve Dunwell, *The Run of the Mill: A Pictorial Narrative of the Expansion, Dominion, Decline and Enduring Impact of the New England Textile Industry* (Boston: David R. Godine, Publisher, 1978), p. 182.

32 Jessie Davis, "My Vacation in a Woolen Mill," *Survey* 40 (Aug. 10, 1918): 541; second quotation in Charles A. Myers and George P. Shultz, *The Dynamics of a Labor Market: A Study of the Impact of Employment Changes on Labor Mobility, Job Satisfactions, and Company and Union Policies* (New York: Prentice-Hall, 1951), p. 36; Gladys L. Palmer, "The Mobility of Weavers in Three Textile Centers," *Quarterly Journal of Economics* 55 (May 1941): 486; Alphonse Parolisi interview, Sept. 23, 1983, Oral History Project: The Mill Workers of Lawrence, MATH; Uttley, *Cotton Manufacturing*, p. 6.

33 *Labor Leader*, March 30, 1889. For more on gender relations in the Law-
    rence textile industry during the period, see Ardis Cameron's *Radicals of the
    Worst Sort: Laboring Women in Lawrence, Massachusetts, 1860–1912* (Urbana:
    University of Illinois Press, 1993), particularly her analysis of the 1882
    strike on pp. 60–65.

34 Massachusetts Legislature, Joint Committee on Labor, *Hearing to Investi-
    gate Recent Reductions of Wages in the Cotton Mills of the Commonwealth*
    (1898), pp. 111–12, transcript at MATH.

35 Marc Scott Miller, *The Irony of Victory: World War II and Lowell, Mas-
    sachusetts* (Urbana: University of Illinois Press, 1988), p. 72; Massachusetts
    Legislature, *Hearing to Investigate Recent Reductions of Wages*, pp. 111–12.
    For more on the family wage doctrine, see the essays in Baron, ed., *Work
    Engendered*; and William F. Hartford, *Working People of Holyoke: Class and
    Ethnicity in a Massachusetts Mill Town, 1850–1960* (New Brunswick, N.J.:
    Rutgers University Press, 1990), 128–32.

36 Fall River newspaper, Jan. 1, 1868, in *Victorian Vistas*, p. 123.

37 This and the next several paragraphs draw heavily on John Cumbler's
    account of the rise of weaver unionism in Fall River. See *Working-Class
    Community*, pp. 184–94.

38 Quotation in Cumbler, *Working-Class Community*, p. 189; Silvia, "Spindle
    City," 465–70; *Labor Leader*, Mar. 23, 1889; Mar. 30, 1889.

39 *Labor Leader*, May 18, 1889; Feb. 27, 1892.

40 Silvia, "Spindle City," pp. 498–502, 505–508; quotation in ibid., pp. 513;
    Cumbler, *Working-Class Community*, p. 194.

41 Robert R. R. Brooks, "The United Textile Workers of America" (Ph.D.
    diss., Yale University, 1935), pp. 41–42; Herbert J. Lahne, *The Cotton Mill
    Worker* (New York: Farrar and Rinehart, 1944), p. 180; U.S. Congress,
    House of Representatives, *Report of the Industrial Commission on the Rela-
    tions and Conditions of Capital and Labor*, 57th Cong., 1st sess., 19 vols.
    (Washington, D.C.: Government Printing Office, 1901), 14:579; Silvia,
    "Spindle City," pp. 545–548, 606.

42 U.S. House of Representatives, *Report of the Industrial Commission*, 14:
    591–92. The New Bedford strike of 1898 is examined in Thomas Austin
    McMullin, "Industrialization and Social Change in a Nineteenth-Century
    Port City: New Bedford, Massachusetts, 1865–1900" (Ph.D. diss., Univer-
    sity of Wisconsin–Madison, 1976), pp. 236–49.

43 Mass, "Technological Change and Industrial Relations," pp. 159, 161–64;
    Robert N. Burnett, "Matthew Chaloner Durfee Borden," *Cosmopolitan* 36
    (Nov. 1903): 62–64.

44 MBSL, *Second Annual Report* (1871), p. 64; Mass, "Technological Change
    and Industrial Relations," pp. 162–64; Smith, *Fall River*, pp. 108–10, 117.

45 Jonathan Thayer Lincoln, *The City of the Dinner-Pail* (Boston: Houghton
    Mifflin Company, 1909), pp. 52–53.

46 U.S. House of Representatives, *Report of the Industrial Commission*, 14:582;
    quotations in ibid., 14:565–66, 579–80.

47 Ibid., 14:566.

48 Ibid., 14:565.

49 Ibid., 14:582.

50 Berthoff, *British Immigrants*, pp. 34–35; MBSL, *Thirteenth Annual Report* (1882), p. 329; U.S. Senate, *Relations between Capital and Labor*, 1:624.

51 Massachusetts Legislature, *Hearing to Investigate Recent Reductions of Wages*, pp. 504–505; first quotation in U.S. House of Representatives, *Report of the Industrial Commission*, 14:577; second and third quotations in Massachusetts Legislature, *Hearing to Investigate Recent Reductions of Wages*, pp. 94–95, 329–30; Gross, *Course of Industrial Decline*, pp. 129–30. The response of Paterson silk weavers to technological change and increased work assignments, which closely resembled that of Fall River cotton weavers, is examined in Steven Golin, *The Fragile Bridge: Paterson Silk Strike, 1913* (Philadelphia: Temple University Press, 1988), pp. 22, 31–34.

52 Irwin Feller, "The Draper Loom in New England Textiles, 1899–1914: A Study of Diffusion of an Innovation," *Journal of Economic History* 26 (Sept. 1966): 320–21; Mass, "Technological Change and Industrial Relations," pp. 65–66, 279.

53 Feller, "The Draper Loom in New England Textiles," pp. 320–47; Mass, "Technological Change and Industrial Relations," pp. 118–21; MBSL, *Labor Bulletin* 36 (June 1905): 63; Silvia, "Spindle City," pp. 587–91; MBSL, *Labor Bulletin* 34 (Dec. 1904): 322–23; Mass, "Technological Change and Industrial Relations," pp. 168–69; "History and Significance of Fall River Strike," *Current Literature* 38 (March 1905): 200; quotation in Gertrude Barnum, "The Story of a Fall River Mill Girl," *Independent* 58 (Feb. 2, 1905): 243.

54 Cumbler, *Working-Class Community*, pp. 201–204; MBSL, *Labor Bulletin* 34 (Dec. 1904): 321–22.

55 Herbert Francis Sherwood, "Negotiating by Habit," *Outlook* 133 (Apr. 18, 1923): 702; MBSL, *Labor Bulletin* 34 (Dec. 1904): 330.

56 MBSL, *Labor Bulletin* 35 (June 1905): 65; "Fall River Strike," *Current Literature*, p. 200; Uttley, *Cotton Manufacturing*, p. 28. Lancashire precedents for weavers' lists, which extend back to the Blackburn agreement of 1853, are discussed in Neville Kirk, *The Growth of Working-Class Reformism in Mid-Victorian England* (Urbana: University of Illinois Press, 1985), pp. 278–79; and H. A. Turner, *Trade Union Growth, Structure, and Policy: A Comparative Study of the Cotton Unions in England* (Toronto: University of Toronto Press, 1985), pp. 128–35.

57 Mass, "Technological Change and Industrial Relations," pp. 170–81; Jonathan Thayer Lincoln, "The Sliding Scale of Wages in the Cotton Industry," *Quarterly Journal of Economics* 23 (May 1909): 450–69; U.S. Congress, Senate, *Final Report and Testimony Submitted to Congress by the Commission on Industrial Relations*, 64th Cong., 1st sess., Senate Document No. 415, 11 vols. (Washington, D.C.: Government Printing Office, 1916), 1:1020; George H. Hills to James Whitehead, July 25, 1907, in MBSL, *Labor*

Bulletin 52 (Sept. 1907): 100; Mass, "Technological Change and Industrial Relations," p. 199, n. 115.

58 Stanley E. Howard, "The Fall River Sliding Scale Experiment of 1905–1910," *American Economic Review* 7 (Sept. 1917): 544–52; Mass, "Technological Change and Industrial Relations," p. 173.

59 Mass, "Technological Change and Industrial Relations," pp. 208–11; Howard, "Fall River Sliding Scale," pp. 547–48, 551.

60 Hartford, *Working People of Holyoke*, pp. 43–44; Blewett, *The Last Generation*, pp. 154–55. The records of the Fall River Loom Fixers Association (FRLFA Rcds.), which cover the period from 1900 to 1918, are at Special Collections and Archives, W. E. B. Du Bois Library, University of Massachusetts–Amherst, Amherst, Massachusetts.

61 "Cecile" to Anthony Valente, Mar. 15, 1938, Mss. 396, box 67, Francis Gorman folder, Textile Workers Union of America Records (TWUA Rcds.), State Historical Society of Wisconsin Archives, Madison, Wisconsin (SHSW); Statement of Mr. Airey, National Loomfixers Association, Conference of Independent Unions, May 21–22, 1921, Mss. 396, box 674, ATWA folder, TWUA Rcds.; quotation in Blewett, *The Last Generation*, p. 190.

62 FRLFA Rcds., June 25, 1900.

63 Ibid., Jan. 22, 1917, May 11, 1914, Mar. 4, 1912, July 27, 1914; quotation in ibid., Feb. 19, 1900.

64 Ibid., Apr. 1, 1912, Dec. 29, 1913, Jan. 5, 1914, Aug. 26, 1912.

65 The Fall River weave-room standards, which were also adopted in New Bedford, are discussed by TWUA research director Solomon Barkin and other union leaders in Minutes, Executive Council, Jan. 22, 1951, pp. 223–33, Mss. 396, box 4, TWUA Rcds. Among the people participating in the discussion were two veteran Fall Riverites, Edward Doolan and Mariano Bishop.

66 Hartford, *Working People of Holyoke*, p. 106; U.S. Immigration Commission, *Immigrants in Industries: Cotton Goods Manufacturing in the North Atlantic States*, 61st Cong., 2d sess., part 3 (Washington, D.C.: U.S. Government Printing Office, 1911), pp. 125–26.

TWO. CULTURAL CONFLICT AND ECONOMIC CRISIS

1 *Textile Worker* (*TW*) 16 (May 1928): 80.

2 U.S. Immigration Commission, *Immigrants in Industries: Cotton Goods Manufacturing in the North Atlantic States*, 61st Cong., 2d sess., part 3 (Washington, D.C.: U.S. Government Printing Office, 1911), p. 125.

3 Gary Gerstle, *Working-Class Americanism: The Politics of Labor in a Textile City* (New York: Cambridge University Press, 1989), pp. 19–41; Massachusetts Bureau of Statistics of Labor (MBSL), *Thirteenth Annual Report* (1882), pp. 206–207; Philip T. Silvia, Jr., "Neighbors from the North: French-Canadian Immigrants vs. Trade Unionism in Fall River, Massachu-

setts," in *The Little Canadas of New England*, ed. Claire Quintal (Worcester, Mass.: French Institute/Assumption College, 1983), pp. 52–55; U.S. Congress, Senate, *Report of the Committee of the Senate upon the Relations between Capital and Labor*, 48th Cong., 2d sess., Senate Report 1262, 5 vols. (Washington, D.C.: Government Printing Office, 1885), 1:66–69; MBSL, *Twelfth Annual Report* (1881), p. 470.

4 Massachusetts Legislature, Joint Committee on Labor, *Hearing to Investigate the Causes of Recent Reductions in the Cotton Mills of the Commonwealth* (1898), pp. 289–90, transcript at Museum of American Textile History, North Andover–Lowell, Massachusetts (MATH); U.S. Immigration Commission, *Immigrants in Industries*, part 3, p. 125.

5 MBSL, *Thirteenth Annual Report* (1882), p. 17; Charles B. Spahr, "The Old Factory Towns in New England," *Outlook* 61 (Feb. 4, 1899): 292. Unlike many French Canadian clergy of the period, this priest supported trade unions because of their efforts to reduce working hours — a matter of no small significance to Catholic leaders, who viewed long hours as detrimental to family life.

6 John T. Cumbler, *Working-Class Community in Industrial America: Work, Leisure, and Struggle in Two Industrial Cities, 1880–1930* (Westport, Conn.: Greenwood Press, 1979), pp. 174–94; Massachusetts Legislature, *Hearing to Investigate Recent Reductions of Wages*, pp. 289–90. Fall River carders' secretary James Tansey expressed similar sentiments in ibid., pp. 265–66.

7 Cumbler, *Working-Class Community*, pp. 200–211.

8 Richard Kelly, *Nine Lives for Labor* (New York: Frederick A. Praeger, 1956), pp. 40–41; *TW* 12 (Dec. 1924): 546; Stephen Wilson, "Immigrant Parish," *Spinner: People and Culture in Southeastern Massachusetts* 3 (1984): 162; Cumbler, *Working-Class Community*, pp. 204–7.

9 U.S. Congress, House of Representatives, *Report of the Industrial Commission on the Relations and Conditions of Capital and Labor*, 57th Cong., 1st sess., 19 vols. (Washington, D.C.: Government Printing Office, 1901), 14:568; U.S. Immigration Commission, *Immigrants in Industries*, part 3, pp. 123–26; Martin Segal, "Interrelationship of Wages under Joint Demand: The Case of the Fall River Textile Workers," *Quarterly Journal of Economics* 70 (Aug. 1956): 469; Aluisio Medeiros da Rosa Borges, "The Portuguese Working Class in the Durfee Mills of Fall River, Massachusetts: A Study of the Division of Labor, Ethnicity, and Labor Union Participation, 1895–1925" (Ph.D. diss., State University of New York at Binghamton, 1990), pp. 262, 318–22.

10 Rosa Borges, "The Portuguese Working Class of Fall River," pp. 127–226; *TW* 12 (Dec. 1924): 546; Donald R. Taft, *Two Portuguese Communities in New England* (rpt.; New York: Arno Press, 1969), p. 255; Cumbler, *Working-Class Community*, p. 212. For a biographical sketch of Campos, who later became an associate commissioner of the Massachusetts Department of Labor and Industries, see *TW* 19 (Feb. 1932): 505–506.

11 *TW* 16 (May 1928): 81.

12 Rowland Tappan Berthoff, *British Immigrants in Industrial America* (Cambridge: Harvard University Press, 1953), p. 98; Melton Alonza McLaurin, *Paternalism and Protest: Southern Cotton Mill Workers and Organized Labor, 1875–1905* (Westport, Conn.: Greenwood Publishing Corporation, 1971), pp. 185–86; Robert R. R. Brooks, "The United Textile Workers of America" (Ph.D. diss., Yale University, 1935), pp. 184–91; Herbert J. Lahne, *The Cotton Mill Worker* (New York: Farrar and Rinehart, 1944), pp. 190–95; Cumbler, *Working-Class Community*, pp. 211–12. Weaver localism in Lancashire is examined in H. A. Turner, *Trade Union Growth, Structure, and Policy: A Comparative Study of the Cotton Unions in England* (Toronto: University of Toronto Press, 1962), pp. 220–21.

13 *TW* 9 (June 1921): 124.

14 Berthoff, *British Immigrants*, p. 100; Cumbler, *Working-Class Community*, pp. 205–206; Brooks, "United Textile Workers of America," p. 135.

15 First quotation in Brooks, "United Textile Workers of America," p. 135; second quotation in U.S. Congress, House of Representatives, *The Strike at Lawrence: Hearings before the Committee on Rules of the House of Representatives on Resolutions 409 and 433*, 62d Cong., 2d sess. (Washington, D.C.: Government Printing Office, 1912), p. 74; *TW* 17 (Oct. 1929): 404.

16 Berthoff, *British Immigrants*, p. 100; Robert W. Dunn and Jack Hardy, *Labor and Textiles* (New York: International Publishers, 1931), pp. 183–84; Lahne, *Cotton Mill Worker*, p. 204.

17 David J. Goldberg, *A Tale of Three Cities: Labor Organization and Protest in Paterson, Passaic, and Lawrence, 1916–1921* (New Brunswick, N.J.: Rutgers University Press, 1989), pp. 83–85; U.S. Immigration Commission, *Immigrants in Industries: Woolen and Worsted Goods Manufacturing*, part 4, p. 741; Donald B. Cole, *Immigrant City: Lawrence, Massachusetts, 1845–1921* (Chapel Hill: University of North Carolina Press, 1963), pp. 60–67.

18 Cole, *Immigrant City*, pp. 68–78; quotations in Massachusetts Legislature, *Hearing to Investigate Recent Reductions of Wages*, pp. 811–12; Goldberg, *Tale of Three Cities*, pp. 86–91; Rudolph J. Vecoli, "Anthony Capraro and the Lawrence Strike of 1919," in *Race and Ethnicity in United States Labor Struggles, 1835–1960*, ed. Robert Asher and Charles Stephenson (Albany: State University of New York Press, 1990), pp. 267–68.

19 Quotations in U.S. Immigration Commission, *Immigrants in Industries*, part 4, p. 772; Vecoli, "Lawrence Strike of 1919," pp. 267–68; U.S. Immigration Commission, *Immigrants in Industries*, part 4, pp. 757–58.

20 Melvyn Dubofsky, *We Shall Be All: A History of the Industrial Workers of the World* (pbk. ed.; New York: Quadrangle, 1969), p. 257; Goldberg, *Tale of Three Cities*, p. 92. On the localistic orientation of Fall River manufacturers, which was just as narrow as that of Spindle City unionists, see Evelyn Knowlton, *Pepperell's Progress: History of a Cotton Textile Company, 1844–1945* (Cambridge: Harvard University Press, 1948), pp. 293–94; and *Transactions of the National Association of Cotton Manufacturers* (*NACM Trans.*) 120 (Apr. 1926): 157–59.

21 Cole, *Immigrant City*, pp. 134–35; Dubofsky, *We Shall Be All*, pp. 233–34; U.S. House of Representatives, *The Strike at Lawrence*, pp. 36, 147–48; *TW* 12 (Dec. 1924): 546. The explanation offered here is by no means the only reason for the IWW's success in Lawrence. A number of the city's Italian, Lithuanian, and Franco-Belgian immigrants were bearers of radical traditions that did not exist among the Portuguese and Poles of Fall River. See Goldberg, *Tale of Three Cities*, pp. 93–96.

22 Dubofsky, *We Shall Be All*, pp. 233–35; U.S. House of Representatives, *The Strike at Lawrence*, pp. 34–35; quotation in Phillips Russell, "The Second Battle of Lawrence," *International Socialist Review* 13 (Nov. 1912): 418. For accounts of the strike, see Dubofsky, *We Shall Be All*, pp. 235–54; and Cole, *Immigrant City*, pp. 1–13, 177–94. Also see Ardis Cameron's examination of how neighborhood-based women's networks helped overcome ethnic differences among newer immigrants and develop a radical critique that combined workplace, community, and family concerns. *Radicals of the Worst Sort: Laboring Women in Lawrence, Massachusetts, 1860–1912* (Urbana: University of Illinois Press, 1993), chap. 4.

23 Cole, *Immigrant City*, pp. 134–35; quotations in U.S. House of Representatives, *The Strike at Lawrence*, pp. 82–83.

24 First quotation in Philip Thomas Silvia, Jr., "The Spindle City: Labor, Politics, and Religion in Fall River, Massachusetts, 1870–1905" (Ph.D. diss., Fordham University, 1973), p. 653; the remaining quotations are from Golden's obituary in *TW* 9 (June 1921): 124–26.

25 Brooks, "United Textile Workers of America," pp. 224–28; O'Sullivan quotation in Herbert Harris, *American Labor* (New Haven: Yale University Press, 1939), p. 323. The following year, in a contest with the IWW for the loyalties of Paterson silk workers, Golden and the UTW would for many of the same reasons again be repudiated by a substantial majority of wage earners. Steve Golin, *The Fragile Bridge: Paterson Silk Strike, 1913* (Philadelphia: Temple University Press, 1988), pp. 82–89.

26 Dubofsky, *We Shall Be All*, pp. 244–45; Vecoli, "Lawrence Strike of 1919," pp. 269–79; Goldberg, *Tale of Three Cities*, pp. 98–122, 199–200.

27 First quotation in John Bruce McPherson, "The Lawrence Strike of 1912," *Bulletin of the National Association of Wool Manufacturers* (*NAWM Bull.*) 42 (1912): 264; Statement of Lawrence Manufacturers, Apr. 11, 1919, box 88, folder 2, National Association of Wool Manufacturers Records (NAWM Rcds.), MATH; Goldberg, *Tale of Three Cities*, pp. 147–51; Federal Council of Churches, "Report on the Strike in the Textile Mills of Lawrence, Massachusetts," p. 15; second quotation in "Minority Report of the Strike in the Textile Mills of Lawrence," Oct. 14, 1919; third quotation in F. Ernest Johnson to William M. Wood, Aug. 4, 1920, all three documents in box 88, folder 3, NAWM Rcds. When the Massachusetts Federation of Churches later recommended that workers and owners hire engineers to determine an appropriate scale of wages, manufacturers dismissed the proposal as impractical. Resolution of the Committee on Industrial Relations

of the Massachusetts Federation of Churches, Mar. 3, 1922; Memo Concerning Proposed Resolutions on New England Textile Situation, both documents in ibid.

28 First quotation in *Boston Herald*, Feb. 23, 1919; second quotation in William M. Leiserson, *Adjusting Immigrant and Industry* (New York: Harper and Brothers Publishers, 1924), p. 204; U.S. House of Representatives, *The Strike at Lawrence*, p. 81; third quotation in Interview with Thomas McMahon, James Starr, and John Golden, Feb. 25, 1919, box 21, David J. Saposs Papers, State Historical Society of Wisconsin Archives, Madison, Wisconsin (SHSW); McMahon quotations in *TW* 9 (Feb. 1922): 532; 10 (Oct. 1922): 410.

29 Goldberg, *Tale of Three Cities*, pp. 152–64; quotation in ibid., p. 110.

30 Cole, *Immigrant City*, pp. 81, 164–65, 197; Goldberg, *Tale of Three Cities*, p. 87; Dubofsky, *We Shall Be All*, p. 257.

31 Cole, *Immigrant City*, pp. 195–96; Henry F. Bedford, *Socialism and the Workers in Massachusetts, 1886–1912* (Amherst: The University of Massachusetts Press, 1966), pp. 273–74; James M. O'Toole, *Militant and Triumphant: William Henry O'Connell and the Catholic Church in Boston, 1859–1944* (Notre Dame, Ind.: University of Notre Dame Press, 1992), pp. 161–62; first quotation in Russell, "Second Battle of Lawrence," p. 421; Federal Council of Churches, "Report on the Lawrence Strike," p. 8; second quotation in *NAWM Bull.* 49 (1919): 264.

32 First quotation in Federal Council of Churches, "Report on the Lawrence Strike," p. 8; second quotation in Cole, *Immigrant City*, pp. 165–66; remaining quotations in *TW* 10 (May 1922): 80; 10 (July 1922): 220. Highlights of the 1922 New England textile strike are surveyed in Leonard E. Tilden, "The New England Textile Strike," *Monthly Labor Review* 16 (May 1923): 13–36; and Dunn and Hardy, *Labor and Textiles*, pp. 220–21.

33 Silvia, "Spindle City," p. 666; quotation in *TW* 11 (Feb. 1932): 499; Herbert Francis Sherwood, "Negotiating by Habit," *Outlook* 133 (Apr. 18, 1923): 701. As a charter member of Father Peter Dietz's militantly antiradical Militia of Christ, John Golden appears to have been particularly influenced by religious considerations. Marc Karson, *American Labor Unions and Politics, 1900–1918* (Carbondale: Southern Illinois University Press, 1958), pp. 244, 253–54. For the social views of one Catholic leader from Fall River, see Bishop William Stang's book, *Socialism and Christianity* (New York: Benziger Brothers, 1905).

34 Stephen Jay Kennedy, *Profits and Losses in Textiles: Cotton Textile Financing since the War* (New York: Harper and Brothers, 1936), p. 128; quotation in William R. Basset and Samuel Crowther, "What's Wrong with Textiles," *World's Work* 59 (Feb. 1931): 45; Solomon Barkin, "Management and Ownership in the New England Cotton Textile Industry," *Journal of Economic Issues* 15 (June 1981): 471; Jules Backman and M. R. Gainsbrugh, *Economics of the Cotton Textile Industry* (New York: National Industrial Conference Board, 1946), p. 173; Lahne, *Cotton Mill Worker*, pp. 90–91.

35   Ernest Lovering to H. L. Sigourney, Mar. 26, 1924, Lyman Mills Papers,
      Vol. PD-22, Baker Library, Harvard Business School, Cambridge, Mas-
      sachusetts; Louis Galambos, *Competition and Cooperation: The Emergence of
      a National Trade Association* (Baltimore: The Johns Hopkins University
      Press, 1966), pp. 89–92, 116–18, 134–36; Lewis L. Lorwin, *The World
      Textile Conference* (New York: National Peace Conference, 1937), pp. 24–
      27; Kennedy, *Profits and Losses*, pp. 196–200; Barkin, "Management and
      Ownership," p. 472.

36   Gavin Wright, *Old South, New South: Revolutions in the Southern Economy
      since the Civil War* (New York: Basic Books, 1986), pp. 135–36; Mas-
      sachusetts Legislature, *Hearing to Investigate Recent Reductions of Wages*,
      p. 53; MBSL, *Labor Bulletin* 36 (June 1905): 63; T. M. Young, *The Ameri-
      can Cotton Industry: A Study of Work and Workers* (New York: Charles
      Scribner's Sons, 1903), pp. 61–62, 68–69, 71, 86, 113; quotation in U.S.
      House of Representatives, *Report of the Industrial Commission*, 14:591. Re-
      gional labor leaders were, if anything, even less concerned about the south-
      ern threat. See, for example, the comments of textile unionists in Mas-
      sachusetts Legislature, *Hearing to Investigate Recent Reductions of Wages*,
      pp. 64–65, 250, 297–98.

37   Wright, *Old South, New South*, pp. 134–55; Alice Galenson, *The Migration
      of the Cotton Textile Industry from New England to the South* (New York:
      Garland Publishing, 1985), pp. 4–7; A. F. Hinrichs, "Historical Review
      of Wage Rates and Wage Differentials in the Cotton-Textile Industry,"
      Monthly Labor Review 40 (May 1935): 1170–76; Barkin, "Management and
      Ownership," p. 472; Backman and Gainsbrugh, *Cotton Textile Industry*,
      p. 26; quotation in Laurence F. Gross, *The Course of Industrial Decline: The
      Boott Cotton Mills of Lowell, Massachusetts, 1835–1955* (Baltimore: The Johns
      Hopkins University Press, 1993), p. 45; President's Cabinet Committee
      on the Cotton Textile Industry, *Report on the Conditions and Problems of
      the Cotton Textile Industry*, 74th Cong., 1st sess., Senate Document No.
      126 (Washington, D.C.: U.S. Government Printing Office, 1935), pp. 115–
      18; George S. Gibb, *The Saco-Lowell Shops: Textile Machinery Building in
      New England, 1813–1949* (Cambridge: Harvard University Press, 1950), pp.
      706–707. T. W. Uttley had warned that southern producers were "gradually
      advancing towards finer work" as early as 1905 in his study, *Cotton Spinning
      and Manufacturing in the United States of America* (Manchester, Eng.: The
      University Press, 1905), pp. 58–59.

38   J. Joseph Huthmacher, *Massachusetts People and Politics, 1919–1933* (pbk. ed.;
      New York: Atheneum, 1973), pp. 59–63; Hinrichs, "Historical Review,"
      pp. 1174–75; Dunn and Hardy, *Labor and Textiles*, pp. 121–31; *TW* 13
      (Jan. 1926): 721–22; quotation in *TW* 12 (March 1925): 719.

39   Brooks, "United Textile Workers of America," pp. 53–54; quotation in *TW*
      15 (Apr. 1927): 49; *TW* 14 (June 1926): 145; Dunn and Hardy, *Labor and
      Textiles*, pp. 221–22; *TW* 14 (Jan. 1927): 619.

40   Sherwood, "Negotiating by Habit," p. 701; Thomas Russell Smith, *The*

Cotton Textile Industry of Fall River, Massachusetts: A Case Study of Industrial Localization (New York: King's Crown Press, 1944), pp. 124–25; Gertrude Springer, "Up from Bankruptcy," *Survey* 66 (June 15, 1931): 344, 361, 364; *TW* 19 (Aug. 1931): 207; McMahon quotation in Louis Adamic,*My America, 1928–1938* (New York: Harper and Brothers Publishers, 1938), p. 271.

41 Smith, *Fall River*, pp. 128–35; quotation in Adamic, *My America*, p. 271; Knowlton, *Pepperell's Progress*, pp. 293–94.

42 *TW* 15 (Feb. 1928): 673; Stephen H. Norwood, *Labor's Flaming Youth: Telephone Operators and Worker Militancy, 1878–1923* (Urbana: University of Illinois Press, 1990), pp. 188–89, 195; quotations in *TW* 12 (Nov. 1924): 466.

43 *TW* 12 (Nov. 1924): 468–69.

44 William Robinson, "Fall River: A Dying Industry," *New Republic* 39 (June 4, 1924): 38–39; first quotation in *TW* 12 (Nov. 1924): 466; second quotation in *TW* 15 (Feb. 1928): 672; third quotation in *TW* 12 (Jan. 1925): 621; *TW* 18 (Feb. 1931): 660.

45 *TW* 12 (Nov. 1924): 467; quotation in *TW* 11 (Feb. 1928): 673; Springer, "Up from Bankruptcy," p. 361.

46 Quotation in *TW* 12 (Nov. 1924): 462; *TW* 11 (Apr. 1923): 11–13; 12 (Dec. 1923): 543; 13 (Apr. 1925): 22; 15 (Feb. 1928): 651.

47 First quotation in *TW* 18 (Dec. 1930): 568; Adamic,*My America*, pp. 263–78; second quotation in *TW* 18 (May 1930): 80; third quotation in *TW* 19 (June 1931): 117.

THREE. THE EMERGENCE OF THE TWUA

1 *New York Times* (*NYT*), Aug. 16, 1934, p. 6; Aug. 17, 1934, pp. 1, 7; Irving Bernstein, *Turbulent Years: A History of the American Worker, 1933–1941* (Boston: Houghton Mifflin Company, 1969), p. 300.

2 Janet Irons, "Testing the New Deal: The General Textile Strike of 1934" (Ph.D. diss., Duke University, 1988), pp. 299–324; Robert R. R. Brooks, "The United Textile Workers of America" (Ph.D. diss., Yale University, 1935), p. 154. Early UTW organizational efforts in the South are examined in Brooks, "United Textile Workers of America," pp. 144–48, 303–307, 312–19; F. Ray Marshall, *Labor in the South* (Cambridge: Harvard University Press, 1967), pp. 83–85, 122–35; and Irons, "Testing the New Deal," pp. 29–51.

3 Bernstein, *Turbulent Years*, pp. 301–303; Irons, "Testing the New Deal," pp. 324–73; James A. Hodges, *New Deal Labor Policy and the Southern Cotton Textile Industry* (Knoxville: University of Tennessee Press, 1986), pp. 64–78, 90–99; Louis Galambos, *Competition and Cooperation: The Emergence of a National Trade Association* (Baltimore: The Johns Hopkins University Press, 1966), pp. 230–32, 243–46. The grievances of southern textile workers are summarized in *Textile Worker* (*TW*) 22 (May 1934): 169–73; 22 (June 1934): 266–69.

4   *NYT*, Aug. 17, 1934, pp. 1, 7.
5   *NYT*, Aug. 28, 1934, p. 3; Aug. 31, 1934, p. 2; Sept. 8, 1934, p. 2; Sept. 11,
    1934, p. 8; Sept. 12, 1934, pp. 1, 3; Sept. 13, 1934, pp. 1, 4; Sept. 22, 1934,
    p. 6; Gary Gerstle, *Working-Class Americanism: The Politics of Labor in
    a Textile City, 1914–1960* (Cambridge, Eng.: Cambridge University Press,
    1989), pp. 127–38; Bernstein, *Turbulent Years*, pp. 307–309.
6   Bernstein, *Turbulent Years*, pp. 311–12; Irons, "Testing the New Deal," pp.
    423–77.
7   Solomon Barkin, "Notes Respecting Presentations and Discussions at the
    Rieve-Pollock Foundation Commemoration of the 1934 General Strike
    and the 1939 Founding of the TWUA," Nov. 12, 1984, pp. 1–2, box 23,
    Solomon Barkin Papers (SBP), Special Collections and Archives, W. E. B.
    Du Bois Library, University of Massachusetts–Amherst, Amherst, Mas-
    sachusetts; Bernstein, *Turbulent Years*, pp. 313–14. Janet Irons presents
    evidence indicating that substantial numbers of southern workers wished
    to continue the strike. It is unlikely, though, that remaining out another
    week—or even another month—would have made any difference, given
    the unfavorable economic conditions that the strikers faced. "Testing the
    New Deal," pp. 460–77.
8   Quotations in Comments on the Winant Report, Sept. 21, 1934, box 7A,
    folder 72, National Association of Cotton Manufacturers/Northern Textile
    Association Records (NACM/NTA Rcds.), Museum of American Textile
    History, North Andover–Lowell, Massachusetts (MATH); Hodges, *New
    Deal Labor Policy*, pp. 120–26. The Winant Report is reprinted in *Bulletin of
    the National Association of Wool Manufacturers (NAWM Bull.)* 63 (1934):
    271–93.
9   Bernstein, *Turbulent Years*, p. 315; Jacquelyn Dowd Hall et al., *Like a
    Family: The Making of a Southern Cotton Mill World* (Chapel Hill: Univer-
    sity of North Carolina Press, 1987), pp. 350–54; Hodges, *New Deal Labor
    Policy*, pp. 117–18; Irons, "Testing the New Deal," pp. 500–524; first quo-
    tation in W. T. Lawson to Emil Rieve, March 10, 1939, Mss. 396, box 67,
    James Starr folder, Textile Workers Union of America Records (TWUA
    Rcds.), State Historical Society of Wisconsin Archives, Madison, Wiscon-
    sin (SHSW); Gerstle, *Working-Class Americanism*, pp. 138–39; second
    quotation in Barkin, "Notes Respecting the 1934 General Textile Strike,"
    pp. 2–3; third quotation in *Textile Labor (TL)*, Jan. 12, 1952, p. 12. In an
    interesting comment on how union politics shapes the writing of labor
    history, Barkin observed that interpretations emphasizing the utter useless-
    ness of the 1934 general strike stemmed in part from a dispute between
    Sidney Hillman and Francis J. Gorman. The Textile Workers Organizing
    Committee, Barkin states, "added to this condemnation because Hillman
    was determined to set Gorman and the old leadership aside and shift them
    out of the control." "Notes Respecting the 1934 General Textile Strike,"
    p. 3.
10 *NACM Bulletin*, Sept. 24, 1934, box 7A, folder 72, NACM/NTA Rcds.;

"Industrial Disputes," *Monthly Labor Review* 41 (Nov. 1935): 1287–88; *NAWM Bull.* 65 (1935): 47–51; Minutes, UTW Executive Council, Sept. 13, 1935, p. 29; Mss. 396, box 674, TWUA Rcds.

11 First quotation in *TW* 20 (July 1932): 23; second quotation in Minutes, UTW Executive Council, Sept. 13, 1935, p. 25, Mss. 396, box 674, TWUA Rcds.; Edmund Wilson, *The American Earthquake: A Documentary of the Twenties and Thirties* (rpt.; Garden City, N.Y.: Anchor Books, 1964), pp. 428–29; third quotation in Minutes, UTW Executive Council, Nov. 12, 1936, p. 7, Mss. 396, box 674, TWUA Rcds.

12 Ellis W. Hawley, *The New Deal and the Problem of Monopoly* (Princeton: Princeton University Press, 1966), p. 223; *NYT*, Aug. 8, 1935, p. 32; quotation in U.S. Congress, House of Representatives, *To Regulate the Textile Industry*, 75th Cong., 1st sess. (Washington, D.C.: U.S. Government Printing Office, 1937), p. 121.

13 Hawley, *New Deal and the Problem of Monopoly*, pp. 223–24; quotation in U.S. House of Representatives, *To Regulate the Textile Industry*, pp. 128–29.

14 Bernstein, *Turbulent Years*, pp. 318–571; Daniel Nelson, *American Rubber Workers and Organized Labor* (Princeton: Princeton University Press, 1988), pp. 170–220.

15 Steven Fraser, *Labor Will Rule: Sidney Hillman and the Rise of American Labor* (New York: The Free Press, 1991), pp. 380–81; Hodges, *New Deal Labor Policy*, pp. 148–53; Bernstein, *Turbulent Years*, pp. 616–19.

16 Bernstein, *Turbulent Years*, pp. 616–17; Fraser, *Labor Will Rule*, pp. 384–86; Michael A. Bernstein, *The Great Depression: Delayed Recovery and Economic Change in America, 1929–1939* (Cambridge, Eng.: Cambridge University Press, 1987), pp. 75–79, 96.

17 Conference of Independent Unions, May 21–22, 1921, Mss. 396, box 674, ATWA folder, TWUA Rcds.; Irons, "Testing the New Deal," pp. 308–10.

18 Abstract, Solomon Barkin interview, pp. 1–2, Mss. 467, TWUA Rcds.; Donald R. Stabile, *Activist Unionism: The Institutional Economics of Solomon Barkin* (Armonk, N.Y.: M. E. Sharpe, 1993), pp. 8–14; Herbert Harris, *American Labor* (New Haven: Yale University Press, 1938), pp. 346–47; *TL*, Jan. 1963, p. 22; Russell T. Fisher to Seabury Stanton, Dec. 1, 1938, box 11, folder 126, NACM/NTA Rcds.

19 *TL*, May 1942, pp. 1, 3; Richard Kelly, *Nine Lives for Labor* (New York: Frederick A. Praeger, 1956), pp. 96–97; "Cecile" to Anthony Valente, Mar. 21, 1938; May 9, 1938, Mss. 396, box 67, Francis Gorman folder; Horace Riviere to Solomon Barkin, Oct. 9, 1937, Mss. 396, box 38, Chicopee Manufacturing folder, all three items in TWUA Rcds.

20 Barkin, "Notes Respecting the 1934 General Textile Strike," p. 2; *TL*, Apr. 1942, p. 3; Chupka quotation in *TL*, Nov. 1967; *Boston Traveller*, Feb. 29, 1952, in Biographical File, reel P68-1975, TWUA Rcds.; *TL*, May 10, 1952, pp. 1, 15; Kelly, *Nine Lives for Labor*, pp. 40–64. Although the post–Golden UTW was more sensitive to the needs and feelings of newer immigrants than it had earlier been, union leaders continued to have their doubts

about the newcomers. In a 1930 interview, Thomas McMahon was asked, "Do you find certain nationalities hard to organize [and] therefore dangerous to the standards of wages and labor conditions? Which ones?" McMahon replied: "Yes. Tell you which ones? I could, and you could, too, but not on your life." Interview with Thomas McMahon, Feb. 27, 1930, box 21, David J. Saposs Papers, SHSW.

21   Solomon Barkin to Donald Stabile, June 30, 1992, copy in author's possession.

22   *NYT*, May 30, 1937, pp. 4, 6; *TWOC News Letter for Regional Directors*, Oct. 15, 1937, box 4, SBP; Fraser, *Labor Will Rule*, pp. 396, 399–401; Bernstein, *Turbulent Years*, pp. 620–21; quotation in Solomon Barkin, Report Presented to the Second Meeting of the TWOC Advisory Council, Jan. 4, 1939, p. 4, Mss. 396, box 1, TWUA Rcds. Events arising from the 1937 recession also created a breach between TWOC and the New Bedford Textile Council, which we will examine in the next section of the chapter.

23   Solomon Barkin to Cletus Daniel, Nov. 8, 1991, copy in author's possession; Solomon Barkin to author, Sept. 11, 1990.

24   Herbert J. Lahne, *The Cotton Mill Worker* (New York: Farrar and Rinehart, 1944), pp. 267–68; Solomon Barkin to Joseph Sylvia, June 22, 1938, Mss. 129A, file 10A, box 22, UTW folder, TWUA Rcds.

25   Bernstein, *Turbulent Years*, p. 301; A. J. Muste to Francis J. Gorman, May 13, 1921, Mss. 396, box 674, ATWA folder, TWUA Rcds.; *TW* 11 (May 1923): 80–81; Brooks, "United Textile Workers of America," p. 380; Irons, "Testing the New Deal," pp. 308–10.

26   Abstract, Solomon Barkin interview, p. 9, Mss. 467, TWUA Rcds.; Barkin, "Notes Respecting the 1934 General Textile Strike," p. 3; Fraser, *Labor Will Rule*, pp. 421–22; Francis J. Gorman to Emil Rieve, Feb. 8, 1938; quotation in Francis J. Gorman to All Unions of the United Textile Workers of America, Dec. 22, 1938, both items in Mss. 396, box 67, TWUA Rcds.; Lahne, *Cotton Mill Worker*, pp. 267–68, 274.

27   Quotation in *TL*, Feb.–Mar. 1975, p. 24; Biographical Sketch of Emil Rieve, Sept. 1934, Mss. 396, box 16, TWUA Rcds.; Fraser, *Labor Will Rule*, pp. 278, 421–23; Philip Scranton, *Figured Tapestry: Production, Markets, and Power in Philadelphia Textiles, 1885–1941* (Cambridge, Eng.: Cambridge University Press, 1989), pp. 419–20, 424–25, 480–94; Nelson Lichtenstein, "Great Expectations: The Promise of Industrial Jurisprudence and Its Demise," in *Industrial Democracy in America: The Ambiguous Promise*, ed. Nelson Lichtenstein and Howell John Harris (Cambridge, Eng.: Cambridge University Press, 1993), pp. 116–20; Thomas Kennedy, *Effective Labor Arbitration: The Impartial Chairmanship of the Full-Fashioned Hosiery Industry* (Philadelphia: University of Pennsylvania Press, 1948), pp. 23, 205, 209.

28   Quotation in *TL*, Mar. 1939, pp. 1, 8; May 1945, p. 12. Although TWOC won an election at the Wood and Ayer mills in September 1937, the victory was nullified when American Woolen laid off three-fourths of its workforce

during a recession that began the following month. Bernstein, *Turbulent Years*, pp. 620–21.

29 Notes on the Woolen and Worsted Conference, Dec. 6–7, 1941, pp. 16–17, Mss. 129A, file 1A, box 20; Emil Rieve to Robert Montgomery, Aug. 31, 1942, Mss. 396, box 34, American Woolen Company folder; first quotation in George Baldanzi to Emil Rieve, Mar. 10, 1945, Mss. 129A, file 1A, box 1; second quotation in Synopsis of the New England Staff Meeting, May 25, 1946, p. 4, Mss. 129A, file 1A, box 18, all four items in TWUA Rcds.

30 *TL*, Apr. 1, 1940, pp. 1, 4; Nov. 7, 1941, p. 1; Oct. 1942, p. 1.

31 Solomon Barkin, Report Presented to the Second Meeting of the TWOC Advisory Council, Jan. 4, 1939, p. 6, Mss. 396, box 1, TWUA Rcds.; Memo to Joseph L. Miller, Aug. 7, 1951, box 37, folder 460, NACM/NTA Rcds.

32 Biographical profile of Edward Doolan, n.d., in Biographical File, reel P68-1975, TWUA Rcds.; Solomon Barkin to author, Mar. 18, 1993; quotations in transcript of radio address by Edward Doolan, Dec. 4, 1941, Mss. 129A, file 10A, box 12, Fall River folder, TWUA Rcds. The Fall River folders in this box contain an extensive assortment of the campaign literature used by both sides in the representation elections of the early 1940s.

33 Kelly, *Nine Lives for Labor*, p. 56; Notes on Executive Council Meeting, Nov. 13–14, 1941, p. 6, Mss. 396, box 5, TWUA Rcds.; *TL*, Oct. 1, 1941, p. 1; Dec. 3, 1941, p. 2; Jan. 1942, pp. 1, 11; *NYT*, Mar. 28, 1942, p. 6; *TL*, Apr. 1942, p. 9; *NYT*, June 20, 1942, p. 8; Feb. 8, 1944, p. 26; Feb. 12, 1944, p. 24; Feb. 14, 1944, p. 17; *TL*, Mar. 1944, pp. 1–2; Mariano Bishop to Emil Rieve, Mar. 1, 1944, Mss. 129A, file 1A, box 7; Minutes, Executive Council Meeting, Mar. 13–14, 1944, pp. 22–24; Mss. 396, box 5, both items in TWUA Rcds.

34 *TL*, Sept. 1942, p. 8; June 1945, p. 3.

35 Thomas Austin McMullin, "Industrialization and Social Change in a Nineteenth-Century Port City: New Bedford, Massachusetts, 1865–1900" (Ph.D. diss., University of Wisconsin–Madison, 1976), pp. 12–23, 57–58.

36 Caroline Ware, *The Early New England Cotton Manufacture: A Study in Industrial Beginnings* (Boston: Houghton Mifflin Company, 1931), pp. 107–108; T. W. Uttley, *Cotton Spinning and Manufacturing in the United States of America* (Manchester, Eng.: The University Press, 1905), p. 34; *TW* 16 (May 1928): 80; quotation in U.S. Congress, House of Representatives, *Report of the Industrial Commission on the Relations and Conditions of Capital and Labor*, 57th Cong., 1st sess., 19 vols. (Washington, D.C.: Government Printing Office, 1901), 14:536; Patrick J. Hearden, *Independence and Empire: The New South's Cotton Mill Campaign* (DeKalb: Northern Illinois University Press, 1982), pp. 99–100; Walker D. Hines to Robert Amory, June 5, 1930, box 2, folder 18; Brief on Behalf of Greater New Bedford, 1938, pp. 10–11, box 13B, folder 146, both items in NACM/NTA Rcds.

37 Fred Beal, *Proletarian Journey: New England, Gastonia, Moscow* (New York: Hillman-Curl, Inc., 1937), pp. 98–106; Michael W. Santos, "Community

and Communism: The 1928 New Bedford Textile Strike," *Labor History* 26 (Spring 1985): 230–49; Sam Bass Warner, Jr., *Province of Reason* (Cambridge: Harvard University Press, 1984), pp. 150–53; Lahne, *Cotton Mill Worker*, pp. 212–14; Robert W. Dunn and Jack Hardy, *Labor and Textiles* (New York: International Publishers, 1931), pp. 225–27.

38   *TW* 16 (June 1928): 150–51; 17 (July 1929): 216; 16 (May 1928): 81; 16 (Aug. 1928): 268–69; Brooks, "United Textile Workers of America," pp. 265–69; Hyman Blumberg to W. E. G. Batty, Oct. 16, 1937, Mss. 396, box 67, TWUA Rcds.

39   *TW* 16 (Sept. 1928): 347.

40   *TW* 19 (Feb. 1932): 499–500.

41   *TW* 17 (Feb. 1930): 656–57; quotation in *Daily News Record* (*DNR*), Jan. 27, 1939; *DNR*, Feb. 11, 1938, both items in Mss. 129A, file 10A, box 15, TWUA Rcds. Copies of the *Weave Room News Sheet* from the late 1930s can be found in Mss. 396, box 67, TWUA Rcds.

42   Emil Rieve to William E. Batty, Feb. 10, 1938, Mss. 129A, file 10A, box 15, TWUA Rcds.

43   W. E. G. Batty to Emil Rieve, May 4, 1939; Jan. 12, 1939; W. E. G. Batty to George Baldanzi, June 29, 1939, Mss. 396, box 67; Jason quotations in Statement of Toby Mendes, n.d., Mss. 129A, file 10, box 15, all four items in TWUA Rcds.; final quotation in Memo to Joseph L. Miller, Aug. 7, 1951, box 37, folder 460, NACM/NTA Rcds.

44   *TL*, Aug. 1942, pp. 1–2; Rieve quotations in Minutes, Executive Council, Nov. 5, 1942, pp. 9–10, Mss. 396, box 1, TWUA Rcds.; *TL*, May 10, 1952, pp. 1, 15; Feb. 19, 1949, pp. 1, 10; Apr. 1943, p. 2.

45   *TL*, Apr. 1943, p. 2; Aug. 1942, pp. 1–2. An extensive assortment of the campaign literature used by both sides in the New Bedford drive can be found in Mss. 129A, file 10A, box 16, TWUA Rcds.

46   *TL*, Apr. 1943, pp. 1–2, 6.

47   Report of Joseph Simas, Aug. 9, 1943, box 13, folder 192, New Bedford Joint Board, TWUA, Records (NB Jt. Bd. Rcds.), Archives and Special Collections, W. E. B. Du Bois Library, University of Massachusetts–Amherst, Amherst, Massachusetts; *TL*, Jan. 1944, p. 2; New Bedford Joint Board, TWUA, Board of Directors Minutes, June 12, 1947, Aug. 3, 1947, box 1, NB Jt. Bd. Rcds.; *TL*, Aug. 1945, p. 1; Mar. 3, 1951, p. 12; Mar. 21, 1953, p. 1; "A true member of your local" to Antonio England, May 1945; Business Agent's Report, Wamsutta Mills, May 5, 1945, both in box 15, folder 226, NB Jt. Bd. Rcds. For evidence concerning the amount of time TWUA officials devoted to UTW-related matters, see box 26, TWUA Collection, MATH; and Mss. 129A, file 2A, boxes 7, 14, TWUA Rcds., SHSW.

48   First quotation in Transcript of Arbitration Hearing, Aug. 17, 1943, p. 7, box 10, folder 148, NB Jt. Bd. Rcds.; second quotation in Memo to Joseph L. Miller, Aug. 7, 1951, NACM/NTA Rcds.; Memo for Mr. Rugg, Aug. 25, 1955, box 51, folder 599, NACM/NTA Rcds.; Isadore Katz to Emil Rieve, Apr. 7, 1943, Mss. 129A, file 1A, box 11, New Bedford Negotiations

folder, TWUA Rcds.; Brief Submitted by the NBCMA and Nashawena Mills, Aug. 24, 1949, pp. 5–12, box 8, folder 100, NB Jt. Bd. Rcds.

49 A. F. Hinrichs, "Historical Review of Wage Rates and Wage Differentials in the Cotton Textile Industry," *Monthly Labor Review* 40 (May 1935): 1170–80. The development of the southern woolen and worsted industry is examined in James A. Morris, *Woolen and Worsted Manufacturing in the Southern Piedmont* (Columbia: University of South Carolina Press, 1952).

50 F. Ray Marshall, *Labor in the South* (Cambridge: Harvard University Press, 1967), pp. 169–71; Paul David Richards, "The History of the Textile Workers Union of America, CIO, in the South, 1937 to 1945" (Ph.D. diss., University of Wisconsin–Madison, 1978), pp. 64–68, 174.

51 Robert Sidney Smith, *Mill on the Dan: A History of the Dan River Mills, 1882–1950* (Durham, N.C.: Duke University Press, 1960), pp. 243–94, 491–93; *TL,* July 1942, pp. 2–3; May 1943, p. 1; Richards, "TWUA in the South," pp. 168–70.

52 Dolores E. Janiewski, *Sisterhood Denied: Race, Gender, and Class in a New South Community* (Philadelphia: Temple University Press, 1985), pp. 163–65, 168–71; *TL,* Apr. 1945, p. 12; Richards, "TWUA in the South," pp. 164–67, 174.

53 U.S. Congress, Senate, Subcommittee on Labor-Management Relations of the Committee on Labor and Public Welfare, *Hearings on Labor–Management Relations in the Southern Textile Manufacturing Industry,* 81st Cong., 2d sess. (Washington, D.C.: U.S. Government Printing Office, 1950), pp. 10–11; *TL,* Nov. 1939, p. 2; July 1, 1940, p. 2; Oct. 1, 1940, p. 7; Richards, "TWUA in the South," pp. 105–108, 114; Margaret Terrell Parker, *Lowell: A Study of Industrial Development* (rpt.; Port Washington, N.Y.: Kennikat Press, 1970), p. 212.

54 Solomon Barkin, "Labour Relations in the United States Textile Industry," *International Labour Review* 75 (Mar. 1957): 407; Barkin, "Wage Policies of Industrial Unions," *Harvard Business Review* 19 (Spring 1941): 346–47.

55 Fraser, *Labor Will Rule,* pp. 391–94, 411–12; George B. Tindall, *The Emergence of the New South, 1913–1945* (Baton Rouge: Louisiana State University Press, 1967), pp. 533–35; William E. Leuchtenberg, *Franklin D. Roosevelt and the New Deal, 1932–1940* (New York: Harper Torchbooks, 1963), pp. 261–62.

56 Leuchtenberg, *Roosevelt and the New Deal,* p. 261; Fraser, *Labor Will Rule,* pp. 392–93; Pamphlet Concerning Black-Connery Bill (Southern-Mid-Western Industry Committee) in box 9, folder 112, NACM/NTA Rcds.; 73rd Annual Meeting, National Association of Wool Manufacturers, Feb. 16, 1938, p. 108, National Association of Wool Manufacturers Records (NAWM Rcds.), MATH.

57 Burton E. Oppenheim to E. E. Andrews, Dec. 22, 1938, box 13A, folder 142; E. F. Walker to E. E. Andrews, Oct. 21, 1938, box 11, folder 125; Lewis Morley to Russell T. Fisher, June 15, 1939, box 13B, folder 148; Statement of Russell T. Fisher, box 14, folder 150, all in NACM/NTA Rcds.

58 Statement of the Minority of Industry Committee No. 1 Submitted to the Administrator of the FLSA of 1938, box 13A, folder 144; Russell T. Fisher to Fred W. Steele, June 9, 1939, box 13B, folder 148; Brief on Behalf of Greater New Bedford, box 13B, folder 146; Russell T. Fisher to E. M. Philippi, June 5, 1939, box 13B, folder 145; Statement of American Thread Company, June 21, 1939, box 13B, folder 149; Statement of Dwight Billings, Pacific Mills, box 13B, folder 148; Statement of Pepperell Manufacturing Company, box 13B, folder 148, all in NACM/NTA Rcds.

59 Gavin Wright, *Old South, New South: Revolutions in the Southern Economy since the Civil War* (New York: Basic Books, 1986), p. 219; Remarks of Russell T. Fisher, NACM meeting, Mar. 17, 1941, box 16, folder 182, NACM/NTA Rcds.

60 Statement before War Labor Board, May 1942, pp. 1–2, 11–12, Bound Notebook 1 (BN-1), SBP.

61 Statement of Charles B. Rugg, Aug. 5, 1942, pp. 17–18, 23–25, box 18, folder 196, NACM/NTA Rcds.

62 NWLB, Directive Order, Aug. 20, 1942, box 18, folder 197, NACM/NTA Rcds.; *NYT*, Nov. 18, 1943, p. 36; Mar. 28, 1944, p. 14; Richards, "TWUA in the South," p. 193; Statement before NWLB, Mar. 1944, box 5, SBP; U.S. Congress, Senate, Subcommittee of the Committee on Education and Labor, *Hearings on Substandard Wages Pursuant to S. Con. Res. 48*, 78th Cong., 2d sess. (Washington, D.C.: U.S. Government Printing Office, 1945), pp. 271–361.

63 Brief Comparative Wage Study for the Cotton Textile Industry, Jan. 31, 1944; Meeting of Northern Mill Executives, Mar. 3, 1944, both in box 22, folder 240, NACM/NTA Rcds.; *TL*, Oct. 1944, p. 1; Feb. 1945, p. 1.

64 *TL*, Mar. 1945, pp. 1–3, 10; Nelson Lichtenstein, *Labor's War at Home: The CIO in World War II* (Cambridge, Eng.: Cambridge University Press, 1982), pp. 210–12; Lloyd G. Reynolds and Cynthia H. Taft, *The Evolution of Wage Structure* (New Haven: Yale University Press, 1956), pp. 75–78; *Report on the Textile Industry by Committee Appointed by the New England Governors* (1952), pp. 33, 130.

FOUR. YEARS OF HOPE, 1945–1949

1 This and the next two paragraphs are based on Nelson Lichtenstein, *Labor's War at Home: The CIO in World War II* (Cambridge, Eng.: Cambridge University Press, 1982), pp. 216–32; Lichtenstein, "From Corporatism to Collective Bargaining: Organized Labor and the Eclipse of Social Democracy in the Postwar Era," in *The Rise and Fall of the New Deal Order, 1930–1980*, ed. Steve Fraser and Gary Gerstle (Princeton: Princeton University Press, 1989), pp. 128–33, 140–44; David Brody, *Workers in Industrial America: Essays on the 20th Century Struggle* (New York: Oxford University Press, 1980), pp. 173–214; Robert Zieger, *American Workers, American Unions, 1920–1985* (Baltimore: The Johns Hopkins University Press, 1986), pp.

100–108, 147–58; and Howell John Harris, *The Right to Manage: Industrial Relations Policies of American Business in the 1940s* (Madison: University of Wisconsin Press, 1982), pp. 91–104, 129–58.

2 *New York Times* (*NYT*), Oct. 6, 1945, p. 2; *Textile Labor* (*TL*), Nov. 1945, p. 1; Dec. 1945, p. 1; Minutes, Executive Council, Dec. 3–5, 1945, pp. 15–18, Mss. 396, box 5, Textile Workers Union of America Records (TWUA Rcds.), State Historical Society of Wisconsin Archives, Madison, Wisconsin (SHSW).

3 Seabury Stanton to Ray R. Murdock, Oct. 20, 1950, box 35, folder 423, National Association of Cotton Manufacturers / Northern Textile Association Records (NACM/NTA Rcds.), Museum of American Textile History, North Andover–Lowell, Massachusetts (MATH); "Textron," *Fortune* 35 (May 1947): 133; "The Bolt in Cotton Textiles," *Fortune* 36 (July 1947): 61; "The Nation's Most Prosperous Industry: An Accounting of the Postwar Financial Expenditures of American Textile Manufacturers," TWUA Research Department Economic Report, Jan. 1948, p. 3.

4 *NYT*, Sept. 1, 1946, 4:8; Solomon Barkin, "The Regional Significance of the Integration Movement in the Southern Textile Industry," *Southern Economic Journal* 15 (Apr. 1949): 406–409; "South Carolina Textiles: Southern Workers, Northern Bosses — A Study of Industrial Concentration and Locale of Ownership," TWUA Research Department Economic Report, 1949, pp. 3–4; U.S. Congress, Senate, Subcommittee on Antitrust and Monopoly of the Committee on the Judiciary, *Hearings to Study the Antitrust Laws of the United States, and Their Administration, Interpretation, and Effect Pursuant to S. Res. 61*, 84th Cong., 1st sess. (Washington, D.C.: U.S. Government Printing Office, 1955), pp. 765–67.

5 Donald N. Anderson, " The Decline of the Woolen and Worsted Industry of New England, 1947–1958: A Regional Economic History" (Ph.D. diss., New York University, 1971), pp. 132–37; U.S. Congress, Senate, Subcommittee of the Committee on Interstate and Foreign Commerce, *Investigation of Closing of Nashua, New Hampshire Mills and Operations of Textron, Inc.*, 80th Cong., 2d sess. (Washington, D.C.: U.S. Government Printing Office, 1948), p. 80; "The Bolt in Cotton Textiles," pp. 64–66, 178; L. D. Howell, *The American Textile Industry: Competition, Structure, Facilities, Costs*, Agricultural Economic Report No. 58 (Washington, D.C.: U.S. Government Printing Office, 1964), p. 39; Jesse W. Markham, "Integration in the Textile Industry," *Harvard Business Review* 28 (Jan. 1950): 83; *NYT*, Aug. 19, 1958, p. 42.

6 "The Bolt in Cotton Textiles," pp. 67, 178; Markham, "Integration in the Textile Industry," pp. 83–84.

7 Minutes, Columbia University Seminar on Labor, Dec. 12, 1956, p. 3, in Bound Notebook 10, Solomon Barkin Papers, (BN-10, SBP), Special Collections and Archives, W. E. B. Du Bois Library, University of Massachusetts–Amherst, Amherst, Massachusetts; U.S. Congress, Senate, Subcommittee on Labor-Management Relations of the Committee on Labor and

Public Welfare, *Hearing on Labor-Management Relations in the Southern Textile Industry Pursuant to S. Res. 140*, 81st Cong., 2d sess. (Washington, D.C.: U.S. Government Printing Office, 1951), p. 68.

8 "Textron," pp. 133–64; Steve Dunwell, *The Run of the Mill: A Pictorial Narrative of the Expansion, Dominion, Decline and Enduring Impact of the New England Textile Industry* (Boston: David R. Godine, Publisher, 1978), pp. 161–62; U.S. Senate, *Investigation of Textron*, pp. 68–81.

9 William F. Hartford, *Working People of Holyoke: Class and Ethnicity in a Massachusetts Mill Town, 1850–1960* (New Brunswick, N.J.: Rutgers University Press, 1990), p. 196; *TL*, Feb. 21, 1948, p. 4.

10 Jerome Campbell, "Berkshire Hathaway's Brave New Voyage," *Modern Textiles Magazine* (Dec. 1957), in Mss. 396, box 363, Berkshire-Hathaway folder, TWUA Rcds.; Address by Seabury Stanton before the Rhode Island Textile Association, Oct. 24, 1951, box 35, folder 414; Address by Seabury Stanton before the NACM, Sept. 13, 1951, box 37, folder 463, both items in NACM/NTA Rcds.

11 Seabury Stanton to Solomon Barkin, Sept. 18, 1951, box 35, folder 423, NACM/NTA Rcds.; *Report on the New England Textile Industry by Committee Appointed by the New England Governors* (1952), p. 112; Campbell, "Berkshire Hathaway's Brave New Voyage"; *TL*, Sept. 3, 1949, p. 6.

12 Memo to WFS re NTA mill identification, 1953, box 44, folder 542, NACM/NTA Rcds.

13 Summary Evaluation, Textile Trade Conference, Geneva, Switzerland, Jan. 29–Feb. 6, 1962, pp. 7–8, BN-16, SBP.

14 First quotation in William F. Sullivan, Draft of Address, Feb. 6, 1951, box 38, folder 473, NACM/NTA Rcds.; second quotation in *TL*, Apr. 3, 1948, p. 8.

15 Hartford, *Working People of Holyoke*, p. 197; NACM Annual Meeting, Report of the Industrial Relations Department, Sept. 16–17, 1948, box 30, folder 348, NACM/NTA Rcds.; *TL*, Mar. 19, 1949, pp. 1, 12; quotation in Seabury Stanton to Ray R. Murdock, Oct. 20, 1950, box 35, folder 423, NACM/NTA Rcds.

16 Seabury Stanton to Henry Cabot Lodge, Jr., Mar. 2, 1949; Seabury Stanton to Joseph W. Martin, Jr., Apr. 12, 1949, both letters in Mss. 396, box 53, Hathaway Manufacturing Company folder, TWUA Rcds.

17 Barbara S. Griffith, *The Crisis of American Labor: Operation Dixie and the Defeat of the CIO* (Philadelphia: Temple University Press, 1988), pp. 23, 36, 46–48; "Labor Drives South," *Fortune* 34 (Nov. 1946): 237; Axelrod quotation from Hartford, *Working People of Holyoke*, p. 196.

18 *NYT*, Nov. 18, 1943, p. 36; Mar. 28, 1944, p. 14; June 21, 1945, p. 20; quotations in *NYT*, Mar. 20, 1948, p. 24; Glenn E. McLaughlin and Stefan Robock, *Why Industry Moves South: A Study of Factors Influencing the Recent Location of Manufacturing Plants in the South*, National Planning Association Committee of the South, Report No. 3 (Kingsport, Tenn.: Kingsport Press, 1949), p. 69.

19 Evaluation of Hathaway Mfg. Company's People, Aug. 1950, in Mss. 396, box 364, Hathaway Manufacturing Company folder, TWUA Rcds.

20 "Reconversion in New England," *Monthly Labor Review* 63 (July 1946): 8–10.

21 Work History of Raymond Dupont, box 8, folder 99, New Bedford Joint Board, TWUA, Records (NB Jt. Bd. Rcds.), Special Collections and Archives, W. E. B. Du Bois Library, University of Massachusetts–Amherst, Amherst, Massachusetts.

22 "Reconversion in New England," pp. 10, 13; Tamara K. Hareven, *Family Time and Industrial Time: The Relationship between the Family and Work in a New England Industrial Community* (Cambridge, Eng.: Cambridge University Press, 1982); Fall River Textile Manufacturers Association (FRTMA); New Bedford Cotton Manufacturers Association (NBCMA) and TWUA, Arbitration Decision No. 9, June 3, 1947, p. 2, box 9, folder 99, NB Jt. Bd. Rcds.

23 "Reconversion in New England," pp. 12–14; *TWOC Weekly News Letter for Regional Directors*, June 30, 1937, in box 4, SBP.

24 *TWOC Weekly News Letter for Regional Directors*, June 30, 1937; FRTMA; NBCMA and TWUA, Arbitration Decision No. 9, June 3, 1947. As it turned out, the union was not able to help Dupont. The case resulted in his dismissal on charges of insubordination.

25 Unless otherwise noted, the following discussion of the persisters' children is based on Hartford, *Working People of Holyoke*, pp. 200–204. For an examination of similar developments among the children of southern textile workers, see Douglass Flamming, *Creating the Modern South: Millhands and Managers in Dalton, Georgia, 1884–1984* (Chapel Hill: The University of North Carolina Press, 1992), pp. 270–72.

26 John P. Hoerr, *And the Wolf Finally Came: The Decline of the American Steel Industry* (Pittsburgh: University of Pittsburgh Press, 1988), p. 192; final quotation in Paul Charles Whitehead, "The Assimilation of the Portuguese in Fall River, Massachusetts" (M.A. thesis, University of Massachusetts at Amherst, 1966), p. 68.

27 Marc S. Miller, *The Irony of Victory: World War II and Lowell, Massachusetts* (Urbana: University of Illinois Press, 1988), pp. 89–90, 118; Claire Lefebvre interview, June 1988, Shifting Gears Project (SGP), Massachusetts Foundation for the Humanities and Public Policy, South Hadley, Massachusetts.

28 *TL*, July 5, 1947, p. 12.

29 Frequent mention of the types of programs discussed in the paragraph can be found in the pages of *Textile Labor*. See, for example, *TL*, Aug. 1943, p. 3; Sept. 1945, p. 12; July 1946, pp. 3, 9; May 17, 1947, p. 8.

30 *TL*, Jan. 1945, p. 3; Jan. 8, 1949; Minutes, Lawrence Joint Board, TWUA, May 9, 1948, Sept. 15, 1948, box 86, TWUA Collection, MATH.

31 Solomon Barkin, "Economic Problems," unpublished ms., Sept. 14, 1956, BN-10, SBP.

32 Solomon Barkin, "Labor's Code for a Free Enterprise Economy," *Labor Law Journal* 3 (1952): 843–44.

33 Barkin, "Economic Problems"; Anna Sullivan interview, Spring 1974, American International College Oral History Collection, Springfield, Massachusetts (AICOHC); Massachusetts House of Representatives, "Report of the Unpaid Special Commission Relative to the Investigation and Study of the Textile Industry and to Prevent the Removal Thereof from the Commonwealth," *Document No. 2590*, 1950, p. 34; Solomon Barkin, "Dissenting Opinion on Bates Manufacturing Decision," June 1952, BN-6, SBP.

34 Richard C. Nyman, *Union-Management Cooperation in the "Stretch-Out"* (New Haven: Yale University Press, 1934); Horace Riviere, "Speeding Up Machinery Is Shortening Workers' Lives," in NACM Bulletin, Sept. 24, 1934, box 7A, folder 72, NACM/NTA Rcds.; *NYT*, May 30, 1937, 4:6.

35 Address by Mariano Bishop, Jan. 26, 1952, box 6, Officer Installations folder, NB Jt. Bd. Rcds.; Solomon Barkin, "Handling Work Assignment Changes," *Harvard Business Review* 25 (Summer 1947): 478–82. Barkin's views on workloads and technological change are more fully examined in Donald R. Stabile, *Activist Unionism: The Institutional Economics of Solomon Barkin* (Armonk, N.Y.: M. E. Sharpe, 1993), pp. 93–104, 128–35.

36 Barkin, "Handling Work Assignment Changes," pp. 479–80, 482; Arthur A. Bright, Jr., and George H. Ellis, eds., *The Economic State of New England: Report of the Committee of New England of the National Planning Association* (New Haven: Yale University Press, 1954), p. 382; Minutes, Columbia University Seminar on Labor, Dec. 12, 1956, pp. 7–8, BN-10, SBP.

37 *TL*, 1945–1950, passim; Solomon Barkin to Emil Rieve, Oct. 12, 1948, Mss. 129A, file 1A, TWUA Rcds. The research department later developed a guidebook to help workers and shop stewards analyze job duties: Solomon Barkin, et al., *Textile Workers' Job Primer* (TWUA Research Department Technical Report, 1953).

38 Gabe LaDoux interview, Nov. 4, 1983, Oral History Project: The Mill Workers of Lawrence, MATH; Diamentina quotations in Donna Huse, et al., "Vizinhanca: Neighborhood," *Spinner: People and Culture in Southeastern Massachusetts* 1 (1981): 17.

39 Quotation in *TL*, Mar. 21, 1953, p. 3. These grievances, together with related business agents' reports, are filed chronologically by mill in boxes 13 through 15 of the New Bedford Joint Board records at the W. E. B. Du Bois Library, University of Massachusetts–Amherst, Amherst, Massachusetts. To reduce the length of footnotes, the following citations will only specify the mill involved and date of grievance.

40 Solomon Barkin, "Workers Must Have Job Specifications," *TL*, June 1, 1941, p. 6.

41 Kilburn Mill, Feb. 11, 1944; Naushon Mill, Jan. 11, 1944; Soule Mill, Jan. 11, 1944, all in NB Jt. Bd. Rcds.; Seabury Stanton to Solomon Barkin, Apr. 20, 1945, Mss. 396, box 53, Hathaway Manufacturing Company folder, TWUA Rcds.

42 Wamsutta Mills, Nov. 29, 1944; Naushon Mill, May 23, 1944; Soule Mill, May 4, 1948; Kilburn Mill, Feb. 12, 1945; quotation in Naushon Mill, July 28, 1943, all in NB Jt. Bd. Rcds.

43 Wamsutta Mills, Mar. 21, 1944; Quissett Screen Print, Nov. 22, 1943; Naushon Mill, Mar. 31, 1944; Soule Mill, Dec. 13, 1944; Fisk Mill, Oct. 11, 1946; Wamsutta Mills, Aug. 15, 1945; Naushon Mill, Nov. 10, 1945; Fisk Mill, July 24, 1946; Soule Mill, Feb. 6, 1947, all in NB Jt. Bd. Rcds. H. A. Turner found that the majority of shop-floor disputes in twentieth-century English mills centered on similar grievances. *Trade Union Growth, Structure, and Policy: A Comparative Study of the Cotton Unions in England* (Toronto: University of Toronto Press, 1962), p. 338.

44 Minutes of Conference between Fred W. Steele, NBCMA, and NB Jt. Bd., TWUA, Feb. 11, 1947, box 14, folder 195, NB Jt. Bd. Rcds.

45 New Bedford Rayon Company, Oct. 14, 1947; Kilburn Mill, Dec. 8, 1947; Kilburn Mill, Oct. 20, 1947; Kilburn Mill, Feb. 11, 1947; Kilburn Mill, Apr. 17, 1948, all in NB Jt. Bd Rcds.

46 Quotations in complaint of Mary Travers and Alice Gomes, Kilburn Mill, summer 1943; Kilburn Mill, Feb. 8, 1944; Wamsutta Mills, Dec. 2, 1944; Fisk Mill, May 25, 1946; Kilburn Mill, May 21, 1948; Kilburn Mill, Sept. 2, 1948; Wamsutta Mills, Oct. 14, 1948, all in NB Jt. Bd. Rcds.

47 Quissett Screen Print, Jan. 21, 1944; Soule Mill, Jan. 27, 1944; Wamsutta Mills, Jan. 11, 1945; Soule Mills, Feb. 14, 1945; Kilburn Mill, Apr. 19, 1945; Soule Mill, Aug. 4, 1947; Quissett Screen Print, Nov. 4, 1943; Fisk Mill, Mar. 10, 1945; Naushon Mill, Nov. 2, 1945, all in NB Jt. Bd. Rcds.

48 Naushon Mill, Mar. 17, 1945; Fisk Mill, Oct. 9, 1945; Kilburn Mill, July 14, 1944; Kilburn Mill, Aug. 8, 1944; New Bedford Rayon Company, Apr. 6, 1945, all in NB Jt. Bd. Rcds.; Barkin quotation in Minutes, Columbia University Seminar on Labor, Jan. 20, 1954, p. 5, BN-8, SBP.

49 Stanton quotation in Hartford, *Working People of Holyoke*, p. 205; Arthur H. Gulliver, "Present Day Relations between the Foreign Born Operative and the Mill Management," *Transactions of the National Association of Cotton Manufacturers* 93 (Sept. 1912): 125–26; Minutes, Executive Council, Feb. 7–11, 1949, Mss. 396, box 6, TWUA Rcds.

50 This and the next paragraph are based on Solomon Barkin to Emil Rieve, Oct. 12, 1948, Mss. 129A, file 1A, box 14; Barkin to Rieve, June 27, 1949, Mss. 129A, file 7A, box 15; Barkin to Mariano Bishop, Dec. 18, 1952, file 7A, box 16, all in TWUA Rcds. The first two items are detailed memos on the workload question in New England.

51 Minutes, Columbia University Seminar on Labor, Dec. 9, 1960, p. 7, BN-14, SBP. For an insightful recent discussion of the cooperation-participation question, see the articles in the fall 1989 issue of *Labor Research Review*.

52 Solomon Barkin, "Union's Viewpoint on Human Engineering and Relations," p. 16, Address Delivered at Meeting of the Society for the Advancement of Management, 1949–1950 lecture series, BN-3, SBP.

53 Author interview with Solomon Barkin, Aug. 7, 1991.

54 Quotations in proposed draft of letter from Mariano Bishop, the union's cotton and rayon director, to Seabury Stanton, Jan. 2, 1947, Mss. 129A, file 7A, box 14, Research Reports folder; abstract, Solomon Barkin interview, p. 25, Mss. 467, both items in TWUA Rcds. The draft response cited above was written by Solomon Barkin and sent to Stanton without any substantial changes. Solomon Barkin to author, Dec. 8, 1992.

55 Quotation in Barkin, "Union's Viewpoint on Human Engineering and Relations," p. 10; Solomon Barkin to author, Dec. 8, 1992; Howell John Harris, *The Right to Manage.*

56 Solomon Barkin to Seabury Stanton, June 27, 1947, July 16, 1947, Mss. 396, box 53, Hathaway Manufacturing Company folder, TWUA Rcds.; *TL*, Feb. 21, 1948, p. 4; quotation in Statement of the TWUA in the Matter of Arbitration with FRTMA and NBCMA, Jan. 3, 1949, pp. 14–15, 30, box 8, folder 113, NB Jt. Bd. Rcds. Other successful instances of union-management cooperation are discussed in George S. Paul, *American Velvet Company and Textile Workers Union of America* (Washington, D.C.: National Planning Association, 1953); *TL*, Dec. 20, 1947, p. 4; and Solomon Barkin to Emil Rieve, Oct. 12, 1948, Mss. 129A, file 1A, box 14, TWUA Rcds.

57 Quotation in Solomon Barkin to Emil Rieve, Oct. 12, 1948, Mss. 129A, file 1A, box 14, TWUA Rcds.; author interview with Solomon Barkin, June 22, 1992.

58 National Association of Wool Manufacturers, Meeting of the Executive Committee, Oct. 16, 1945, box 15, National Association of Wool Manufacturers Records (NAWM Rcds.), MATH; *TL*, Dec. 20, 1947, p. 1; Nov. 8, 1947, pp. 1, 3; Nashua plant manager quotation in Charles A. Myers and George P. Shultz, *The Dynamics of a Labor Market: A Study of the Impact of Employment Changes on Labor Mobility, Job Satisfactions, and Company and Union Policies* (New York: Prentice-Hall, Inc., 1951), pp. 161–62; NACM Annual Meeting, Report of the Industrial Relations Department, Sept. 16–17, 1948, box 30, folder 348, NACM/NTA Rcds.

59 "New England Textile Problems: An Outline for Discussion by TWUA Representatives," TWUA Research Department, Jan. 29, 1952, p. 6, Mss. 129A, file 1A, box 16, TWUA Rcds.; Bright and Ellis, eds., *State of the New England Economy*, p. 544; Massachusetts H. R., "Study of the Textile Industry," 1950, pp. 45–46.

FIVE. CRISIS YEARS, 1949–1952

1 "They Said It Couldn't Be Done: A History of the Textile Workers Union of America, AFL-CIO, CLC," TWUA, n.d., p. 10.

2 Arthur Besse to Board of Directors, Oct. 21, 1947, box 16, National Association of Wool Manufacturers Records (NAWM Rcds.), Museum of American Textile History, North Andover–Lowell, Massachusetts (MATH);

"The Nation's Most Prosperous Industry: An Accounting of the Postwar Financial Expenditures of American Textile Manufacturers," TWUA Research Department Economic Report, Jan. 1948, p. 7.

3 William H. Miernyk, *New England Textile Employment in 1970* (Federal Reserve Bank of Boston Research Report, Dec. 1959), p. 2; "They Said It Couldn't Be Done," p. 10; Robert W. Eisenmenger, *The Dynamics of Growth in New England's Economy, 1870–1964* (Middletown, Conn.: Wesleyan University Press, 1967), p. 68; quotations in *Textile Labor (TL)*, Sept. 3, 1949, pp. 6–7.

4 *TL*, Apr. 1948, pp. 1, 3; *CIO News*, Apr. 26, 1948, p. 8; quotation in "Naushon Mills, Inc.," TWUA Research Department, Mar. 19, 1948, p. 20, Mss. 396, box 329, Textile Workers Union of America Records (TWUA Rcds.), State Historical Society of Wisconsin Archives, Madison, Wisconsin (SHSW).

5 Statement of the TWUA, CIO, at Stockholders Meeting, Wm. Whitman Co., Inc., Nov. 12, 1952, p. 3; *Daily News Record (DNR)*, Dec. 17, 1946; quotation in John Harriman to Solomon Barkin, July 28, 1949, all three items in Mss. 396, box 353, William Whitman folder, TWUA Rcds.; *TL*, Sept. 3, 1949, p. 6.

6 Minutes, New Bedford Joint Board, Sept. 18, 1949, box 1, New Bedford Joint Board, TWUA, Records (NB Jt. Bd. Rcds.), Special Collections and Archives, W. E. B. Du Bois Library, University of Massachusetts–Amherst, Amherst, Massachusetts; Jack Gross to Emil Rieve, Jan. 5, 1950, Mss. 129A, file 1a, Letters: People Outside of Organization folder, TWUA Rcds.; Steve Dunwell, *The Run of the Mill: A Pictorial Narrative of the Expansion, Dominion, Decline and Enduring Impact of the New England Textile Industry* (Boston: David R. Godine, Publisher, 1978), pp. 161–62; *TL*, Oct. 2, 1948, p. 5. For a listing of the numerous mills Textron liquidated between 1947 and 1957, see the table compiled by the TWUA research department in Mss. 396, box 419, Textron folder, TWUA Rcds.

7 *TL*, July 3, 1948, p. 1; Aug. 21, 1948, p. 11; U.S. Congress, Senate, Subcommittee of the Committee on Interstate and Foreign Commerce, *Investigation of Closing of Nashua, New Hampshire Mills and Operations of Textron, Inc.*, 80th Cong., 2d sess. (Washington, D.C.: U.S. Government Printing Office, 1948), p. 76; *TL*, Jan. 8, 1949, p. 2; Textron, Inc., Esmond Mills, and TWUA, Arbitration Decision, 1949, box 31, folder 369, National Association of Cotton Manufacturers/Northern Textile Association Records (NACM/NTA Rcds.), MATH.

8 U.S. Senate, *Investigation of Textron Operations*, pp. 68–72, 110–11.

9 Margaret Terrell Parker, *Lowell: A Study of Industrial Development* (rpt.; Port Washington, N.Y.: Kennikat Press, 1970), pp. 183–85; Gary Gerstle, *Working-Class Americanism: The Politics of Labor in a Textile City, 1914–1960* (Cambridge, Eng.: Cambridge University Press, 1989), pp. 97–101; L. D. H. Weld, "Specialization in the Woolen and Worsted Industry," *Quarterly Journal of Economics* 27 (Nov. 1912): 77–78; *Report on the New*

England Textile Industry by Committee Appointed by the New England Governors (1952), p. 97.

10 Donald N. Anderson, "The Decline of the Woolen and Worsted Industry of New England, 1947–1958" (Ph.D. diss., New York University, 1971), pp. 35–37; James A. Morris, *Woolen and Worsted Manufacturing in the Southern Piedmont* (Columbia: University of South Carolina Press, 1952), pp. 47–61; "New England Textile Problems: An Outline for Discussion by TWUA Representatives," TWUA Research Department, Jan. 29, 1952, p. 6; quotation in Sumner D. Charm, "Textile Twilight, New England," p. 3, last two items in Mss. 129A, file 1A, box 16, Research Department 1952 folder, TWUA Rcds.

11 First quotation in Council of Economic Advisors, Committee on the New England Economy, *The New England Economy: A Report to the President* (Washington, D.C.: U.S. Government Printing Office, 1951), p. 164; Edward G. Roddy, *Mills, Mansions, and Mergers: The Life of William M. Wood* (North Andover, Mass.: Merrimack Valley Textile Museum, 1982), p. 115; remaining quotations in Dero A. Saunders, "The Twilight of American Woolen," *Fortune* 49 (March 1954): 198. Although published in 1954, the Saunders article, as the author made clear, described problems that had plagued American Woolen for some time.

12 Charm, "Textile Twilight, New England," p. 1. Obsolete plant was also a major problem for New England cotton manufacturers. See, for example, Royal Little's observations in *New England Governors' Report* (1952), p. 118.

13 Saunders, "Twilight of American Woolen," pp. 198, 94–96.

14 NAWM, Meeting of the Executive Committee, Dec. 21, 1950, box 17, NAWM Rcds.; Saunders, "Twilight of American Woolen," p. 198; quotation in NAWM, Meeting of the Executive Committee, June 17, 1947, box 16, NAWM Rcds.; Notes on the Woolen and Worsted Conference, Dec. 6–7, 1941, p. 18, Mss. 129A, file 1A, box 20, TWUA Rcds.

15 "Mill Closings: Their Causes and Consequences," TWUA Research Department, July 20, 1954, pp. 4–6, Mss. 396, box 104; Economic Notes, TWUA Woolen and Worsted Industry Conference, May 27, 1950, pp. 1–5, Mss. 129A, file 1A, box 21; H. A. Griffin to A. B. Walls, Jr., Mar. 5, 1948; A. B. Walls, Jr., to Emil Rieve, Mar. 9, 1948, both letters in Mss. 396, box 34, American Woolen folder; Minutes, TWUA Executive Council, Oct. 22–25, 1949, pp. 7, 20–21; June 19–22, 1950, p. 21, Mss. 396, box 6, all items in TWUA Rcds.; Arthur A. Bright, Jr., and George H. Ellis, eds., *The Economic State of New England: Report of the Committee on New England of the National Planning Association* (New Haven: Yale University Press, 1954), p. 342; John A. Hogan, "Employment and Collective Bargaining Problems in the American Woolen and Worsted Industry" (Ph.D. diss., Harvard University, 1952), p. 342; Charm, "Textile Twilight, New England," pp. 1–2; Morris, *Woolen and Worsted Manufacturing*, pp. 60, 71, 103–104, 109, 115–17.

16 Statement of Solomon Barkin before the Subcommittee of the Senate In-

terstate and Foreign Commerce Committee Investigating the Textile Industry, July 9, 1958, table 6, Bound Notebook 12, Solomon Barkin Papers (BN-12, SBP), Special Collections and Archives, W. E. B. Du Bois Library, University of Massachusetts–Amherst, Amherst, Massachusetts; *TL*, Jan. 8, 1949, pp. 1, 12; Fall River Textile Manufacturers Association (FRTMA), New Bedford Cotton Manufacturers Association (NBCMA), and TWUA, Arbitration Decision, Jan. 15, 1949, box 31, folder 372, NACM/NTA Rcds.; *TL*, Feb. 5, 1949, pp. 1, 3; Minutes, New Bedford Joint Board, Sept. 18, 1949, box 1, NB Jt. Bd. Rcds.; quotation in Minutes, Cotton and Rayon Conference, Jan. 6, 1950, p. 3, Mss. 129A, file 1A, box 4, TWUA Rcds.

17 Industrial Relations Notes and Comments, July 5, 1949, box 116, NAWM Rcds.

18 First quotation in *Investigation of Textron Operations*, pp. 12–13; Dunwell, *Run of the Mill*, pp. 161–62; William F. Sullivan to W. J. Ryan, Dec. 17, 1951, box 37, folder 462, NACM/NTA Rcds.; Massachusetts House of Representatives, "Report of the Unpaid Special Commission Relative to the Investigation and Study of the Textile Industry and to Prevent Removal Thereof from the Commonwealth," *Document No. 2590*, 1950, p. 32; second quotation in Seabury Stanton to Ray R. Murdock, Oct. 20, 1950, box 35, folder 423, NACM/NTA Rcds.

19 First quotation in *TL*, June 18, 1949, p. 5; Charles A. Myers and George P. Shultz, *The Dynamics of a Labor Market: A Study of the Impact of Employment Changes on Labor Mobility, Job Satisfactions, and Company and Union Policies* (New York: Prentice-Hall, Inc., 1951), pp. 149–51; *Bulletin of the National Association of Wool Manufacturers* (*NAWM Bull.*) 64 (1934): 287–88; 65 (1935): 400–401; J. F. Morrissey to R. T. Fisher, July 3, 1933, box 4, folder 35, NACM/NTA Rcds.; Hathaway Manufacturing Company and TWUA, General Statement by Francis Vaas, June 10, 1952, p. 11, box 7, folder 77, NB Jt. Bd. Rcds.

20 First quotation in *TL*, Sept. 17, 1949, p. 4; Minutes, Executive Council, Oct. 22–25, 1949, p. 21, Mss. 396, box 6; "New England Textile Problems: An Outline for Discussion by TWUA Representatives," TWUA Research Department, Jan. 29, 1952, p. 9, Mss. 129A, file 1A, box 16; second quotation in Solomon Barkin to Emil Rieve, Oct. 20, 1949, Mss. 129A, file 1A, box 14, all three items in TWUA Rcds.; final quotation in Minutes, Columbia University Seminar on Labor, Dec. 12, 1956, pp. 7–8, BN-10, SBP. Woolen manufacturers later agreed to give workers technological severance pay.

21 Arthur Besse, Address before the Seminar on Labor Relations, Philadelphia Textile Institute, July 11, 1946, in *NAWM Bull.* 76 (1946): 488; William F. Sullivan to John A. Hogan (draft letter), July 1951, box 35, folder 422; William F. Sullivan to Seabury Stanton, Dec. 12, 1950, box 35, folder 423, both items in NACM/NTA Rcds.; Robert Sidney Smith, *Mill on the Dan: A History of Dan River Mills, 1882–1950* (Durham, N.C.: Duke University Press, 1960), p. 499.

22 Brief Submitted by the NBCMA and Nashawena Mills, Aug. 24, 1949, box 8, folder 100, NB Jt. Bd. Rcds.

23 Reply of TWUA to Association's Written Statement, Sept. 26, 1949, box 8, folder 100, NB Jt. Bd. Rcds.

24 Union/Company Agreements, appendix C, box 17, folder 235; FRTMA, NBCMA, and TWUA, Arbitration Decision No. 10, Sept. 27, 1949, box 10, folder 156; FRTMA, NBCMA, and TWUA, Arbitration Decision No. 22, June 13, 1949, box 9, folder 117; FRTMA, NBCMA, and TWUA, Arbitration Decision No. 25, Sept. 3, 1949, box 11, folder 158; FRTMA, NBCMA, and TWUA, Arbitration Decision No. 2, April 26, 1950, box 11, folder 170; Fisk Cord Mills and TWUA, Arbitration Decision, Nov. 14, 1952, box 11, folder 166, all items in NB Jt. Bd. Rcds. For an earlier decision requiring maintenance of average hourly earnings, see FRTMA, NBCMA, and TWUA, Arbitration Decision No. 11, Sept. 29, 1947, box 31, folder 368, NACM/NTA Rcds.

25 FRTMA, NBCMA, and TWUA, Arbitration Decision No. 1, March 23, 1950, box 11, folder 170, NB Jt. Bd. Rcds.; FRTMA (Pepperell) and TWUA, Arbitration Decision #FR 1, box 36, folder 441, NACM/NTA Rcds. Not all arbitrators accepted management contentions about the nature of worker resistance to workload increases. Discussion with union leaders led woolen arbitrator John Hogan to conclude that employer contentions "that opposition to work assignment changes is based on custom, unwillingness to venture change and laziness have been greatly exaggerated." "Employment and Collective Bargaining Problems," pp. 279–80.

26 First quotation in Minutes of the American Woolen Company Advisory Council, July 8, 1950, Mss. 396, box 34, TWUA Rcds.; second quotation in *New England Governors' Report* (1952), p. 173; 1951 Overseers Seminar, part II, pp. 10–11, box 214, NAWM Rcds.; final quotation in Minutes, Executive Council, Oct. 22–25, 1949, p. 21, Mss. 396, box 6, TWUA Rcds.; Hogan, "Employment and Collective Bargaining Problems," pp. 311–12.

27 FRTMA, NBCMA, and TWUA, Arbitration Decision No. 30, Mar. 7, 1950, box 8, folder 100; Cluett, Peabody, and Co., Inc., and TWUA, Arbitration Decision, Sept. 5, 1950, box 7, folder 77, both cases in NB Jt. Bd. Rcds. Two important earlier rulings on the wage-productivity question are FRTMA and TWUA, Case No. L-676, Aug. 14, 1944, box 21, folder 235; and Statement of Policy Adopted by Agreement of the Textile Directive Steering Committee and TWUA, June 1, 1945, box 24, folder 261, both in NACM/NTA Rcds. In the 1944 case, an arbitrator urged that workers be given part of the savings made possible by new machinery; the 1945 policy statement endorsed employer claims that the practice was unsound, and "that the benefits should be shared by all workers through general wage increases."

28 Solomon Barkin to Emil Rieve, Jan. 13, 1949, Mss. 129A, file 7A, box 15; Franklin G. Bishop to George Carignan, Mar. 23, 1949, Mss. 396, box 328, Nashawena Mills folder; Solomon Barkin to John Chupka, Aug. 3, 1951,

Mss. 129A, file 7A, box 15; Mariano Bishop to Northern State Directors and Cotton and Rayon Joint Board Managers, July 17, 1952, Mss. 129A, file 1A, box 1; final quotation in Report of Field Investigation, Berkshire Hathaway Inc., Nov. 29, 1960, Mss. 396, box 363, all five items in TWUA Rcds.; author interview with Solomon Barkin, June 22, 1992. Hugh G. J. Aitken provides an excellent critique of the reputed objectivity of time studies in *Scientific Management in Action: Taylorism at Watertown Arsenal, 1908–1915* (rpt.; Princeton: Princeton University Press, 1985), pp. 23–27. The difficulties hosiery arbitrators faced in assessing time studies are discussed in Thomas Kennedy, *Effective Labor Arbitration: The Impartial Chairmanship of the Full-Fashioned Hosiery Industry* (Philadelphia: University of Pennsylvania Press, 1948), pp. 72–77.

29 Quotations in "An Evaluation of the Arbitration of TWUA Cases," TWUA Research Department, Oct. 1949, pp. 6, 12, BN-3, SBP; Solomon Barkin to Herbert Payne, Mariano Bishop, and John Chupka, Jan. 8, 1951, Mss. 129A, file 7A, box 15, TWUA Rcds.

30 Robert H. Zieger, *American Workers, American Unions, 1920–1985* (Baltimore: The Johns Hopkins University Press, 1986), pp. 108–14; Christopher L. Tomlins, *The State and the Unions: Labor Relations, Law, and the Organized Labor Movement, 1880–1960* (Cambridge, Eng.: Cambridge University Press, 1985), pp. 282–316; Nelson Lichtenstein, "From Corporatism to Collective Bargaining: Organized Labor and the Eclipse of Social Democracy in the Postwar Era," in *The Rise and Fall of the New Deal Order, 1930–1980*, ed. Steve Fraser and Gary Gerstle (Princeton: Princeton University Press, 1989), p. 134.

31 Abstract, Lawrence Rogin interview, p. 22, Mss. 467; Minutes, Executive Council, May 21, 1949, pp. 61, 67–68, Mss. 396, box 6; Abstract, Joseph Heuter interview, p. 14, Mss. 467, all three items in TWUA Rcds.; *TL*, May 13, 1950, pp. 1–4.

32 William F. Hartford, *Working People of Holyoke: Class and Ethnicity in a Massachusetts Mill Town, 1850–1960* (New Brunswick, N.J.: Rutgers University Press, 1990), pp. 199–200; Bruce Saxon, "Fall River and the Decline of the New England Textile Industry, 1949–1954," *Historical Journal of Massachusetts* 16 (Jan. 1988): 56, 65; *TL*, Oct. 7, 1950, p. 4.

33 *TL*, Oct. 7, 1950, p. 4; Sept. 16, 1950, pp. 1, 3; quotation in *TL*, Jan. 6, 1951, pp. 1, 3.

34 *TL*, Oct. 7, 1950, p. 1; *American Wool and Cotton Reporter* (Oct. 19, 1950), in Mss. 396, box 419, Textron folder, TWUA Rcds.; quotations in William F. Sullivan to Walter Neale, Jan. 22, 1951, box 35, folder 414, NACM/NTA Rcds.; *TL*, Sept. 16, 1950, pp. 1, 3; Mar. 17, 1951, pp. 1, 3. In a later memo, William Sullivan shed light on the extent to which the strike threat influenced manufacturers during the March negotiations. "A certain mill," Sullivan noted, "figures that a six weeks' strike beginning on March 15, would have cost it $836,000. The cost per week of the new wage increase is $7736. In other words it would have taken 108 weeks . . . to off-set the loss

of a six-week strike, providing that the result of the strike was no wage increase whatsoever." Memo from WFS to WFS, Sept. 17, 1951, box 35, folder 423, NACM/NTA Rcds.

35   *TL*, Oct. 7, 1950, p. 1; NAWM, Meeting of the Executive Committee, Oct. 17, 1950, box 17; Jan. 16, 1951, box 18, NAWM Rcds.; *TL*, Mar. 17, 1951, pp. 1, 4.

36   Minutes, Executive Council, June 29, 1951, pp. 2493–97, Mss. 396, box 3, TWUA Rcds.; *TL*, Apr. 7, 1951, p. 4.

37   Minutes, Executive Council, Jan. 22, 1951, pp. 173–74, Mss. 396, box 4, TWUA Rcds.; William F. Sullivan, memo, Nov. 28, 1950, box 38, folder 468, NACM/NTA Rcds.; first quotation in Mariano Bishop to Emil Rieve, Jan. 31, 1951, Mss. 129A, file 1A, box 4, Northern Cotton, Silk, and Rayon folder; George Baldanzi to Emil Rieve, Jan. 19, 1951, Mss. 129A, file 1A, box 1; final quotation in Minutes, Executive Council, Jan. 22, 1951, p. 179, Mss. 396, box 4, all three items in TWUA Rcds.

38   *TL*, Oct. 21, 1950, p. 6; Report on Southern Strike, June 26, 1951, p. 1, Mss. 129A, file 5A, box 1, TWUA Rcds.; Seabury Stanton to Ray R. Murdock, Oct. 20, 1950, box 35, folder 423, NACM/NTA Rcds.; *TL*, Apr. 7, 1951, pp. 1, 3.

39   Barbara S. Griffith, *The Crisis of American Labor: Operation Dixie and the Defeat of the CIO* (Philadelphia: Temple University Press, 1988), pp. 36, 42–43, 161–62; Minutes, New Bedford Joint Board, Dec. 5, 1948, Jan. 15, 1949, box 1, NB Jt. Bd. Rcds.; Minutes, Lawrence Joint Board, Dec. 5, 1948, box 86, TWUA Collection, MATH.

40   Solomon Barkin, *The Decline of the Labor Movement and What Can Be Done about It* (Santa Barbara, Calif.: Center for the Study of Democratic Institutions, 1961), p. 21; "Textile Barons Keep Southern Mill Hands in Their 'Place,'" TWUA Research Department, June 28, 1949, BN-3, SBP; U.S. Congress, Senate, Subcommittee on Labor-Management Relations of the Committee on Labor and Public Welfare, *Hearing on Labor-Management Relations in the Southern Textile Industry Pursuant to S. Res. 140*, 81st Cong., 2d sess. (Washington, D.C.: U.S. Government Printing Office, 1951), pp. 84–85, 101–46, Morse quotation on pp. 363–64.

41   Mary Sperling McAuliffe, *Crisis on the Left: Cold War Politics and American Liberals, 1947–1954* (Amherst: The University of Massachusetts Press, 1978), pp. 51–62; Griffith, *Crisis of American Labor*, p. 155; Michael K. Honey, *Southern Labor and Black Civil Rights: Organizing Memphis Workers* (Urbana: University of Illinois Press, 1993), chap. 9. For a different perspective on this question, see Solomon Barkin's observations in "'Operation Dixie': Two Points of View," *Labor History* 31 (Summer 1990): 384.

42   Minutes, Executive Council, Oct. 22–25, 1949, pp. 49–52, Mss. 396, box 6, TWUA Rcds.

43   Minutes, Northern Cotton and Rayon Conference, Jan. 6, 1950, Mss. 129A, file 1A, box 4, TWUA Rcds.; quotation in William F. Sullivan, memo, Jan. 24, 1951, box 38, folder 468, NACM/NTA Rcds.

44 Seabury Stanton, draft of a statement on wage competition, Jan. 2, 1951, box 35, folder 423; William F. Sullivan, memo, Jan. 24, 1951, box 38, folder 468, both items in NACM/NTA Rcds.

45 Quotation in Minutes, Executive Council, June 26, 1951, pp. 1818–19, Mss. 396, box 3, TWUA Rcds.; William F. Sullivan, memo, Apr. 2, 1951, box 38, folder 468, NACM/NTA Rcds.

46 Quotation in Minutes, Executive Council, June 27, 1951, p. 2045, Mss. 396, box 3; abstract, Solomon Barkin interview, p. 27, Mss. 467; abstract, William Gordon interview, p. 10, Mss. 467, all three items in TWUA Rcds.

47 Quotation in Report on Southern Strike, June 26, 1951, p. 4, Mss. 129A, file 5A, box 1; Minutes, Meeting of the Cotton Rayon Policy Committee, Apr. 18, 1951, pp. 11, 13–14, Mss. 129A, file 1A, box 20, both items in TWUA Rcds.

48 First quotation in *TL*, Apr. 21, 1951; Minutes, Meeting of the Cotton Rayon Policy Committee, Apr. 18, 1951, pp. 4–6, second quotation on p. 4; Report on Southern Strike, pp. 6–7.

49 Ken Kramer to Emil Rieve, May 15, 1951, Mss. 129A, file 1A, box 20, TWUA Rcds.; Report on Southern Strike, pp. 7–8, 13; Minutes, Meeting of the Cotton Rayon Policy Committee, Apr. 18, 1951, pp. 3–4, 6–7, 11–12, quotations on pp. 3–4.

50 Quotation in William F. Sullivan to Seabury Stanton, May 8, 1951, box 35, folder 423, NACM/NTA Rcds.; *TL*, Nov. 17, 1951, p. 5; Report on Southern Strike, pp. 9–16.

51 Rubinstein quotation in Minutes, Executive Council, June 28, 1951, p. 2257; Minutes, Executive Council, June 26, 1951, pp. 1803–1804, both items in Mss. 396, box 3, TWUA Rcds.; *TL*, May 19, 1951, p. 5; abstract, William Gordon interview, p. 11, Mss. 467, TWUA Rcds.

52 Bishop quotation in Minutes, Executive Council, June 28, 1951, p. 2303; Minutes, Executive Council, June 26, 1951, p. 1810, both items in Mss. 396, box 3, TWUA Rcds.; William F. Sullivan to Seabury Stanton, May 8, 1951, box 35, folder 423; Report of the President and Secretary, NACM annual meeting, Sept. 25–26, 1952, both items in NACM/NTA Rcds.

53 T. M. Stanback, Jr., "The Textile Cycle: Characteristics and Contributing Factors," *Southern Economic Journal* 25 (Oct. 1958): 174–88; Seabury Stanton to Emil Rieve, June 29, 1951, box 35, folder 423, NACM/NTA Rcds.

54 Address by Seabury Stanton before the NACM, Sept. 13, 1951, box 37, folder 463; Address by Seabury Stanton before the Rhode Island Textile Association, Oct. 24, 1951, box 35, folder 414, both items in NACM/NTA Rcds.; Seabury Stanton to Solomon Barkin, Sept. 18, 1951; Solomon Barkin to Seabury Stanton, Sept. 24, 1951; Seabury Stanton to All Employees of the Rayon Division, Dec. 3, 1951, all three items in box 35, folder 423, NACM/NTA Rcds.; Hathaway Manufacturing Company and TWUA, General Statement, June 10, 1952, box 7, folder 77, NB Jt. Bd. Rcds.

55 A. W. Macy to Albert A. List, Apr. 9, 1952, box 42, folder 516, NACM/NTA Rcds.; Solomon Barkin to Emil Rieve and Mariano Bishop, July 2,

1952, Mss. 129A, file 1A, box 16, TWUA Rcds.; Walter B. Gallant, Jr., to Kenneth B. Cook, Oct. 8, 1951, box 34, folder 441, NACM/NTA Rcds.; *NYT*, Oct. 28, 1951, 3:1; Mar. 6, 1952, p. 38; Oct. 2, 1952, p. 43; *New England Governors' Report* (1952), p. 121; final quotation in memo from LA to WFS, Feb. 1, 1955, box 54, folder 629, NACM/NTA Rcds.

56 *Boston Evening Globe*, Dec. 26, 1951, in J. William Belanger Scrapbooks (JWB Scrapbooks), Special Collections and Archives, W. E. B. Du Bois Library, University of Massachusetts–Amherst, Amherst, Massachusetts; Address by Mariano Bishop, Jan. 26, 1952, box 6, Officer Installations folder, NB Jt. Bd. Rcds.

57 Bates Manufacturing Company and TWUA, Arbitration Decision, June 15, 1952, box 7, folder 77, NB Jt. Bd. Rcds.; FRTMA, NBCMA, Berkshire Fine Spinning Associates, Inc., and TWUA, Arbitration Decision, July 15, 1952, box 40, folder 496, NACM/NTA Rcds.

58 Stetin and Belanger quotations in Minutes, Executive Council, June 17, 1952, pp. 26–27, Mss. 396, box 7, TWUA Rcds.; TWUA Executive Council Resolution on Bates Arbitration Decision, June 17, 1952, box 7, folder 77, NB Jt. Bd. Rcds.

59 Minutes, Executive Council, June 28, 1951, pp. 2297, 2273, Mss. 396, box 3, TWUA Rcds.

60 Abstract, William Gordon interview, p. 10, Mss. 467; Minutes, Executive Council, June 28, 1951, p. 2216, Mss. 396, box 3; "The Boston Meeting That Baldanzi Didn't Hold," ca. Aug. 1951, pp. 2–3, Mss. 129A, file 3A, box 4; Chupka quotation in Minutes, Executive Council, June 29, 1951, pp. 2502–2503, Mss. 396, box 3; Minutes of the Woolen and Worsted Policy Committee, July 11, 1951, pp. 48–49, Mss. 396, box 584, all items in TWUA Rcds.

61 Abstract, Kenneth Fiester interview, pp. 15, 12; abstract, Solomon Barkin interview, p. 15; abstract, Lawrence Rogin interview, pp. 11, 21–22, all three items in Mss. 467, TWUA Rcds.

62 *Boston Traveler*, Feb. 28, 1952; *New Bedford Standard-Times*, Mar. 25, 1951, both items in Biographical File, reel P68-1977; *Retail Clerks Advocate*, Nov. 1957, in Biographical File, reel P68-1978; abstract, Solomon Barkin interview, p. 7, Mss. 467; abstract, Sol Stetin interview, p. 19, Mss. 467, all items in TWUA Rcds.; Donald R. Stabile, *Activist Unionism: The Institutional Economics of Solomon Barkin* (Armonk, N.Y.: M. E. Sharpe, 1993), pp. 136–37.

63 Abstract, William Gordon interview, p. 8; abstract, Sol Stetin interview, pp. 17–18; abstract, Lawrence Rogin interview, p. 22; abstract, Joseph Heuter interview, p. 14, all four items in Mss. 467, TWUA Rcds.

64 Abstract, William Gordon interview, p. 8; abstract, Solomon Barkin interview, p. 27, both items in Mss. 467; Charles Hughes to Sam Baron, Mar. 13, 1951, Mss. 396, box 11, Baldanzi folder; abstract, Lawrence Rogin interview, p. 22, Mss. 467, all four items in TWUA Rcds. Rieve supporters

had a much different view of the Baldanzi team, especially Hughes and Baron. One report observed, "Around Baldanzi have rallied two ambitious and unhappy fellow travelers of the labor movement[:] . . . Hughes, a failure as a staff member and a known anti-Semite, and Baron, former theater manager and a person who has managed to get himself fired from the staffs of three unions." Eyewitness Report of the Baldanzi "Rump" Conference, July 21–22, 1951, Mss. 129A, file 3A, box 4, TWUA Rcds.

65 Abstract, Solomon Barkin interview, p. 27, Mss. 467; *Saturday Night* (Apr. 11, 1950); quotation in *New Liberty* (Dec. 1951), both items in Biographical File, reel P68-1975; Minutes, Executive Council, June 8, 1951, Mss. 396, box 1, all four items in TWUA Rcds.

66 *Saturday Night* (Apr. 11, 1950); *New Liberty* (Dec. 1951); quotations in Minutes, Executive Council, June 7, 1951, pp. 552–53, Mss. 396, box 3, all three items in TWUA Rcds.

67 Analysis of Baldanzi's Paper, Feb. 11, 1952; Analysis of Structural Changes Proposed by the Opposition, Sept. 17, 1951; first quotation in The Pre-Convention Committee for a Democratic TWUA, Statement of Policy, 1952, all three items in Mss. 129A, file 3A, box 4; second quotation in Reba Gilpin to Emil Rieve, Sept. 7, 1951, Mss. 396, box 11, Political folder, all four items in TWUA Rcds.

68 Abstract, Kenneth Fiester interview, p. 13, Mss. 467; Minutes, Executive Council, June 7, 1951, p. 492, Mss. 396, box 3; Minutes, New England Staff Meeting, Feb. 7, 1942, Mss. 129A, file 1A, box 11, all three items in TWUA Rcds.

69 *TL*, July 7, 1951, p. 1; Baldanzi quotation in *TL*, Sept. 8, 1951, p. 2; abstract, William Gordon interview, p. 10, Mss. 467, TWUA Rcds. It should be added that some Baldanzi supporters took the democracy issue very seriously. See, for example, Sam Fiore to Sol Stetin, ca. May 1951, Mss. 396, box 11, Baldanzi folder, TWUA Rcds.

70 William F. Sullivan, memo, Nov. 28, 1950, box 38, folder 468, NACM/NTA Rcds.; Minutes, Lowell Joint Board, Aug. 2, 1951, Sept. 6, 1951, box 119, TWUA Collection, MATH; *Berkshire County Eagle*, Mar. 14, 1951, in JWB Scrapbooks; Minutes, New Bedford Joint Board, Aug. 5, 1951, box 1, NB Jt. Bd. Rcds.

71 *TL*, May 10, 1952, pp. 1, 12.

72 *TL*, May 10, 1952, p. 12; abstract, William Gordon interview, p. 11, Mss. 467, TWUA Rcds.

73 Minutes, Executive Council, May 25–28, 1953, p. 24, Mss. 396, box 7; Kenneth Fiester to Solomon Barkin, Dec. 29, 1952, Mss. 129A, file 7A, box 16; Emanuel Boggs to John Harkins, et al., July 17, 1952, Mss. 396, box 11, Secession Movement folder, all three items in TWUA Rcds.; *TL*, Nov. 8, 1952, p. 2; May 2, 1953, p. 8.

74 Minutes, Executive Council, May 25–28, 1953, p. 24, Mss. 396, box 7, TWUA Rcds.

SIX. THE COLLAPSE, 1952–1960

1   U.S. Congress, Senate, Committee on Interstate and Foreign Commerce, *Report Made by a Special Subcommittee Pursuant to S. Res. 287 on Problems of the Domestic Textile Industry*, 86th Cong., 1st sess. (Washington, D.C.: U.S. Government Printing Office, 1959), pp. 2–4, 7–8; Bernard Nossiter, "Slump in Textiles," *New Republic* 181 (Dec. 22, 1955): 72; "The Substitution of Plastic and Paper Products for Textiles in the United States," TWUA Research Department, Apr. 1957, in Bound Notebook 11, Solomon Barkin Papers (BN-11, SBP), Special Collections and Archives, W. E. B. Du Bois Library, University of Massachusetts–Amherst, Amherst, Massachusetts; Solomon Barkin, Statement before the Joint Committee of the Economic Report on the Textile Industry as a Depressed Industry, Jan. 27, 1955, pp. 8–9, BN-9, SBP.

2   Steve Dunwell, *The Run of the Mill: A Pictorial Narrative of the Expansion, Dominion, Decline and Enduring Impact of the New England Textile Industry* (Boston: David R. Godine, Publisher, 1978), p. 147; Seymour E. Harris, *The Economics of New England: Case Study of an Older Area* (Cambridge: Harvard University Press, 1952), p. 130; Harris, "The Merger Movement in Textiles," July 7, 1955, pp. 5–7, 13, 15–16, in box 54, folder 632, National Association of Cotton Manufacturers/Northern Textile Association Records (NACM/NTA Rcds.), Museum of American Textile History, North Andover–Lowell, Massachusetts (MATH); U.S. Congress, Senate, Subcommittee on Antitrust and Monopoly of the Committee on the Judiciary, *Hearings to Study the Antitrust Laws of the United States, and Their Administration, Interpretation, and Effect Pursuant to S. Res. 61*, 84th Cong., 1st sess. (Washington, D.C.: U.S. Government Printing Office, 1955), pp. 765–80; Barkin, Statement on the Textile Industry as a Depressed Industry, p. 10.

3   Harris, "Merger Movement in Textiles," pp. 6–12; U.S. Senate, *Hearings to Study the Antitrust Laws*, pp. 765–66, 770–77; Seymour Harris to Emmanuel Cellar, June 28, 1955, in U.S. Congress, House of Representatives, Subcommittee No. 5 of the Committee on the Judiciary, *Staff Report on the Merger Movement in the Textile Industry*, 84th Cong., 1st sess. (Washington, D.C.: U.S. Government Printing Office, 1955), pp. 36–37; Dunwell, *Run of the Mill*, p. 160. Union efforts to reform tax laws that facilitated mill liquidations will be examined in Chapter Seven.

4   Memo re Collins and Aiken, 1953, box 44, folder 542, NACM/NTA Rcds.; *CIO News*, Feb. 4, 1952, p. 2; *Boston Record*, Feb. 23, 1952; *Kennebec Journal*, June 21, 1954; *Fall River Herald News*, May 15, 1957, all three items in J. William Belanger Scrapbooks (JWB Scrapbooks), Special Collections and Archives, W. E. B. Du Bois Library, University of Massachusetts–Amherst, Amherst, Massachusetts; Arthur A. Bright, Jr., and George H. Ellis, eds., *The Economic State of New England: Report of the Committee of New England of the National Planning Association* (New Haven: Yale University

Press, 1954), pp. 439–41; abstract, Lawrence Rogin interview, p. 28, Mss. 467; Minutes, Executive Council, Jan. 22, 1952, pp. 180–81, Mss. 396, box 4, both items in Textile Workers Union of America Records (TWUA Rcds.), State Historical Society of Wisconsin Archives, Madison, Wisconsin (SHSW); William H. Miernyk, *Inter-Industry Labor Mobility: The Case of the Displaced Textile Worker* (Boston: Northeastern University, 1955), pp. 5–6; final quotation in William F. Sullivan to Member Mills, General Bulletin No. 2, Feb. 2, 1956, p. 4, box 55, folder 644, NACM/NTA Rcds.

5   Minutes, Greater Lawrence Citizens' Committee for Industrial Development (GLCCID), June 13, 1950, p. 2, Immigrant City Archives, Lawrence, Massachusetts; first quotation in notes on Public Relations, Jan. 1951, box 38, folder 468; second quotation in William F. Sullivan, draft address, "The New England Textile Industry," Nov. 1955, box 51, folder 600, both items in NACM/NTA Rcds.; Solomon Barkin to William Pollock, July 16, 1954, Mss. 129A, file 7A, box 17, TWUA Rcds.

6   "They Said It Couldn't Be Done: A History of the Textile Workers Union of America, AFL-CIO, CLC," TWUA, n.d., p. 11; William H. Miernyk, *New England Textile Employment in 1970* (Federal Reserve Bank of Boston Research Report, Dec. 1959), p. 2; U.S. Senate, *Report on Problems of Textile Industry*, pp. 6–7, 20–21.

7   Ken Fiester to Solomon Barkin, Dec. 29, 1952, Mss. 129A, file 7A, box 16; Barkin quotation in Minutes, Staff Meeting, Dec. 18, 1952, Mss. 129A, file 1A, box 5, both items in TWUA Rcds. Between 1951 and 1958, the union lost 164,770 members. Solomon Barkin, *The Decline of the Labor Movement and What Can Be Done about It* (Santa Barbara, Calif.: Center for the Study of Democratic Institutions, 1961), p. 11.

8   Minutes, Meeting of the Executive Committee, Dec. 16, 1947, box 16, National Association of Wool Manufacturers Records (NAWM Rcds.), MATH; Minutes, Meeting of the Executive Committee, Sept. 18, 1951, June 17, 1952, box 18, NAWM Rcds.

9   Economic Notes: TWUA Woolen and Worsted Conference, Jan. 9, 1954, pp. 1, 3–4, Mss. 396, box 103, Solomon Barkin folder; Economic Notes: TWUA Woolen and Worsted Conference, June 27, 1953, pp. 1–4, Mss. 396, box 34, American Woolen Folder; quotation from *Boston Herald*, Feb. 10, 1952, in Statement of the TWUA, CIO, in the Matter of Arbitration with American Woolen Company, Mar. 25, 1953, p. 12, Mss. 396, box 580, all three items in TWUA Rcds.

10   Economic Notes: TWUA Woolen and Worsted Conference, June 27, 1953, pp. 5–7; Economic Notes: TWUA New England Staff Conference, Sept. 30, 1954, pp. 1, 5, Mss. 396, box 103, Cotton-Rayon Conference folder, both items in TWUA Rcds.

11   Miernyk, *Inter-Industry Mobility*, pp. 56–57; Royal Little, *How to Lose $100,000,000 and Other Valuable Advice* (Boston: Little, Brown and Company, 1979), pp. 136–37; Statement of the TWUA, CIO, in the Matter of Arbitration with American Woolen Company, Mar. 25, 1953, pp. 11–16.

12 Statement of the TWUA, CIO, in the Matter of Arbitration with American Woolen Company, Mar. 25, 1953, pp. 17–20.

13 American Woolen Company v. TWUA, Arbitration Decision, May 19, 1953, pp. 7–8, New Bedford Joint Board Records (NB Jt. Bd. Rcds.), Special Collections and Archives, W. E. B. Du Bois Library, University of Massachusetts–Amherst, Amherst, Massachusetts; quotation in NAWM, memo to members, May 25, 1953, box 43, folder 525, NACM/NTA Rcds.

14 TWUA press release, Jan. 14, 1954, in JWB Scrapbooks.

15 *Textile Labor* (*TL*), Jan. 23, 1954, p. 2; Minutes, Executive Council, Oct. 17, 1950, pp. 284–87, Mss. 396, box 3; Minutes of the Woolen and Worsted Conference, Jan. 6, 1952, p. 8, Mss. 129A, file 1A, box 21; Minutes, Executive Council, Feb. 23–26, 1954, p. 14, Mss. 396, box 7, all three items in TWUA Rcds. Mill owners appear to have been well aware of the advantages dealing with the UTW offered them. In a letter to Seabury Stanton, one Lawrence manufacturer remarked, "Pacific has the AFL and a very favorable situation from what I am told." Kurtz M. Hanson to Seabury Stanton, Jan. 11, 1955, box 51, folder 598, NACM/NTA Rcds.

16 *TL*, Mar. 6, 1954, p. 1; Mar. 20, 1954, p. 1; May 15, 1954, p. 16; June 12, 1954, pp. 1, 3; Minutes, Meeting of the Board of Directors, June 9, 1954, box 19, NAWM Rcds.

17 Greater Lawrence Joint Board Monthly Report, Mar. 16, 1954, Mss. 129A, file 2A, box 18, TWUA Rcds.

18 Solomon Barkin to John Chupka, June 3, 1953, Mss. 129A, file 7A, box 16, TWUA Rcds.; Dero A. Saunders, "The Stormiest Merger Yet," *Fortune* 51 (Apr. 1955): 137, 171; quotations in *TL*, Apr. 3, 1954, pp. 1–2.

19 Saunders, "Stormiest Merger," p. 137; *New York Times* (*NYT*), Apr. 13, 1956, p. 33; draft of letter to individual New England senators, Mar. 9, 1954, Mss. 129A, file 1A, box 16, Solomon Barkin folder, TWUA Rcds.

20 First quotation in Saunders, "Stormiest Merger," p. 137; *NYT*, Apr. 13, 1956, pp. 33, 39; Dunwell, *Run of the Mill*, pp. 162–64; Little, *How to Lose $100,000,000*, pp. 137, 144–45, final quotation on p. 145.

21 Barkin quotation in Minutes, Woolen and Worsted Conference, Jan. 5, 1957, pp. 5–6, Mss. 396, box 610, TWUA Rcds.; NAWM, memo to members, Feb. 14, 1956, box 58, folder 676, NACM/NTA Rcds.; Solomon Barkin to Ken Fiester, Dec. 26, 1956, Mss. 396, box 610, Woolen and Worsted Negotiations folder, TWUA Rcds. Deering-Milliken and J. P. Stevens were especially vehement in their opposition to unions. Where on one occasion the former liquidated a Darlington, South Carolina, mill after workers voted to join the TWUA, J. P. Stevens refused to join the Northern Textile Association because "it wanted no formal connection with an organization that worked with unions." *NYT*, Oct. 18, 1956, p. 18; Oct. 23, 1958, p. 23; D. D. Gordon to William F. Sullivan, Feb. 8, 1961, box 108, folder 1180, NACM/NTA Rcds.

22 Solomon Barkin to Ken Fiester, Dec. 26, 1956, Mss. 396, box 610, Woolen and Worsted Negotiations folder; Greater Lawrence Joint Board Monthly

Report, Feb. 15, 1955, Mar. 16, 1954, Mss. 396, box 581, all three items in TWUA Rcds.; Minutes, Lawrence Joint Board, Dec. 3, 1954, Sept. 19, 1953, Apr. 3, 1955, Jan. 5, 1955, Sept. 9, 1956, TWUA Collection, MATH.

23 Solomon Barkin's Comments before TWUA Board, Nov. 28, 1955, Mss. 129A, file 1A, box 16; Greater Lawrence Joint Board Monthly Report, Feb. 15, 1955, Mss. 396, box 581, both items in TWUA Rcds.

24 *America's Textile Reporter* (May 14, 1954), in Mss. 129A, file 1A, box 21, Woolen and Worsted folder, TWUA Rcds.; Kurtz M. Hanson to Seabury Stanton, Jan. 11, 1955, box 51, folder 598, NACM/NTA Rcds.

25 Solomon Barkin, Statement before Subcommittee of the Senate Interstate and Foreign Commerce Committee Investigating the Textile Industry, July 9, 1958, table 6, BN-12, SBP; Miernyk, *Inter-Industry Mobility*, pp. 92, 110–12; Robert W. Eisenmenger, *The Dynamics of Growth in New England's Economy, 1870–1964* (Middletown, Conn.: Wesleyan University Press, 1967), p. 71; Harold Kuptzin, "Chronic Labor Surplus Areas: Characteristics and Trends," *Monthly Labor Review* 82 (Nov. 1959): 1212–14; Statement of Fall River–New Bedford Manufacturers, Mar. 24, 1955, p. 3, box 51, folder 598, NACM/NTA Rcds.

26 Bruce Saxon, "Fall River and the Decline of the New England Textile Industry, 1949–54," *Historical Journal of Massachusetts* 16 (1988): 71; quotation in *TL*, Apr. 4, 1953, p. 1; Eugene J. Audet to Emil Rieve, Oct. 14, 1954, Mss. 396, box 103, Denis Blais folder; Solomon Barkin to William Pollock, Aug. 16, 1954, Mss. 129A, file 7A, box 16, both items in TWUA Rcds.

27 *North Adams Transcript*, Jan. 12, 1953; *Fall River Herald News*, Feb. 10, 1954, both items in JWB Scrapbooks; New England Cotton-Rayon Mills, Wage Picture–1954, Dec. 23, 1953, box 44, folder 542, NACM/NTA Rcds.; Pepperell Manufacturing Company and TWUA, Arbitration Decision, May 17, 1954, box 7, folder 79, NB Jt. Bd. Rcds.

28 Harris, "Merger Movement in Textiles," p. 6; Jerome Campbell, "Berkshire Hathaway's Brave New Voyage," *Modern Textiles Magazine* (Dec. 1957): 57, 60, in Mss. 396, box 363, TWUA Rcds.

29 Seabury Stanton to Emil Rieve, Apr. 14, 1955, Mss. 396, box 105, TWUA Rcds.; Statement of Fall River–New Bedford Manufacturers, Mar. 24, 1955, pp. 14–15, box 52, folder 598; press release, Berkshire-Hathaway, Inc., Apr. 24, 1955, box 52, folder 620, both items in NACM/NTA Rcds.

30 Rieve quotation in Minutes, Executive Council, Apr. 26–29, p. 12, Mss. 396, box 7, TWUA Rcds.; *TL*, June 1955, p. 22; George Carignan to Victor Canzano, Feb. 8, 1955, Mss. 396, box 106, Wamsutta folder, TWUA Rcds.

31 *TL*, May 1955, pp. 22, 24; Seabury Stanton to Joseph L. Miller, Apr. 18, 1955, box 51, folder 599, NACM/NTA Rcds.; Janet Thompson Burns, "Textile Strike: 1955 Style," *New Republic* 133 (July 25, 1955): 11–12; quotations in undated memo, ca. May 1955, box 54, folder 630, NACM/NTA Rcds.; Berkshire Hathaway, Inc. to Our Employees, May 17, 1955, box 2, NB Jt. Bd. Rcds. This ambivalence was no doubt a reflection of what

William Miernyk described as the "curious mixture of optimism and pessimism" exhibited by textile workers whom he interviewed during the period. Miernyk, *Inter-Industry Mobility*, p. 53.

32 Solomon Barkin to Emil Rieve and Mariano Bishop, July 2, 1952, Mss. 129A, file 1A, box 16; Minutes, Executive Council, Apr. 26–29, 1955, pp. 8, 12, Mss. 396, box 7, both items in TWUA Rcds.; *TL*, May 1955, pp. 22, 24; June 1955, p. 24; Summary—New England Strike, Aug. 16, 1955, pp. 1–2, Mss. 396, box 105, TWUA Rcds.; Statement of Seabury Stanton, May 26, 1955, box 52, folder 620; Stanton quotation in Seabury Stanton to Brackett Parsons, Aug. 16, 1955, box 51, folder 599, both items in NACM / NTA Rcds.; final quotation in Notes on Department Directors Meetings, June 10, 1955, Mss. 129A, file 7A, box 17, TWUA Rcds.

33 Summary—New England Strike, Aug. 16, 1955, p. 2, TWUA, Mss. 396, box 105, TWUA Rcds.; *NYT*, July 24, 1955, p. 24; NTA to Member Mills, July 25, 1955, box 52, folder 620; Seabury Stanton to Brackett Parsons, Aug. 16, 1955, box 51, folder 599; Statement of Seabury Stanton, May 26, 1955, box 52, folder 620; William F. Sullivan to F. J. Vaas, Sept. 8, 1955, box 51, folder 599; final quotation in Memo for Mr. Rugg, Aug. 2, 1955, box 51, folder 599, all five items in NACM / NTA Rcds. The Rugg memo, which was most likely written by William Sullivan, contains an assessment of the advantages and disadvantages of Berkshire-Hathaway continuing its membership in the Fall River association.

34 Solomon Barkin to William Pollock, July 16, 1954, Mss. 129A, file 7A, box 17, TWUA Rcds.; Miernyk, *Inter-Industry Mobility*, p. 106.

35 Paul A. Tiffany, *The Decline of American Steel: How Management, Labor, and Government Went Wrong* (New York: Oxford University Press, 1988), pp. 84–86; Rieve and Payne quotations in Minutes, Executive Council, Oct. 17, 1950, pp. 199, 214, Mss. 396, box 2, TWUA Rcds.; final quotation in WFS, memo, Nov. 28, 1950, NACM / NTA Rcds.; Paul Mulkern, "Wages and Personal Income," *Monthly Labor Review* 80 (Mar. 1957): 299–300; "Earnings in the Cotton Textile Industry, August 1960," *Monthly Labor Review* 84 (May 1961): 479.

36 Ruhm quotations in Solomon Barkin to Emil Rieve and Mariano Bishop, July 2, 1952, Mss. 129A, file 1A, box 16, TWUA Rcds.; Little, *How to Lose $100,000,000*, p. 106; Leonard Arnold, "Labor Turnover in Textile Mills," *Monthly Labor Review* 80 (March 1957): 306; Douglas Pidgeon, "New England Textile Mills Face Skilled Labor Dearth," *Journal of Commerce*, Oct. 3, 1952, in Mss. 129A, file 7A, box 16, TWUA Rcds. By decade's end, Berkshire-Hathaway was looking to workers displaced by Canadian mill liquidations and southern textile strikes for skilled help. Seabury Stanton to Joseph Miller, Dec. 23, 1960, box 101, folder 1011, NACM / NTA Rcds.

37 U.S. Senate, *Report on Problems of Textile Industry*, p. 22; Solomon Barkin to Irving Kahn, ca. 1957, Mss. 129A, file 7A, box 18; quotations in Minutes, Cotton Rayon Conference, Dec. 4, 1955, pp. 3–6, Mss. 129A, file 1A, box 4, both items in TWUA Rcds.

38 TL, Aug. 1955, pp. 19, 24; Address by Emil Rieve, Sept. 1955, box 51, folder 599; William F. Sullivan, draft address, "The New England Textile Industry," Nov. 1955, p. 10, box 51, folder 600, both items in NACM/NTA Rcds.

39 TL, Oct. 1956, p. 24; May 1959, p. 24; abstract, George Perkel interview, p. 27, Mss. 467; William Pollock to Solomon Barkin, Oct. 30, 1958, Mss. 129A, file 7A, box 18; William Pollock to Roland H. Benoit, Feb. 26, 1959, Mss. 396, box 112, all three items in TWUA Rcds.; William Pollock to TWUA Local Unions and Joint Boards, Nov. 7, 1963, box 1, NB Jt. Bd. Rcds.; quotation in L. T. Barringer to William F. Sullivan, Feb. 17, 1959, box 83, folder 902, NACM/NTA Rcds.

40 Barkin quotation in Minutes, Columbia University Seminar on Labor, Feb. 21, 1962, p. 17, BN-16, SBP; William F. Sullivan to Seabury Stanton, Jan. 23, 1959, box 83, folder 903, NACM/NTA Rcds.

41 Frank C. Mawby to William Pollock, Jan. 23, 1957; TWUA press release, Mar. 22, 1957, both items in Mss. 396, box 109, TWUA Rcds.; quotation in Bates Manufacturing Company and TWUA, Arbitration Decision, 1957, p. 21, box 64, folder 726, NACM/NTA Rcds.; W. Stanley Devino et al., *A Study of Textile Mill Closings in Selected New England Communities* (Orono: University of Maine Press, 1966), pp. 8–9.

42 NYT, June 6, 1958, p. 68; Memo for Mr. Pollock's use, Jan. 24, 1958, Mss. 396, box 111, Berkshire-Hathaway folder; Solomon Barkin to William Pollock, Feb. 4, 1958, Mss. 129A, file 7A, box 18; Minutes of Meeting Held Sept. 13, 1957, Berkshire Hathaway, Inc., Mss. 396, box 109; Minutes, Executive Council, Feb. 17–20, 1958, pp. 24–28, Mss. 396, box 8, all four items in TWUA Rcds.

43 Minutes, Executive Council, Feb. 17–20, 1958, p. 30, Mss. 396, box 8, TWUA Rcds.

44 Anna Sullivan to Victor Canzano, May 25, 1959, Mss. 396, box 113, Chicopee Manufacturing folder; first quotation in Minutes, Cotton-Rayon Policy Committee, Feb. 8, 1957, p. 1, Mss. 396, box 611; Minutes, Executive Council, Feb. 17–20, 1958, p. 26, Mss. 396, box 8, all three items in TWUA Rcds.; Memo, Mar. 4, 1959, box 89, folder 980, NACM/NTA Rcds.; second quotation in William Pollock to George Carignan, Sept. 10, 1964, box 4, NB Jt. Bd. Rcds.

45 Quotation in TL, Dec. 1956, p. 9; Solomon Barkin to William Pollock, July 16, 1954, Mss. 129A, file 7A, box 17, TWUA Rcds.; William F. Sullivan, draft address, "The New England Textile Industry," Nov. 1955, p. 8, box 51, folder 600, NACM/NTA Rcds.

46 Bennett Harrison, *Rationalization, Restructuring, and Industrial Reorganization in Older Regions: The Economic Transformation of New England since World War II* (Joint Center for Urban Studies of MIT and Harvard University, Working Paper No. 72, Feb. 1982), pp. 89–95; William H. Miernyk, *Depressed Industrial Areas—A National Problem* (Washington, D.C.: National Planning Association, Planning Pamphlet No. 98, Jan. 1957),

p. 13; second quotation in Charles A. Myers and George P. Shultz, *The Dynamics of a Labor Market: A Study of the Impact of Employment Changes on Labor Mobility, Job Satisfactions, and Company and Union Policies* (New York: Prentice-Hall, Inc., 1951), p. 36; Miernyk, *Inter-Industry Mobility*, pp. 87–88. For more on the different long-term experiences of displaced textile workers of varying ages, see the interviews in Mary H. Blewett, *The Last Generation: Work and Life in the Textile Mills of Lowell, Massachusetts, 1910–1960* (Amherst: University of Massachusetts Press, 1990), pp. 139, 164, 191–92, 199–200, 207, 213, 227–28, 223.

47 Blewett, *The Last Generation*, p. 164; Miernyk, *Inter-Industry Mobility*, pp. 18–21, 29, 141, quotation on p. 141.

48 Miernyk, *Inter-Industry Mobility*, pp. 13–16, 73, 87, 106, 122, quotations on pp. 87, 122, 106; Minutes, GLCCID, Oct. 20, 1952, p. 3; *TL*, Dec. 20, 1952, p. 7.

49 U.S. Senate, *Report on Problems of Textile Industry*, pp. 20–21; *Report on the New England Textile Industry by Committee Appointed by the New England Governors* (1952), pp. 308–10; A. W. Macy to A. A. List, Apr. 9, 1952, box 42, folder 516, NACM/NTA Rcds.; *TL*, Dec. 20, 1952, p. 7; Dec. 1956, pp. 8–9; *Boston Morning Globe*, Feb. 4, 1956, in JWB Scrapbooks; Miernyk, *Inter-Industry Mobility*, pp. 23–24, 72, first quotation on p. 72; Minutes, GLCCID, Sept. 13, 1954, pp. 5–6; Blanche Sciacca interview, Sept. 25, 1983, Oral History Project: The Mill Workers of Lawrence (OHP: Mill Workers), MATH. Father McQuade was still expressing these concerns three years later. Minutes, GLCCID, Sept. 30, 1957, p. 3.

50 Minutes, Columbia University Seminar on Labor, Dec. 9, 1960, BN-14, SBP; Miernyk, *Inter-Industry Mobility*, pp. 52–53, 73, 104, 107, quotation on p. 107.

51 Miernyk, *Inter-Industry Mobility*, pp. 72, 104, quotation on p. 104; John Bodnar, "Power and Memory in Oral History: Workers and Managers at Studebaker," *Journal of American History* 75 (Mar. 1989): 1219; Mary H. Blewett, "Introduction," in *Surviving Hard Times: The Working People of Lowell*, ed. Mary H. Blewett (Lowell: Lowell Museum, 1982), p. 8; second quotation in Ernie Marquis interview, Oct. 31, 1983; final quotation in Blanche Sciacca interview, Sept. 25, 1983, both items in OHP: Mill Workers; Lucienne Adams interview, June 3, 1988, Shifting Gears Project interviews, Immigrant City Archives, Lawrence, Massachusetts.

52 Harrison, *Rationalization, Restructuring, and Industrial Reorganization*, pp. 48–52; Ralph E. Corderre to Paul Swaity, Dec. 6, 1974, box 9, Anglo Fabrics folder, TWUA Collection, MATH.

53 Seabury Stanton to Solomon Barkin, Dec. 27, 1962, BN-16, SBP.

SEVEN. THE POLITICS OF DEINDUSTRIALIZATION

1 Paul Jacobs, *The State of the Unions* (New York: Atheneum, 1963), p. 264; *CIO News*, May 8, 1950, p. 6.

2   Abstract, Kenneth Fiester interview, p. 15, Mss. 467, Textile Workers Union of American Records (TWUA Rcds.), State Historical Society of Wisconsin Archives, Madison, Wisconsin (SHSW); Len DeCaux, *Labor Radical: From the Wobblies to CIO* (Boston: Beacon Press, 1970), pp. 285–88.

3   Solomon Barkin, "Can We Maintain the Democratic Middle Course in the United States?" unpublished ms., 1947, p. 4, Bound Notebook 2, Solomon Barkin Papers (BN-2, SBP), Special Collections and Archives, W. E. B. Du Bois Library, University of Massachusetts–Amherst, Amherst, Massachusetts. Barkin's application of the concept of social costs is more fully examined in Donald R. Stabile, *Activist Unionism: The Institutional Economics of Solomon Barkin* (Armonk, N.Y.: M. E. Sharpe, 1993), chap. 2.

4   Emil Rieve to Wayne Morse, Sept. 17, 1952, Mss. 396, box 16, TWUA Rcds.; David Brody, *Workers in Industrial America: Essays on the 20th Century Struggle* (New York: Oxford University Press, 1980), pp. 215–57; Nelson Lichtenstein, "From Corporatism to Collective Bargaining: Labor and the Eclipse of Social Democracy in the Postwar Era," in *The Rise and Fall of the New Deal Order, 1930–1980*, ed. Steve Fraser and Gary Gerstle (Princeton: Princeton University Press, 1989), pp. 134–40.

5   Alan Brinkley, "The New Deal and the Idea of the State," in *The Rise and Fall of the New Deal Order*, pp. 85–121, quotation on p. 112.

6   Solomon Barkin to Emil Rieve, Jan. 4, 1943, Mss. 129A, file 1A, box 14, TWUA Rcds.; Steven Fraser, *Labor Will Rule: Sidney Hillman and the Rise of American Labor* (New York: The Free Press, 1991), pp. 506–17; Lichtenstein, "From Corporatism to Collective Bargaining," pp. 137–45; Lichtenstein, *Labor's War at Home: The CIO in World War II* (Cambridge, Eng.: Cambridge University Press, 1982), pp. 234–38.

7   First quotation in Minutes, Columbia University Seminar on Labor, Dec. 12, 1956, p. 2, BN-10, SBP; U.S. Congress, Joint Committee on the Economic Report, *Hearings on the January 1955 Economic Report of the President Pursuant to Sec. 5 (a) of Public Law 304*, 84th Cong., 1st sess. (Washington, D.C.: U.S. Government Printing Office, 1955), p. 40.

8   Solomon Barkin, "Meeting the Problems of the Shifting Location of American Industries," unpublished address, Jan. 16, 1958, pp. 1, 3, Mss. 396, box 109, TWUA Rcds.

9   This and the next two paragraphs are based on information in U.S. Congress, Senate, Subcommittee of the Committee on Interstate and Foreign Commerce, *Investigation of Closing of Nashua, New Hampshire Mills and Operations of Textron, Inc.*, 80th Cong., 2d sess. (Washington, D.C.: U.S. Government Printing Office, 1948), pp. 76–77, 222, 1026–29.

10 This and the next two paragraphs are based on information in ibid., pp. 68–73, 86–87, 218–20.

11 Little later claimed that Rieve could not persuade workers to accept the new work assignments. Royal Little, *How to Lose $100,000,000 and Other Valuable Advice* (Boston: Little, Brown and Company, 1979), p. 73.

12 John A. Hogan, "Employment and Collective Bargaining Problems in the

American Woolen and Worsted Industry" (Ph.D. diss., Harvard University, 1952), p. 279; Cotton Report, Mss. 129A, Jan. 11, 1953, file 1A, box 4, TWUA Rcds.

13 U.S. Senate, *Investigation of Textron Operations*, pp. 1033–36, 1040–42; Little, *How to Lose $100,000,000*, p. 99; William H. Miernyk, "The Problem of Depressed Areas," *Monthly Labor Review* 80 (Mar. 1957): 302; Sar A. Levitan, *Federal Aid to Depressed Areas: An Evaluation of the Area Redevelopment Administration* (Baltimore: The Johns Hopkins University Press, 1964), p. 215; W. Stanley Devino et al., *A Study of Textile Mill Closings in Selected New England Communities* (Orono: University of Maine Press, 1966).

14 Solomon Barkin to Emil Rieve, Nov. 5, 1948, Mss. 129A, file 7A, box 15; Statement of the TWUA at Stockholders Meeting, Wm. Whitman, Inc., Nov. 12, 1952, Mss. 396, box 353, both items in TWUA Rcds.; Rieve quotation in *CIO News*, Dec. 24, 1951, p. 9; second quotation in *New York Times* (*NYT*), Oct. 9, 1951, p. 41; *Report on New England Textile Industry by Committee Appointed by the New England Governors* (1952), pp. 282–84.

15 First quotation in Solomon Barkin to John Chupka, Mar. 9, 1954; draft of letter to individual New England senators, Mar. 9, 1954, both items in Mss. 129A, file 1A, box 16, TWUA Rcds.; *TL*, Apr. 1955, p. 3; Dero A. Saunders, "The Stormiest Merger Yet," *Fortune* 51 (Apr. 1955): 137.

16 Solomon Barkin to William Pollock, Jan. 10, 1955, Mss. 129A, file 1A, box 16, TWUA Rcds.; Solomon Barkin, Statement before the Joint Committee of the Economic Report on the Textile Industry as a Depressed Industry, Jan. 27, 1955, pp. 9–10, 13–14, BN-9, SBP; United States Congress, Senate, Subcommittee on Antitrust and Monopoly of the Committee on the Judiciary, *Hearings to Study the Antitrust Laws of the United States, and Their Administration, Interpretation, and Effect Pursuant to S. Res. 61*, 84th Cong., 1st sess. (Washington, D.C.: U.S. Government Printing Office, 1955), pp. 764, 770–77, quotations from p. 764. The proposal to levy special taxes on liquidating corporations had apparently been under discussion for some years. In 1952, for example, the New Bedford Joint Board sent a similar recommendation to the Massachusetts legislature. Minutes, Board of Directors, Nov. 2, 1952, box 1, New Bedford Joint Board Records (NB Jt. Bd. Rcds.), Special Collections and Archives, W. E. B. Du Bois Library, University of Massachusetts–Amherst, Amherst, Massachusetts.

17 Solomon Barkin to Colin Stam, Nov. 7, 1957; Remarks by Solomon Barkin, unpublished ms., n.d., both items in BN-11, SBP; U.S. Congress, Joint Committee on the Economic Report, *January 1959 Economic Report of the President*, 86th Cong., 1st sess. (Washington, D.C.: U.S. Government Printing Office, 1959), p. 306.

18 *New England Governors' Report* (1952), 118; Steve Dunwell, *The Run of the Mill: A Pictorial Narrative of the Expansion, Dominion, Decline, and Enduring Impact of the New England Textile Industry* (Boston: David R. Godine, Publisher, 1978), p. 160. Laurence F. Gross provides an able examination

of the plant obsolescence problem at a major Lowell firm in *The Course of Industrial Decline: The Boott Cotton Mills of Lowell, Massachusetts, 1835–1955* (Baltimore: The Johns Hopkins University Press, 1993), pp. 44–45, 102–103, 125, 176–79, 210–11. There is a large and growing literature on American industry during the 1980s. Two perceptive books by Barry Bluestone and Bennett Harrison anticipated and summarized the decade's central economic developments: *The Deindustrialization of America: Plant Closings, Community Abandonment, and the Dismantling of Basic Industry* (New York: Basic Books, 1982); and *The Great U-Turn: Corporate Restructuring and the Polarizing of America* (New York: Basic Books, 1988). The best case study of a leveraged buyout is Max Holland, *When the Machine Stopped: A Cautionary Tale from Industrial America* (Boston: Harvard Business School Press, 1989). Also see Walter Adams and James W. Brock, *Dangerous Pursuits: Mergers and Acquisitions in the Age of Wall Street* (New York: Pantheon Books, 1989); Bryan Burrough and John Helyar, *Barbarians at the Gate: The Fall of RJR Nabisco* (New York: Harper and Row, 1990); and George Anders, *Merchants of Debt: KKR and the Mortgaging of American Business* (New York: Basic Books, 1992).

19   Solomon Barkin, "Management and Ownership in the New England Cotton Textile Industry," *Journal of Economic Issues* 15 (June 1981): 475.

20   Sar A. Levitan, *Federal Aid to Depressed Areas*, pp. 9, 17–20; Minutes, Columbia University Seminar on Labor, Dec. 12, 1956, pp. 6–7, BN-10, SBP; Roger H. Davidson, "The Depressed Areas Controversy: A Study in the Politics of American Business" (Ph.D. diss., Columbia University, 1963), pp. 85–96; Paul H. Douglas to Kenneth O'Donnell, Apr. 24, 1961, BN-15, SBP.

21   Solomon Barkin and J. Raymond Walsh, Memorandum for Mr. Murray, Feb. 26, 1944, Mss. 129A, file 1A, box 14, TWUA Rcds. The economic developments to which the memo referred are examined in Jack Temple Kirby, *Rural Worlds Lost: The American South, 1920–1960* (Baton Rouge: Louisiana State University Press, 1987), chap. 2; and Pete Daniel, *Breaking the Land: The Transformation of Cotton, Tobacco, and Rice Cultures since 1880* (Urbana: University of Illinois Press, 1985), chaps. 11–12.

22   First quotation in Solomon Barkin to Emil Rieve, Nov. 16, 1944; Barkin to Rieve, Jan. 4, 1943, both items in Mss. 129A, file 1A, box 14; Barkin to Rieve, Nov. 5, 1948, Mss. 129A, file 7A, box 15, all three items in TWUA Rcds.; Minutes, Columbia University Seminar on Labor, Dec. 9, 1960, p. 6, BN-14, SBP.

23   Solomon Barkin to Emil Rieve, Aug. 1, 1947, Mss. 129A, file 1A, box 14, TWUA Rcds.

24   *CIO News*, July 31, 1950, p. 2; McMahon quotation in *TL*, Jan. 24, 1950; *Massachusetts CIO News*, Mar. 1955, in J. William Belanger Scrapbooks (JWB Scrapbooks), Special Collections and Archives, W. E. B. Du Bois Library, University of Massachusetts–Amherst, Amherst, Massachusetts; *NYT*, Nov. 26, 1952, p. 35.

25 Solomon Barkin to Emil Rieve, Dec. 5, 1949, Mss. 129A, file 1A, box 15, TWUA Rcds.; quotation in Minutes, Columbia University Seminar on Labor, Dec. 12, 1956, p. 7, BN-10, SBP. The two studies mentioned in the text are: Council of Economic Advisors, Committee on the New England Economy, *The New England Economy: A Report to the President* (Washington, D.C.: U.S. Government Printing Office, 1951); and Arthur A. Bright, Jr., and George H. Ellis, eds., *The Economic State of New England: Report of the Committee of New England of the National Planning Association* (New Haven: Yale University Press, 1954).

26 Solomon Barkin to Emil Rieve, Jan. 7, 1949, Mss. 129A, file 1A, box 14; quotations in Memorandum on New England Textile Commission, Jan. 11, 1949, Mss. 129A, file 1A, box 15, both items in TWUA Rcds.

27 Emil Rieve to Solomon Barkin, Jan. 14, 1949, Mss. 129A, file 1A, box 14, TWUA Rcds.; Statement of Solomon Barkin to Massachusetts Special Commission on Textile Industry, Oct. 31, 1949, pp. 1–4, BN-3, SBP; Seabury Stanton to Solomon Barkin, Mar. 20, 1950, Mss. 396, box 53, Hathaway Manufacturing Company folder; Solomon Barkin to Seymour Harris, Oct. 30, 1952, Mss. 129A, file 7A, box 16, both items in TWUA Rcds.

28 *New England Governors' Report* (1952); Minutes, Department Heads Meeting, Apr. 29, 1953, Mss. 129A, file 1A, box 5, TWUA Rcds.; quotation in *New England Textiles and the New England Economy: Report to the Conference of New England Governors* (1956), p. 16.

29 Solomon Barkin to Edward Doolan, Oct. 2, 1952, Mss. 129A, file 7A, box 16; Minutes, Staff Meeting, Oct. 27, 1952, pp. 1–4, Mss. 129A, file 1A, box 11, both items in TWUA Rcds.

30 Minutes, Department Directors Meeting, Nov. 5, 1954, Mss. 129A, file 1A, box 5, TWUA Rcds.; Solomon Barkin, Testimony on Behalf of TWUA before the House Committee on Ways and Means on H.R. 2893, Apr. 12, 1949, BN-3; Solomon Barkin, "Older Workers in Textile Industry Desperately Need Improved Social Security," Testimony before the Senate Committee on Finance, June 28, 1954, BN-8; final quotation in Solomon Barkin, "Economic Problems," unpublished ms., Sept. 1956, BN-10, all three items in SBP.

31 Levitan, *Federal Aid to Depressed Areas*, pp. 7–9; Davidson, "Depressed Areas Controversy," pp. 222–52.

32 Davidson, "Depressed Areas Controversy," pp. 86–87; quotation in Solomon Barkin, "Principles of Area Development Legislation," *Labor Law Journal* 10 (Aug. 1959): 525.

33 Quotation in Statement of Solomon Barkin on "Minority Views" Expressed on S. 3683 Area Redevelopment Act, May 8, 1958, p. 1, BN-12, SBP; Transcript of Second Annual Conference on the Economic Outlook Sponsored by Editorial Committee, Magazine Publishers Association, Mar. 18, 1959, pp. 54–55, BN-13, SBP; U.S. Congress, House of Representatives, Subcommittee No. 3 of the Committee on Banking and Currency, *Hearings on the Area Redevelopment Act*, 86th Cong., 1st sess. (Washington,

D.C.: U.S. Government Printing Office, 1959), pp. 20–21; Levitan, *Federal Aid to Depressed Areas*, pp. 8–14.

34 Levitan, *Federal Aid to Depressed Areas*, p. 9; Stephen Amberg, "The Triumph of Industrial Orthodoxy: The Collapse of Studebaker-Packard," in *On the Line: Essays in the History of Auto Work*, ed. Nelson Lichtenstein and Stephen Meyer (Urbana: University of Illinois Press, 1989), pp. 205–206; Davidson, "Depressed Areas Controversy," pp. 100–101; Minutes, Columbia University Seminar on Labor, Dec. 9, 1960, p. 3, BN-14, SBP; Solomon Barkin to Ray Marshall, Apr. 15, 1984, box 1, series 2, SBP. That the threat foreign competition posed to U.S. steel producers was already evident by 1960 is a central theme of Paul A. Tiffany, *The Decline of American Steel: How Management, Labor, and Government Went Wrong* (New York: Oxford University Press, 1988).

35 Memo from Joseph Miller to William F. Sullivan, Jan. 4, 1956, box 59, folder 680; William F. Sullivan to Seabury Stanton, Dec. 7, 1955, box 51, folder 600; William F. Sullivan to William H. Miernyk, Mar. 6, 1957, box 66, folder 745; John F. Kennedy to Seabury Stanton, May 27, 1960, box 92, folder 1016; Seabury Stanton to William F. Sullivan, Dec. 8, 1958; William F. Sullivan to Seabury Stanton, Dec. 15, 1958, both items in box 72, folder 800, all six items in National Association of Cotton Manufacturers/Northern Textile Association Records (NACM/NTA Rcds.), Museum of American Textile History, North Andover–Lowell, Massachusetts (MATH).

36 William H. Miernyk, "The Problem of Distressed Areas," p. 305; Minutes, Greater Lawrence Citizens' Committee for Industrial Development (GLCCID), Dec. 12, 1955, pp. 1–3; Jan. 9, 1956, p. 3, Immigrant City Archives, Lawrence, Massachusetts; William H. Miernyk, *Depressed Industrial Areas—A National Problem* (Washington, D.C.: National Planning Association, Planning Pamphlet No. 98, 1957), p. 66; Davidson, "Distressed Areas Controversy," p. 202.

37 Robert W. Eisenmenger, *The Dynamics of Growth in New England's Economy, 1870–1964* (Middletown, Conn.: Wesleyan University Press, 1967), p. 71; William J. Byron, "*Needed:* Local Leadership in Depressed Areas," *Harvard Business Review* 38 (July–Aug. 1960): 118; Miernyk, *Depressed Industrial Areas*, p. 18; Solomon Barkin, Statement to the Subcommittee on Production and Stabilization, Senate Banking and Currency Committee Hearings on Area Assistance Legislation, May 8, 1957, pp. 12–13, BN-11, SBP.

38 Charles A. Myers and George P. Shultz, *The Dynamics of a Labor Market: A Study of the Impact of Employment Changes on Labor Mobility, Job Satisfactions, and Company and Union Policies* (New York: Prentice-Hall, Inc. 1951), pp. 155–56; Kurtz M. Hanson to Seabury Stanton, Jan. 11, 1955, box 55, folder 598, NACM/NTA Rcds.; Minutes, GLCCID, Sept. 13, 1954, pp. 6–7; Nov. 5, 1956, p. 3.

39 William H. Miernyk, *Inter-Industry Mobility: The Case of the Displaced Textile Worker* (Boston: Northeastern University, 1955), pp. 146–50; Mier-

nyk, *Depressed Industrial Areas*, pp. 19, 22–25; Minutes, GLCCID, Oct. 15, 1951, pp. 2–3; Mar. 3, 1952, pp. 2–3; Sept. 13, 1954, pp. 5–6.

40 Levitan, *Federal Aid to Depressed Areas*, pp. 10–13, 165–67, 191–95.

41 Solomon Barkin to Juanita Kreps, Sept. 7, 1977; Solomon Barkin to Ray Marshall, Apr. 15, 1984, both items in box 1, series 2, SBP; Levitan, *Federal Aid to Depressed Areas*, pp. 25–26, 250–53.

42 "Disarmament Economics in the Limelight," Panel Discussion Sponsored by Regional Science Association, Dec. 25, 1959, BN-13, SBP; "The Labor Market and Social Security," Proceedings of the Fourth Annual Social Security Conference, Jan. 23–24, 1962, BN-16, SBP; Barkin, "Principles for Area Redevelopment Legislation," p. 529; Miernyk, "The Problem of Depressed Areas," p. 304. William Byron also emphasized the importance of regional planning in "*Needed:* Local Leadership in Depressed Areas," pp. 119–21.

43 Solomon Barkin to William Pollock, Aug. 16, 1954, Mss. 129A, file 7A, box 16, TWUA Rcds.

44 Staughton Lynd, *The Fight Against Shutdowns: Youngstown's Mill Closings* (San Pedro, Calif.: Singlejack Books, 1982), chap. 6; William Serrin, *Homestead: The Glory and Tragedy of an American Steel Town* (New York: Times Books, 1992), pp. 333–40, 352–57.

45 Minutes, Columbia University Seminar on Labor, Dec. 9, 1960, p. 7, BN-14, SBP; Solomon Barkin, "Economic Problems," unpublished ms., Sept. 1956, BN-10, SBP.

46 U.S. Congress, Senate, Subcommittee of the Committee on Banking and Currency, *Hearings on the Effect of Private Investment on U.S. Employment, Profits, and Markets*, 86th Cong., 1st sess. (Washington, D.C.: U.S. Government Printing Office, 1959), pp. 115–17; *New Bedford Standard Times*, Sept. 2, 1958, in JWB Scrapbooks; Stabile, *Activist Unionism*, pp. 183–85.

CONCLUSION

1 Samuel Bowles, David M. Gordon, and Thomas E. Weisskopf, *After the Waste Land: A Democratic Economics for the Year 2000* (Armonk, N.Y.: M. E. Sharpe, Inc., 1990), pp. 63–79; Kim Moody, *An Injury to All: The Decline of American Unionism* (London: Verso, 1988), chap. 5; Mike Davis, *Prisoners of the American Dream: Politics and Economy in the History of the US Working Class* (London: Verso, 1986), pp. 136–43; Nelson Lichtenstein, *Labor's War at Home: The CIO in World War II* (Cambridge, Eng.: Cambridge University Press, 1982), pp. 244–45.

2 Solomon Barkin, "Selected Aspects of the CIO Experience," *Proceedings of the 38th Annual IRRA Meeting* (1986), p. 192. Katherine Van Wetzel Stone provides a thoroughgoing critique of arbitration and the entire postwar structure of industrial jurisprudence in "The Post-War Paradigm in American Labor Law," *Yale Law Journal* 90 (June 1981): 1509–80.

3 Quotation in Minutes, Columbia University Seminar on Labor, Dec. 12,

1956, p. 6, Bound Notebook 10, Solomon Barkin Papers (BN-10, SBP), Special Collections and Archives, W. E. B. Du Bois Library, University of Massachusetts–Amherst, Amherst, Massachusetts.

4 Barry Bluestone and Irving Bluestone, *Negotiating the Future: A Labor Perspective on American Business* (New York: Basic Books, 1992).

5 Robert Blauner, *Alienation and Freedom: The Factory Worker and His Industry* (Chicago: The University of Chicago Press, 1964), p. 70, n. 32; Dana Frank, "Sleeping with the Enemy," *Nation* (Mar. 8, 1993): 312.

6 Mike Parker, "Industrial Relations Myth and Shop-Floor Reality: The 'Team Concept' in the U.S. Auto Industry," in *Industrial Democracy in America: The Ambiguous Promise*, ed. Nelson Lichtenstein and Howell John Harris (Cambridge, Eng.: Cambridge University Press, 1993), pp. 249–74; Donald M. Wells, *Empty Promises: Quality of Working Life Programs and the Labor Movement* (New York: Monthly Review Press, 1987); John Russo, "Saturn's Wings: What GM's Saturn Project Is Really About," *Labor Research Review* 9 (Fall 1986): 67–77; Frank, "Sleeping with the Enemy," pp. 311–13; Eric Mann, *Taking on General Motors: A Case Study of the UAW Campaign to Keep GM Van Nuys Open* (Los Angeles: Institute of Industrial Relations, University of California, Los Angeles, 1987), pp. 81–88, 121–23.

7 James Parrott, "Fashioning an Industrial Strategy for Garment Workers," *Labor Research Review* 19 (Fall 1992): 55–67; Thomas A. Kochan, Harry C. Katz, and Robert B. McKersie, *The Transformation of American Industrial Relations* (New York: Basic Books, 1986), pp. 187–89; quotations in David Brody, "The Breakdown of Labor's Social Contract: Historical Reflections, Future Prospects," *Dissent* (Winter 1992): 41; Brody, "Workplace Contractualism in Comparative Perspective," in *Industrial Democracy in America*, pp. 202–205.

8 Stone, "The Post-War Paradigm," p. 1580; William Greider, *Who Will Tell the People: The Betrayal of American Democracy* (New York: Simon & Schuster, 1992), pp. 354–55.

9 Quotation in Minutes, Columbia University Seminar on Labor, Dec. 12, 1956, p. 11, BN-10, SBP; Elizabeth Faue, *Community of Suffering and Struggle: Women, Men, and the Labor Movement in Minneapolis, 1915–1945* (Chapel Hill: The University of North Carolina Press, 1991).

10 Some of the best thinking on how labor might deal with the current crisis is regularly surveyed in *Labor Research Review*, a publication of the Midwest Center for Labor Research. See especially the Summer 1983, Fall 1986, and Fall 1992 issues.

11 Brody, "The Breakdown of Labor's Social Contract," p. 41; E. P. Thompson, *The Making of the English Working Class* (pbk. ed.; New York: Vintage Books, 1966), p. 12.

INDEX